TOWARDS LITURGIES THAT RECONCILE

Towards Liturgies that Reconcile reflects upon Christian worship as it is shaped, and mis-shaped, by human prejudice, specifically by racism. African Americans and European Americans have lived together for 400 years on the continent of North America, but they have done so as slave and master, outsider and insider, oppressed and oppressor.

Scott Haldeman traces the development of Protestant worship among whites and blacks, showing that the following exist in tension: African-American and European-American Protestant liturgical traditions are both interdependent and distinct; and that multicultural communities must both understand and celebrate the uniqueness of various member groups while also accepting the risk and possibility of praying themselves into an integrated body, one new culture.

LITURGY, WORSHIP AND SOCIETY

SERIES EDITORS

Dave Leal, Brasenose College, Oxford, UK
Bryan Spinks, Yale Divinity School, USA
Paul Bradshaw, University of Notre Dame, UK and USA
Gregory Woolfenden, St Mary's Orthodox Church, USA
Phillip Tovey, Ripon College Cuddesdon, UK

The Ashgate Liturgy, Worship & Society series forms an important new "library" on liturgical theory at a time of great change in the liturgy and much debate concerning traditional and new forms of worship, suitability and use of places of worship, and wider issues concerning interaction of liturgy, worship and contemporary society. Offering a thorough grounding in the historical and theological foundations of liturgy, this series explores and challenges many key issues of worship and liturgical theology, currently in hot debate within academe and within Christian churches worldwide - issues central to the future of the liturgy, to public and private worship, and set to make a significant impact on changing patterns of worship and the place of the church in contemporary society.

Other titles in the series:

Early and Medieval Rituals and Theologies of Baptism
From the New Testament to the Council of Trent
Bryan D. Spinks

Reformation and Modern Rituals and Theologies of Baptism
From Luther to Contemporary Practices
Bryan D. Spinks

The Liturgies of Quakerism
Pink Dandelion

Inculturation of Christian Worship
Exploring the Eucharist
Phillip Tovey

Towards Liturgies that Reconcile

Race and Ritual among African-American and European-American Protestants

SCOTT HALDEMAN
Chicago Theological Seminary, USA

ASHGATE

BV
198
.H28
2007

Published by
Ashgate Publishing Limited
Gower House
Croft Road
Aldershot
Hampshire GU11 3HR
England

Ashgate Publishing Company
Suite 420
101 Cherry Street
Burlington, VT 05401-4405
USA

Ashgate website: http://www.ashgate.com

British Library Cataloguing in Publication Data
Haldeman, Scott (William Scott)
   Towards liturgies that reconcile : race and ritual among African-American and European-
American Protestants. – (Liturgy, worship and society)
   1. Protestant churches – United States – Liturgy 2. Reconciliation – Religious aspects
– Protestant churches 3. Racism – Religious aspects – Protestant churches
   I. Title
   280.4'0973

Library of Congress Cataloging-in-Publication Data
Haldeman, Scott (William Scott)
   Towards liturgies that reconcile : race and ritual among
African-American and European-American Protestants / Scott Haldeman.
      p. cm. —(Liturgy, worship and society series)
   Includes bibliographical references and index.
   ISBN-13: 978-0-7546-5726-2 (hardcover : alk. paper)
   1. Liturgies—United States. 2. Worship. 3. Race relations—Religious
aspects—Christianity.   I. Title.
   BV198.H28 2007
   264'.0089–dc22

                                                                            2006018849

ISBN 978-0-7546-5726-2

Printed and bound in Great Britain by TJ International Ltd, Padstow, Cornwall.

Contents

List of Figures

Preface

Liturgical theology tends to be both critical and nostalgic. Critical because it begins with dissatisfaction with current practice in a tradition or family of traditions. Nostalgic because proposed solutions to the deficiencies of the present have, almost inevitably, involved a call to return to some golden age of the past when practices were "better". So, in the sixteenth century, Luther and Calvin looked backed to scriptural warrant, the insights of Augustine and other early figures, to curb papal "abuses" and to reshape the Mass and other rites. So, in the nineteenth century, leaders in various American Protestant denominations who had a liturgical bent looked back to Luther, Calvin or some other "founder" to combat what in their view were the shortcomings of revivalist forms of worship then gaining popularity. So, in the twentieth century, Pentecostal leaders looked to the church of the Book of *Acts* to promote ecstatic practices, while participants in the ecumenical liturgical reform movement pored over newly (re)discovered documents such as the *Didache* and *The Apostolic Constitutions* to "fix" so-called mainline worship once again.

Much has been gained by these efforts. Neglected riches of the past—whether particular prayer texts, wholesale musical traditions or an overall pattern of worship that had become obscured—are uncovered and again embraced, enriching a new generation. Yet, the pattern of a lone prophet (or a small school of prophets), whether a Saxon Augustinian monk, a French lawyer in exile, a denominational worship staff, or an ecumenical consultation of experts, correcting contemporary practice by returning to older patterns also has it risks. The main one being that a church, The Church, may adopt patterns of worship that are more suited to another time, another context—and so unable to engage fully the minds and hearts and bodies, the hopes and dreams, the memories and imaginations of this people in this place in this day.

This work attempts a different approach. While I am, undeniably, a scholar hoping to influence practice, and I do turn to history for models, insights, conceptual tools, the work that follows tries to be constructive and suspicious. By constructive, I mean that the project originated around a conference table in one local church where the members and staff were struggling to find ways to communicate about worship from multiple cultural and theological locations. I came to understand my task as less to mount a critique of present practice and more to reach for new and better ways not only to do worship in that particular place but also new language to help them talk to each other about worship—to construct bridges over chasms of historical conflict and misunderstanding. In addition, my turn to history is decidedly not nostalgic but is, instead, suspicious that forms of practice in earlier eras contributed to the divisions and injustices of the present.

While I continue to find it necessary to make more complex the analysis you will find in the pages that follow, the aim of this project is, then, to trace the ways that African-American and European-American Protestants (among other cultural groups) have worshiped (among other kinds of social/ecclesial practices) themselves into a place of separation and distrust that must be confronted if we are to construct pathways towards reconciliation. To tear down walls and build bridges requires that we leave behind practices that we are coming to understand have served as one means to divide us and allow God to do a new thing among us. Patterns of worship that formed us as members of distinct groups and continue to reinforce our differences will not lead us to (re)discover our common humanity and our interdependence as members of the One Body. Instead, rereading the past to trace the paths we have walked, where we diverged, where we went wrong, what we need to preserve, we may be able to speak more honestly with one another and to gain empathy in relation to one another's need to protect some particular style of prayer and praise. And, having begun to understand one another better, we may then be able to develop together new patterns that engage us all even as they reshape us into something new—the one people of God, the Body of Christ, where we recognize ourselves as equals, as sisters and brothers, as no more and no less than adopted children of the Most High. Such is the method attempted and recommended here.

First, then, I must thank the members of The Riverside Church, New York City, several of whom are named below in Chapter 1, who allowed me to witness and to reflect with them on their collective lives, their communal practices and the tensions they experienced as they endeavored to consider reforms.

Material in chapters 2 and 4 were previously published by The Liturgical Conference as "American Racism and the Promise of Pentecost" in *Liturgy* 14:4 (Spring 1998), 34–50 and is reprinted here by permission of The Liturgical Conference. I thank then editor Blair Gilmer Meeks, her colleague, Virginia Sloyan, and past and present Board Members of The Liturgical Conference for this permission and for their encouragement of my explorations.

I thank also those who read my work, provided resources, and challenged me to clarify my thinking during the original research and writing stages and still to this day: Tom F. Driver, Janet R. Walton, James Melvin Washington (of blessed memory), Bob Seaver, Delores Williams, and David Daniels. The members of the African-American Liturgical Traditions Seminar of the North American Academy of Liturgy (especially Melva Wilson Costen, Joseph Donnella, Fred Holper, Mary McGann, and J-Glenn Murray, SJ), have responded to various aspects of the project from its stages as draft dissertation chapters to its present form. Colleagues and students at the Chicago Theological Seminary confront me with new conceptual questions and introduce me to yet more practices for me to consider and integrate into my schematic. Bryan Spinks encouraged me to pursue publication, and I thank him and other members of the advisory board of the Liturgy, Worship and Society series of Ashgate Publishing Limited for recommending the work to the editorial staff. Sarah Lloyd and Ann Newell have provided professional support as editors and improved the work substantially. Many thanks to them and other Ashgate staff. Finally, for her inspiration and because she and others of her generation must pursue the hopes for justice that this book attempts to fuel, I dedicate it to my daughter, Sydney Lynn Sichenze Haldeman.

Scott Haldeman

*For Sydney,
a first book for a first and only child,
in hope that your generation,
more than mine,
may find ways to pray and to live,
which honor all and lead towards peace with justice.*

CHAPTER 1

Liturgical Theology in Context

What follows is a study in liturgical theology. It begins not with a particular, historic example of Christian worship which it then explains theologically. Neither does it begin with a general, some even claim universal, shape of Christian public prayer which is then justified and interpreted. Instead, it begins with a church, The Riverside Church in New York City, a community of respected heritage, monumental property, and people, real people with faith, promise, faults, talent, conflict, difference, commitment, and pain. These people gather for worship in this building on Sunday mornings. They pray, preach, announce, collect money, sing, stand, sit, and listen. A crucial fact of this community is that the people who gather, who make up the membership of this local Body, have many racial, ethnic, and cultural backgrounds. They also all live in a major metropolitan area in the United States in the early twenty-first century. Most speak English with fluency, although the number of languages native to members continues to rise. Most are professionals, although class differences are becoming more apparent in recent years. At a time when the eleven o'clock hour on Sunday morning remains one of the most segregated times in this country, this diverse community gathers regularly for worship, performing multicultural liturgies. This study addresses a small number of the many obstacles they have discovered as they have gathered. It offers historical data to facilitate their continuing conversations and their worship.

Worship at Riverside is explicitly a product of community history and continuing innovation. There are no delusions about praying in a manner based upon strict adherence to apostolic, biblical, or catholic norms. Harry Emerson Fosdick founded Riverside as an "interdenominational, interracial, international" community.[1] Under his resolute leadership, worship was characterized by beauty, awe, liberal thought, and tolerance. Over the years, elements that promote one or another of these values were added to the order of service and the flow of the service became impeded by the clutter. The present generation seeks services of worship that are more coherent and inclusive. This study is intended to provide resources to assist the on-going liturgical reform at Riverside (and similar places). While the worship program at Riverside has many facets, I focus my efforts on issues of cultural diversity, and even more specifically on the polar truths that the worship traditions of African-American and European-American Protestants are both interdependent and distinct. I provide, in the body of this work, historical narratives of the worship patterns among, first, African-American Protestants, second, European-American Protestants, and, third, four examples of previous occasions of biracial worship. I conclude by noting implications of these histories for the discipline of liturgical theology.

Methodological assumptions

The procedure to begin in a local church and not with history, tradition, or bible is a deliberate one. I base it on five convictions. First, the church is the social base of theology.[2] Theology, in its familiar, academic form, is meant to answer the church's questions about what it should teach about an issue at hand. I go purposely to a church to discover what the question of the day might be. I find at Riverside a community concerned about worshiping in ways that celebrate pluralism and contribute to the building of community among diverse members. I hope my reflections shed light on questions of importance to this particular community, and, perhaps, for others.

Second, academic theology is not a primary, but a secondary articulation.[3] I write in response to, and at the service of, questions of a particular church. The questions addressed here arise in a context, the life of this community, and, more precisely, their common life of prayer. Primary theology is the series of encounters between a historical community of peoples and its living God. These encounters depend upon God's initiative and occur in all manner of human experience. However, human communities have created religious institutions and, in particular, religious rites to embody such encounters. As they perform ritual actions such as invoking, meditating, and breaking bread, Christians meet God as Creator, Christ and Spirit, predictably, if not always comfortably. The God of Christians is not confined to worship services but has promised to be with Christians when they pray. In other words, Christians who gather for prayer can expect God to show up. The interaction of God and people, and the change wrought in the community, and, perhaps, in God as well, is first-level theology.[4] Our reflection on the changes that occur and the questions the encounter raises about who we are, who God is, and where we are heading together is an important, but secondary, act. Theology, then, is enacted faith in actual occasions of prayer (and other aspects of a life of faith). Specific, local liturgical acts, more than books that reflect on such acts, are the primary expressions of the character of a community's faith.

Christian worship as a form of human ritualizing is a complex act. Communities may follow ritual texts published by their denomination, but the performance of rites is much more than the script on which it is based. Sometimes rites follow their scripts with such exactitude and conviction that the world the text aims to reflect is represented tangibly. But more often, as rites are performed, life intervenes, mistakes are made, local variances are introduced, or conflicts arise. In either case— whether a worship service is flawless or inept—the convictions, vision, and hopes of a community become manifest in their ritualizing. Local performances of Christian worship rather than published scripts, then, are the basis of authentic liturgical theology. Worship both describes and defines the relationship of people with each other and with God. The meaning of the rite has to do with the quality of these relationships and this can only be discovered "on the ground" as it were.

Third, rites hide the truth that they have been historically constructed. They function most effectively when they present a vision of the cosmos so compelling and coherent that the community accepts them as given, as a tradition beyond question, as a set of sacred directives. Unquestioned rites are effective but are also subject to abuse. Rites which seem to have dropped from heaven imply that the cosmic order is static and, thereby, encourage the acceptance of a static social order as well. Reflecting the hierarchy of divine power, beneficiaries of social privilege remain in charge while the marginal are relegated permanently to lower status. The impetus for protest and change is dissipated as celebrations express that "the way things are" is the way God meant them to be. I study the history of worship not as an exercise in restoration but to find out how the rites we perform came to be. Revealing the process by which rites take shape, communities come to understand the connections between liturgical forms and their consequences. Questioning our rites, we see that they sometimes function to reinforce unjust social relations. If we can identify how rites divide human communities into castes, we are enabled to imagine ways to pray that encourage notions of equality. Tracing liturgical history, we may choose to continue in the trajectory on which we find ourselves. Or, we may choose to proceed in a new direction, like the ancient astronomers who came to understand what it would mean to return to Herod after encountering a Nazarene babe in swaddling clothes and took another road back home.

Fourth, uncritical histories, like unquestioned rites, record the path chosen. Paths not taken are soon forgotten. The paths chosen often look, in retrospect, as the only choice. The choice itself becomes lost in the journey. Sometimes the path upon which Christians walk is wide and flat, without stark alternatives or obstacles, and we proceed with vigor. Sometimes the path is obscure and requires effort. Sometimes we find ourselves at a dead end, and steps need to be retraced. The more we know about the paths traveled thus far—and the ones we might have taken—the better able we are to orient ourselves to step towards the future. Historical narratives, infused with a hermeneutic of suspicion, do not present the past as normative, but, instead, reveal it as the series of choices, accidents, and wanderings of our forebears, and similar to the choices we face. We may find help for the making of present choices by re-visiting times of choice in the past. Both choices that we recognize as good and faithful and those in which the wrong direction was taken hold lessons. By reconstructing a critical history of our rites, we may learn which path to follow into the future or, instead, simply to avoid the wrong one. Either way, the choices of our ancestors never relieve us of the responsibility to choose our own path to follow in our own day.

In a diverse religious community, the paths that lead people to the present time and place where they meet to join together in a common journey are myriad. I choose to map a few of them. In the chapters which follow, I provide narratives that describe the features of paths chosen by African-Americans, European-Americans, and mixed groups. The narratives describe how these liturgical traditions have grown in this country. I am indebted to Robert Taft for examples of questions to ask as one looks at the development of received forms of Christian public prayer. Taft's work focuses on the development of the Byzantine rite.[5] He calls his approach structural and historical. First, he selects a discrete element of the liturgy, such as the series of antiphons in the opening rites, or *enarxis*.[6] Then, he traces these antiphons over time, noting their point of origin, their changing form and position in various periods, and their eventual settlement in the order of today. This method reveals that liturgies grow according to patterns. First, Taft notes, liturgies take shape locally, and therefore, in variety. Then, this original variety is subject to a period of unification as local traditions combine into stable families. He writes:

> Hence, the process of formation of rites is not one of diversification, as is usually held, but of unification. And what one finds in extant rites today is not a synthesis of all that went before, but rather the result of a selective evolution: the survival of the fittest—of the fittest, not necessarily of the best.[7]

As time passes, the families, while most often maintaining their basic contours, are subject to cycles of elaboration and pruning.

Following Taft, I look for changes in the patterns of rites, for the development of liturgical families out of diverse local practices, and for subsequent developments. My subject is, however, not the Byzantine rite, but Protestant worship in North America and, specifically, worship among African-Americans and European-Americans. North America has proven to be fertile soil for liturgical development. Protestant traditions with their proclivity towards schism allow for substantial and frequent innovation and reform. At this stage, the number of traditions involved and the lack of uniformity in either past or current liturgical structures requires general narratives which may serve to encourage more detailed research within the families that I identify. My narratives describe two sibling sub-traditions, or streams, within the families of both African-American and European-American Protestant liturgical traditions. I call these, respectively, the *classical* and *improvisational,* and the *mainline* and *enthusiast.* The narratives reveal that a dialectical relationship between religion and culture has contributed substantially to the shaping of all streams of African-American and European-American Protestant liturgical traditions.

Finally, I subject liturgical traditions to explicit ethical critique. Liturgies are central to Christian formation. Our rites shape our communal identity, our relationship to the world, and our patterns of living. We come together to pray. The ways in which we use our bodies, the texts we read and do not read, the actions we undertake, the words we speak and hear, the music we listen to and create, all form us into a community and form our ways of relating to each other and the world. Liturgies create a time and space in which Christians can experience God's grace, or, better, God's reign. The "liminality" of rites, this quality of standing outside the constraints of daily life and offering an opportunity to perform alternative social relationships, enables them to contribute to the ethical formation of Christians. As Tom Driver has written: "The liminality of ritual can be used by God to weaken the grip of oppressive powers. In fact, God has no other use for it".[8] Liturgies have often been used to perform unethical relationships between groups of people. In regard to the race issue in the US, Christian worship has served most often to divide and oppress rather than to unite and liberate. What the various rites teach about the relationship between racial groups is a central concern of the narratives. How to establish rites that contribute to relations of justice and equality is the central concern of the project as a whole.

These five methodological assumptions guide my study. They are prior commitments of my own, formed before I was invited to observe the Riverside process. They shape what I saw and what I have chosen to offer here in both scope and style. I turn now to Riverside's story and from there to the historical narratives to which the Riverside experience pointed me.

The Context: Worship at The Riverside Church in New York City

The Riverside Church opened its doors on 5 October 1930. Harry Emerson Fosdick was the founding pastor. The congregation consisted primarily of former members of the Park Avenue Baptist Church who supported Fosdick's vision to move to Morningside Heights. In her history of the congregation, Mina Pendo writes:

> Dr. Fosdick … agreed to accept the call with three provisos: first, that affirmation of faith in Christ be the only requirement for worship; second, that all Christians, of whatever denominational background, be freely admitted to membership, thus making the church an inter-denominational congregation, while retaining its historic denominational affiliation for the sake of a continuing relationship with the universal church; third, that a new and larger building be created to house larger congregations and an expanding program.[9]

Because of its eloquent preacher, high-profile members such as John D. Rockefeller, Jr., and centrality in the modernist/fundamentalist controversy, Riverside became widely known. Fosdick led the congregation from 1925 to 1946. During his tenure, he promulgated a faith cast in the terminology of modernity. His theology engaged educated liberals on an intellectual level but also had active social dimensions. Fosdick's cooperation with the national war effort during World War I transformed into a strong pacifist stance as he witnessed the enormity of suffering caused by modern fighting methods. He actively opposed US intervention in World War II. During The Great Depression, Riverside helped the unemployed find jobs and even provided some paid work. In addition, Fosdick developed a myriad of social and educational activities for members.

Riverside is affiliated with the American Baptist Convention and the United Church of Christ. It stands, then, in the liturgical tradition which James White refers to as "Free Churches".[10] Both denominations are committed to "liturgical subsidiarity", giving independence in most matters of belief and policy to individual parishes.[11] Neither denomination mandates specific liturgical practices. Riverside's joint affiliation in two Free church denominations gives the congregation substantial freedom. Practically, such freedom is both a blessing of possibility and a temptation to rootlessness. Pendo describes the principles of worship at Riverside as follows:

> Fosdick understood that his vision of an interdenominational, interracial, and international congregation would necessitate an inclusive, diverse and open-minded worship ethos. Public worship required the same freedom of expression, and once again the members themselves determined the pattern. Every variety of worship was represented in the congregation, ranging from the simple Quaker meeting to the highly ritualized services of the Greek Orthodox Church. In between fell all the denominational preferences that have so fractured rather than enriched Protestantism. Some believed in infant baptism, others in immersion, and others in verbal confession of faith; some were accustomed to the congregational preaching service followed in most nonliturgical churches, while others wanted a liturgical service without sermon, and others simply wanted silence. The

worship program expanded to make room for these variations, and by doing so, actually strengthened the sense of unity, for it dramatized the fact that many rings of worship can revolve around a common center. When members gathered in one body to share the sacrament of the Lord's Supper, they were reminded of this unity of purpose in the following words: "There are in this church many members of many denominations and many faiths. In welcoming you into our membership, we do not ask you to give up any belief or form that is dear to you but rather to bring it to us that we may be enriched thereby. We invite you not to our table or the table of any denomination, but to the Lord's Table".[12]

Fosdick wanted people to bring their own traditions together in the worship life of the congregation. He was committed to freedom of conscience. A preacher by trade, he also wanted to cultivate a broader sense of worship than the Reformed emphasis on the spoken word. He made sure the architecture of the new building created an atmosphere of awe but also wanted people to be active participants in the liturgy. He once wrote:

Beauty is a roadway to God. Our characteristic Protestant tradition has too much neglected that fact and has relied too exclusively on talking. It has often reduced worship to a few exercises of devotion appended to a sermon. Such a starvation diet will not serve rightly the needs of the spiritual life and we should rejoice that we are to have a structure made for worship, conducive to worship, in which worship can be made beautiful and effective.

Too commonly our Protestant congregations come to church, as they go to a lecture, to have somebody talk to them. They do not come to do something themselves—to worship and so be carried out of themselves by something greater than themselves to which they give themselves. They come in the passive voice instead of the active. Worship, however, is not a function which the minister can perform for the congregation—it is a cooperative act in which all the congregation should partake ... Especially in our case, where so many casual visitors are present in our services, we need to lay this matter to heart. We want everyone who enters our church to be hushed and inspired by the spirit which pervades our worship. Let us not be afraid—as so many Protestants are—of outward expression of devotion, kneeling in prayer if we feel like it, and certainly joining actively and heartily in the services.[13]

Fosdick was a theological pragmatist. He crafted sermons to help people with their everyday problems.[14] In fact, he envisioned the preaching event as "individual consultation on a group scale, intended to achieve results".[15] As one of his homiletics professors, Francis Carmody, taught him, a sermon is like a closing argument at a legal trial and so one should "preach for a verdict".[16]

Fosdick was succeeded by Robert J. McCracken, who in turn was followed by Ernest T. Campbell. Each lent his own emphasis to the style of the worship and other programs, but the tradition of wedding intellectual analysis of social issues to direct action on the part of the congregation remained characteristic of the church. At the same time, with all of its liberal leanings, the congregation remained wealthy, mainstream, and white.

The Riverside Church like most other Protestant churches had followed the periodic migrations of its congregations, but it had left the slums, the immigrants, and the lower income classes behind. By the time it reached Riverside, it was not, as public rumor had it, the rich man's as much as the professional man's church—teachers, doctors, students, and white collar workers. Ironically, the slums and immigrants were not far from its doors, but labor's representatives were quite noticeably absent.[17]

George Younger, former chair of the Worship Commission (one of the congregation's five governing bodies) and a "cradle Riversider", identifies the reading of the Black Manifesto by James Forman on Sunday 4 May 1969 as a turning point in relation to the racial composition of the congregation.[18] He contends that Forman's disruption of worship to challenge white churches to recognize their complicity in societal racism and to respond with repentance and monetary reparations brought Riverside to the attention of larger portions of the black community. Whether traceable directly to Forman's action or not, the number of African-American members grows steadily from this period.

William Sloane Coffin, Jr., assumed the position of Senior Pastor in 1977. He was not on the list of candidates during the search after Campbell's retirement. His name was added when he came as a guest preacher and, to the aging congregation's astonishment, filled the room with young people. His commitment to nuclear disarmament provided a focus for the congregation's activism. His dynamic preaching also brought in many new members. Under Coffin, people came to Riverside to participate in the actions to foster social justice, even if they were uncomfortable with traditional faith language. Sally Norris, a Minister for Older Adults and Worship, describes the differences between the ethos of Riverside under Coffin and what one finds today:

> Riverside is changing from a Christ-centered church to a Jesus-centered one. The primary tension in the current diversity is theological and not cultural. Under Coffin, the emphasis was on internal transformation that was expressed in outward and visible works. A majority of those joining today want to worship expressively but are more personal about the consequences of faith.[19]

Riverside remains one of the best known churches in the country. It was the site of Martin Luther King, Jr.'s famous Vietnam sermon on 4 April 1967 in which he "proclaimed America to be the greatest purveyor of violence in the world today".[20] It is the place where Nelson Mandela appeared on 22 June 1990 while on his first visit to the United States after his release after twenty-seven years of imprisonment in South Africa. It is a church home for many denominational leaders. This prominence carries with it a responsibility to set an example for other US mainline Protestant churches. Riverside continued in this leadership role by naming, in 1989, The Rev. Dr. James A. Forbes as Senior Minister. Forbes is the first African-American to receive a call to this prestigious pulpit. With the calling of Forbes, Riverside made an important step in embodying its principles. Barbara Butler, a long-standing member, Day School staff person and Chair of The Usher Board, describes reaction to Forbes in this way:

When Jim came along, it was the right time. Calling a black minister made people feel
good. They thought he would be just like them…but he's not. His being here is making
people face their own racism.[21]

Forbes not only brings a new heritage to the pulpit he also brings different
theological and liturgical leanings than his predecessors. Forbes was raised in
a Pentecostal denomination, The United Holy Church of America. He joined the
American Baptist denomination in conjunction with his acceptance of the position,
but his roots in the younger, charismatic denomination continue to influence his
manner. Susan Chin, former Chair of the Trustees, says:

> I often do not like Jim's preaching but I understand that he is constrained by the situation
> here. I would just like him to be himself. People were surprised by who he turned out to
> be. At the time of the search, there was a cry for more biblically-based, spiritual preaching
> but, now that we have that, there are many who miss the worldly-wise Coffin.[22]

From the time the edifice was completed, Riverside has been a Protestant
pilgrimage site. The sanctuary was meant to welcome, and has always welcomed at
least as many visitors as members each Sunday. Now Riverside has the opportunity
to exemplify good multicultural worship. Barbara Butler, on the Riverside video
Acting on Faith, states: "I want Riverside to stand as a beacon on a hill as a mixed
community, a diverse community".[23]

Multicultural congregations are a relatively new phenomenon. With some
exceptions, since the end of the Civil War, African-Americans and European-
Americans have worshiped in segregated communities and in different styles.
Members of other racial/ethnic groups have also tended to maintain their own distinct
worship traditions. Changing demographics, financial concerns, and the continued
diversification of this nation assure, however, that the number of multicultural
communities will continue to grow. Multicultural communities need examples such
as Riverside to understand the inevitable tensions of living with diversity. Riverside
because of its high visibility can also serve as a place to experiment with and hold
discussion around possible solutions to the tensions. Also on the video, Forbes
states:

> In the last decade, Riverside influenced this country's policy in the area of disarmament.
> Today, we have the opportunity to make an impact on this nation around issues of race and
> class, and in tensions over sexual orientation, to demonstrate that there is a richness and a
> power in diversity. We who are the children of God belong in one family. And, even if we
> have been separated, we come here to discover what has divided us and what the path is
> toward our walking together again. That is vintage Riverside.[24]

In terms of the current worship style, *Prayers from Riverside*, a collection of
prayer texts by each of the senior ministers and two other staff members, reveals
many of the same characteristics that Fosdick bequeathed to Riverside. The prayers
remain occasional, pastoral, activist, practical, and situational. Leo Thorne, who
compiled the collection, writes:

This interdenominational, interracial, international church espouses a social interpretation of the gospel which affirms that the message of Jesus Christ is vitally concerned with all aspects of life, whether they be spiritual, moral, political, economic, or cultural.[25]

The order of service follows a general outline that is recognizably Reformed. It is a formalized preaching order which consists in preparation (entering, calling, confessing), the sharing of scripture and reflection (reading, preaching), and responding (praying, announcing, giving, leaving). Music bridges the various parts, communicates spiritual insight, sets pace and mood, provides beauty to be enjoyed, and is one medium through which a variety of cultural groups can contribute to the worship. The texts of the service are mainly occasional: the rite of confession, the pastoral prayer, the call and benediction are crafted according to the theme or occasion each Sunday. Communion is celebrated monthly. The eucharistic prayer now in use is carefully structured. It is the work of leaders of the ecumenical movement, who attended Riverside while working in various denominational offices in The Interchurch Center just across the street.

Recent changes in the demographics of the membership has called this worship tradition into question. Since Forbes' arrival, the church has attracted a growing number of African-American, Hispanic, and Asian members, while also experiencing some measure of "white flight". Diverse communities need images to help them orient their journey towards a fully inclusive shared life. Forbes reflects on two metaphors that have shaped his own vision of the congregation's life together. The biblical images of a banquet and the pearl of great price provide contrasting perspectives on the dynamics between sub-groups in a mixed congregation.

Forbes notes, first, how Jesus commented on the dynamics in evidence at a meal that he attended, challenging the host to rethink the guest list:

> But when you give a banquet, invite the poor, the crippled, the lame, and the blind. And you will be blessed, because they cannot repay you, for you will be repaid at the resurrection of the righteous. (Luke 14:13)

Jesus's story emphasizes values such as inclusivity, equality, hospitality, and festivity. Encouraging to diverse congregations, the metaphor indicates that all types of people should gather together around the Lord's table.

However, for Forbes, the image stops short of full integration. Jesus challenged those who used their banquet tables to reflect, rather than serve as an alternative to, hierarchies of social status. Today, many who have opened their tables remain stuck in the static roles of host and guest. In one dynamic common in congregations that are shifting from "monocultural" to "multicultural", the host group shares its table, and often its physical plant, out of the security of its bounty upon which the guests are dependent. The guests do not seem to be permanent fixtures at the host's table, much less adopted family members. The poor, crippled, lame, and blind come to dinner because they cannot repay their host. The host is promised great reward later. Yet, what happens to the guests after the meal? They are fed and entertained but then, apparently, they must return to the same struggle for survival from which they came before the meal.

Relating the story to Riverside's situation, Forbes puts it this way:

From the beginning this congregation made a commitment to diversity but did not live
that commitment out. It was a one class and race church and its values kept it that way...
When Bill Coffin came, the congregation was 70% white and 30% black; when he left
the numbers were 60 and 40. Yet, in all this time, essentially, black people were invited
into white ways. Whites felt magnanimous. Blacks felt the elation of assimilation. In
1989, they called me. I was a powerful symbol that ideological commitment had not been
enough. But, when I arrived, it was clear that although people were committed to this
symbolic move, it was still painful for them to accept my differences. I came to an activist
church as one who could add something—a strong faith commitment. People seemed to
want that, but my presence was still disorienting. I meant to offer my talents as a gift, but
it was a gift that was hard to accept. Molding diversity into a new whole sounds good but
is a difficult process for those who are used to being in charge.[26]

As the host of the banquet, white Riversiders welcomed African Americans into
membership. But it was an invitation of assimilation and not true partnership; the
invited remained guests, not family members.

Many parishes face questions about how to structure the interaction of various
groups of people. For those who seek motivation to reach out to neighbors who are
different, the banquet can be a helpful image. But for those who attempt to form a
unified community out of diverse groups, the image may reinforce divisions and
leave untouched differences of power between the older and newer member groups.
If the banquet is the central image of a diverse community, the most likely result is a
multicongregational church rather than an integrated multicultural one.[27]

Forbes suggests that the image of the pearl of great price supports a different
dynamic:

> ... the kingdom of heaven is like a merchant in search of fine pearls; on finding one pearl
> of great value, he went and sold all that he had and bought it. (Matthew 13:45–46)

The story of the pearl addresses the important, but often neglected, issue of cost.
The pearl is not found but bought. In the same way, the creation of community
among people of different races and classes will entail cost. For long-term members
comfortable patterns will need to be left behind. Historic arguments will need to be
replayed. Dynamics of relation will have to be re-tooled. Old wounds will have to
be allowed to heal and forgiveness asked for and granted. New talents may have to
be sought—musicians, dancers, visual artists, speakers, poets. Consultants may also
charge fees. Preparation will grow more complex and time-consuming. What costs
will be considered worth the riches of diverse and authentic community? Who will
pay? Forbes told me this story:

> A child went to the home of a friend for the evening. The host child had a new fire engine
> which, of course, both children wanted to play with. The two of them fought over the toy
> all evening long. The play date ended quickly and with hard feelings. The next week, the
> child returned to her friend's house. This time, however, she brought with her a truck of
> her own. The children got along famously, handing the toys back and forth to each other.
> They both had a wonderful time. Riverside is like these two children. Those who are used
> to being in control experience sharing as giving up unless they see what the "other" brings
> as a gift of value.[28]

In contrast to the image of the heavenly banquet, which disparages any notion of reciprocity, the image of the pearl of great price is about mutual worth. To acquire the pearl, the merchant must sell all he has. Both the merchant's former possessions and the pearl have value. Just so, the toy of the host and the toy of the guest have value. White and black, long-time member and newcomer, must all recognize value in both what was and what might be. Fosdick's eucharistic prayer invited members of many faiths to share rather than leave behind beliefs and forms that were dear to them. Subsequent history has shown how difficult it is to honor a multiplicity of gifts equally.

Riverside has a history of activist faith. As the congregation becomes increasingly diverse, however, this single dominant presupposition becomes increasingly tenuous. Many new members are drawn from sectors of the population that have suffered under oppressive societal structures to a greater degree than Riversiders of old. The emphasis on justice action in the context of the wider city, nation, and world must now be balanced with increased attention to pastoral and community needs. Today, Riverside faces an opportunity to live out the principles of its liturgical and theological heritage in new ways.

The Worship Roundtable: Formation and Process

In the spring of 1993, Forbes asked Union Theological Seminary Professors Robert Seaver (Speech and Drama), Janet Walton (Worship), and James Washington (History) to serve as consultants for a group of lay and clergy who wanted to discuss and plan worship together. Forbes' motivation for analysis was based on some unrest, his own and others, that his style of worship leadership was not compatible with the expectations of some members of the congregation. The Worship Commission, with Sarah Cunningham as chair, agreed that the time was right to look closely at the worship program.

With the agreement of the consultants and approval by the Commission, The Worship Roundtable was established. It included the members of the Worship Commission, clergy representatives, the Director of Music and Organist, and several at-large members.[29] The group included seven people of European-American descent, four African Americans, one Asian American, and one Hispanic American.

The initial proposal indicates an intention to prepare and perform six liturgies in the fall of 1993, but this idea was quickly abandoned as "too much too soon". The group instead began discussing worship and their own devotional preferences. Forbes remembers:

> The first phase provided a unique and much needed opportunity for sustained conversation about the liturgy. Within this, there were some brief glimpses of the oppression that results from cultural elitism. There began to be some recognition that even good intentions could be a problem. It was surely seen that insistence on one's own preferences could get embarrassing. The Roundtable provided an opportunity for all to speak. In a strange twist of fate, this phase actually gave me more freedom to speak my mind than I had yet felt. Riverside is odd in that although the senior pastor has freedom to use the pulpit as he sees fit (still knowing that his teachings will be *considered*, not accepted outright, by

the congregation), he is expected to yield in many other arenas. In the Roundtable, since every one else got to speak their mind, I did too.[30]

Out of these personal conversations grew a new plan to prepare two liturgies: one in February and the other at Pentecost of 1994. These initial efforts were well received. They provided examples of a coherent service that drew upon a wide variety of cultural traditions. The Pentecost service, in particular, generated a lot of enthusiasm. Several members asked if the "first Annual" Pentecost service would be repeated, showing their approval of the effort and their proclivity to turn the unusual into tradition.

In spite of this positive response, the Roundtable failed to reconvene until December of 1994. During this hiatus, discussions about the next phase were occurring, however. Seaver insisted that the planning of services continue and suggested that a series of four services in a row be tried. The Roundtable agreed to this suggestion and took responsibility for four services in February and March 1995. They began the planning process as a large group and formed consensus around a "spine" upon which all the groups would build their services.[31] The large group then divided into four smaller groups to focus on the individual services.

Each planning group met weekly for the four weeks prior to the service. The first meeting consisted of reading the lectionary texts together and brainstorming about what they might mean to the members of Riverside today. The second meeting again focused on the texts but with a goal of choosing an image or theme that would bind the service together. At the third meeting, an order of service had to be drafted and parts assigned to individuals to script. The fourth meeting occurred the day before the service and was a rehearsal of the entire service.

Each of the planning groups consisted of two or three lay members of the Roundtable, two clergy, Walton and Seaver as consultants, and one at-large lay person from outside the Roundtable (to foster a larger base of support for the process among the congregation). Each group was given control of their own service. There was no attempt to create an over-arching theme or progression for the series as a whole. The only restrictions were to begin with the texts as presented by the lectionary, to utilize the schematic structure agreed to in January, and to abide by the established calendar. This required that on 12 February there would be baptisms; 19 February would include a guest preacher and the welcoming of new members; and on 5 March communion would be celebrated. 26 February was the one day free of any prior obligations.

The series of services at Riverside provide a great deal of data for those who would now seek to reformulate Riverside's worship program to meet the needs of the congregation today. Services of worship need to be interpreted in the overlapping contexts of denominational ethos, congregational history, local theology, various cultural norms, and social setting. It is also crucial to interpret not just the text of the liturgy even if it is a complete written record of what was done, but also its performance. Observation of the skill, or lack thereof, of various participants, the ad-libs and miscues, the gestural activity that accompanies the words, and the qualities of the relationships among those present is a vital part of liturgical criticism. Here, I simply note two examples from the Roundtable experience.

In the service of baptism on 12 February 1995, a child was initiated by sprinkling, then an adult was sprinkled, and then five adults were immersed. A place where three different forms of the sacrament can all happen in one service is remarkable. Riverside somehow lives in the tension of difference without getting lost in it. Such variety can also be chaotic, of course. Some services feel more like a series of events than an integrated drama. Yet, each Sunday, Riverside demonstrates how the Body, with all of its many members, somehow manages to function. The ongoing task is to ensure, to the extent possible, that no one part lords itself over others, that all are honored, and that the contribution of each is respected. This can only be accomplished through vigilant observation of what occurs Sunday to Sunday: who speaks, what is sung, how everything fits together, and who controls the decisions. Riverside's ability to function in the midst of theological and cultural multiplicity is an important model for other churches.

Second, members of the Riverside community hold quite disparate attitudes toward liturgical time. There are several Riversiders, a couple of whom sit on the Roundtable, who are clock watchers. They time the service each week and let Forbes know when his sermon or some other part of the service exceeded the allotments they prefer. While the timing of the service should be subject to some standard to which the community can agree, the cultural norms governing the perception of liturgical time must also be clarified. Different cultural groups with different histories and different liturgical sensibilities perceive time differently. In a place like Riverside, it is important to note that the historical experience of African Americans encourages a perception of church as a place of freedom unlike any other available to them in a racist society and so a few extra hours there are welcomed, not resented. Of course, not all African Americans share a desire to spend large portions of their Sunday in church, but less rather than more concern with the number of minutes allocated to worship can be considered a cultural norm for this group. European Americans, especially those in positions of relative socio-economic security, are less inclined to give over control of their calendars to the spontaneous flow of service (which, of course, can be either Spirit- or personality-driven). Forbes offers this perspective:

> Until white people know that Black worship takes time because it is meant to be more than a nod to each other and God and until black people understand how threatening changing the time structure of worship is to white people, we will not come to any common ground about this. I would like to see a series of events based on one-on-one conversations on topics such as time so that we will start to listen to each other more deeply. People will then see that they must all decide what is more important to them, comfort or interaction across difference.[32]

The series of services required an enormous amount of energy from Roundtable members. So much so that they effectively served as the end of the group's life. Follow-up was meager. The Roundtable provided evaluation forms so that the community could respond to the series, but the questions were not sufficiently specific and no demographic information was required of respondents to help in the interpretation of the answers. In any case, the data collected were never analyzed. Further exploration of alternative "spines" did not continue either. The Roundtable experience reveals the difficulty of maintaining the energy necessary for on-going experimentation and evaluation. The worship program was opened a bit. The experiments created more room for subsequent innovation but primarily on a sporadic basis. Both obstacles and the promise of more inclusive forms of public prayer within the Riverside context remain.

A Scholar's Role: Turning to History

George Younger wanted one result of the Roundtable process to be a statement defining worship at Riverside. He contends that a community engaged in worship reform should state a common understanding of what worship is.[33] No consensus statement was developed, however. The Roundtable did agree on a worship schematic of "God, us, and beyond".[34] Little time was spent in discussion about the history of Riverside's worship, and the traditions that lie behind it. Both phenomenological and historical resources are needed to support liturgical adaptation in any community, but such data is crucial in diverse congregations where shared history and vocabulary cannot be assumed.

In addition, the Roundtable process assumed that *a* multicultural order of service could be created and that such an order would allow everyone enough comfort and freedom to worship authentically with everyone else. Observing the process, I came to disagree with the assumption. From my perspective, the order is not the problem nor is a new order the solution. The Riverside spine is a basic three-fold Reformed Service of the Word: preparation, texts and sermon, response. No one disagrees with this basic structure. Black, white, Hispanic, and Asian churches all over the country use this same order. But few services in churches dominated by one group or another feel the same. My suggestion is that factors such as performative style, understandings of time and space, and perspectives shaped by a group's social location, rather than preferences about the order, distinguish the cultural style of a community's service. At a place like Riverside, there are many aspects of culture (such as language and geography) shared among all groups. There are also important aspects of each cultural tradition (such as music and art) that are distinct.

The existence of distinct, and competing, cultural understandings of time in worship, noted above, is but one question that begs for elaboration and reconciliation in diverse communities that wish to share public prayer together. Such questions also harbor assumptions about why distinctions exist between, and among, members of various racial/ethnic groups. It is to these deeper questions that I turn and a historical response that I seek to provide.

African-American and European-American liturgical traditions have grown up together. Their attributes are based, in part, on their mutual influence. Both African-American and European-American Protestant liturgical traditions are adaptations of Western European Christianity. Both remain loyal to many of the received practices. They also made some similar adjustments to the shared environment of colonial North America. There are also examples of times and places where blacks and whites worshiped together, and these interactions resulted in mutual influence between the two.

At the same time, there are many differences between black and white traditions. Distinctions between the worldviews of African Americans and European Americans derives, in part, from the manner in which the two groups have combined the shared resources of Western Christianity with other religious and cultural traditions, and, most importantly, the values of African Traditional Religion. US Christianity, like all other manifestations of religions, combines inherited traditions and cultural values and idioms. As I noted above, the interaction of blacks and whites has resulted in cultural borrowings so that even the most uptight white church has traces, however minute, of African-American cultural idioms. Certainly, the Black Church(es), and especially southern Afro-Baptist and Pentecostal traditions, exhibit significant African survivals. African influences pervade US Protestantism but the concentrations vary considerably between various churches. Further, white racism stratifies US society and has ensured that despite mutual influence, the contrast between African-American and European-American worldviews, modes of expression, and theo-ethical norms has been exacerbated.

Communities with African-American and European-American members have to contend with the tension that these groups have both a shared and distinct cultures. African Americans and European Americans have lived together on this continent for 400 years. But they have done so from different social locations. Because they live on the underside of this history, African-American traditions embody an ethical critique of European-American worship, and while not free from their own flaws, stand as an alternative interpretation of how Christians might pray. The narratives which follow attempt to highlight contrasting characteristics of the two families of traditions in order to help communities with black and white members understand and negotiate the barriers to communication across lines of difference. Praying together will entail acceptance of difference, the risk of further mutual influence, and the necessity of further ethical critique of the norms of each culture. Shared worship implies that the community aims for the promised unity of the baptized community, one new culture, a local manifestation of the multicultural Body of Christ.

The text which follows traces the development of Protestant worship among whites and blacks. I intend to show that: (1) African-American and European-American Protestant liturgical traditions are both interdependent and distinct; and (2) multicultural communities must both understand and celebrate the uniqueness of various member groups and accept the risk and possibility of praying themselves into an integrated Body, one new culture. To this end, I offer narratives of the history of African-American Protestant worship, European-American Protestant worship, and four examples of previous occasions of biracial worship. I conclude by reflecting on the implications of these narratives for the discipline of liturgical theology.

Chapter 2 traces the contours of African-American Protestant liturgical traditions. After introducing the religious innovations of slaves in the "invisible institution", I identify the two major sub-divisions which exist to this day. The first I call the *classical*. This stream originates in the independent churches founded by free blacks in the North in the late eighteenth century and is characterized by tensions between poles such as integration and nationalism, African and European norms, protest and accommodation. The second stream, the *improvisational,* preserves the ritual legacy of the "invisible institution" in southern Afro-Baptist communities, and has flowered again in the Pentecostal movement. This stream is more fiercely independent, more prone to ecstatic forms of ritualizing, and aims more often to heal and shelter members of marginal communities than to engage in direct political or social action. I conclude by noting both the interdependence and distinctiveness of these sub-traditions and important characteristics of African-American religious practice, such as the ability to weave cultural materials into new cloth, the ubiquity of both substantial congregational participation and demonstrative responses to God's presence, and the prophetic critique of religious justifications of racism.

Chapter 3 offers a parallel analysis of the history of European-American Protestant liturgical practice. Again, I identify two major sub-traditions, the *mainline* and the *enthusiast*. The former comprises churches that were founded as traditions of protest in the context of European Christianity but became the central religious institutions of the North American colonies. The worship of these traditions is characterized by stable orders, relatively restrained responses by the laity to Word and Sacrament, and cycles of restoration and innovation in response to shifting cultural norms. The *enthusiast* tradition is linked to American evangelicalism and assumes a more experiential approach to religious practice, is highly adaptable to new cultural situations, and exhibits a high degree of pragmatism in liturgical reform efforts. Again, the streams are shown to be interdependent and distinct. In sum, European-American Protestant liturgical traditions are characterized by their ability to adjust to historical and cultural changes, to maintain themselves as hegemonic ideologies in the face of criticism as they uphold structures of race and class privilege, and to function as a bolster for US mainstream culture by forging a racial group (so-called "unhyphenated whites") out of a variety of ethnic sub-cultures and by forming individualistic and consumption oriented citizens.

Chapter 4 considers the relationship of the four streams defined in Chapter 2 and Chapter 3 and discusses four examples of previous occasions of biracial worship. In the frontier camp meetings, the antebellum Baptist and Methodist churches, the plantation missions, and the early stages of the Pentecostal movement, blacks and whites worshiped together. While fleeting, and, for the most part, not based upon notions of racial equality, these occasions do contain important lessons for communities in the present day with both African-American and European-American members.

I conclude, in Chapter 5, by returning to the discipline of liturgical theology. The journey from Riverside back into the past to find lessons for multicultural communities who seek to worship authentically takes us full circle. I begin with a church struggling with the difficult issues of how to address the reality of growing cultural diversity in worship. I end by arguing that liturgical theology should serve the development of a plurality of local authentic worship traditions instead of imposing any one "shape" of Christian public prayer onto the traditions of local communities. The Body of Christ is multicultural both in an ideal and an empirical sense. It is this Body that worship serves as Christians celebrate God's activity among them. The local Body that is, or desires to be, faithfully multicultural, despite the obstacles of cultural difference and the history of oppression that has divided us for so long, steps in a new and risky direction, relying on God's promises to break down the dividing wall and make many into one.

CHAPTER 2

"Once You were No People ... Now You are God's People":
An Analytical Narrative of the Construction of African-American Protestant Liturgical Traditions

African-American worship is the ritualized legacy of persons who have lived for nearly four hundred years in a nation in which they persevere and thrive even as they continue to suffer discrimination and scorn because of the color of their skin. Africans were brought to this country as chattel, beasts of burden. Their captors tore them from their families, land, and religious traditions, forcing them to construct anew the meaning-making structures of human existence. A random group of individuals thrown together in the terror of kidnapping, sale and bondage, Africans in the North American colonies of Great Britain forged themselves into a people.[1] Together they established new religious practices that reflected their condition, provided comfort and healing in the midst of daily trauma, and offered a vision of an alternative future that empowered them to join and sustain their struggle for liberation.

The analysis that follows cannot convey the full richness of African-American Protestant liturgical traditions. The aim of this chapter is to describe the contours of the history of African-American liturgical traditions crucial to interracial understanding. I identify major sub-divisions and themes of African-American Protestant practices, primarily, to help multicultural communities with African-American members craft inclusive liturgies. By generalizing, I risk caricaturing those I seek to honor. I accept the risk that naming common traits among African-American worship traditions may be interpreted as stereotyping and proceed.

In this chapter, I limit my analysis to African-American Protestants in the US. Africans on the continent and elsewhere in Diaspora practice a variety of religious traditions with contrasting and yet related ritual traditions. Comment on the complexity of African ritual traditions is beyond the scope of this project, however.[2] I also must narrow the scope of investigation among African-American Protestants. While some interdenominational and nondenominational exceptions exist, generally, African-American local churches belong either to denominations controlled by African Americans or to institutions belonging to European Americans. Independent black denominations best represent the African-American adaptations of Protestant worship. I concentrate on these churches, acknowledging that both similarities and differences exist in relation to the worship of black congregations in institutions that are majority white. Lincoln and Mamiya utilize similar principles to limit the scope of their sociological study of African-American religious institutions. They, and I following them, call the historically independent African-American denominations the "Black Church", and focus on these institutions in their work.[3]

African Americans created their own version of Christianity as they developed a sense of themselves as black people, a people destined not for continued victimization but for freedom and dignity as full citizens of their new land. African-American Protestant worship has served the needs of the African-American community, while, in fact, forging the community itself out of a variety of peoples. African-American Protestant worship traditions are distinct from those of other Christians because they have been created for and by an oppressed group in a racist society. African-American Protestant worship combines practices from both Africa and Europe into a unique and coherent whole that produces meaning and power for its participants.

Two major streams exist within the history of African-American Protestant worship. I designate them: the *classical* and the *improvisational*.[4] The history of independent African-American Protestant worship begins with the so-called Second Great Awakening circa 1790.[5] At this time, European and European-American missionaries begin to attract significant numbers of slaves to the Christian religion. The slaves, and free blacks, adapted the religion of their masters to suit their own ends. These adaptations took two primary forms. The *classical* stream straddles the characteristic divide of African-American existence, supporting racial pride and solidarity while also participating fully in the wider society, being both African and American. The liturgies of this stream reveal a marked ambiguity toward African and slave practices. They both celebrate African-American uniqueness and cultivate mainstream values in the cause of assimilation. The *classical* stream balances spontaneity and order, exuberance and discipline. The *improvisational* stream emphasizes more of the distinct attributes of African-American culture, especially modes of spirit possession. The liturgies of this stream preserve and celebrate the African and slave traditions that survive within African-American culture and are less concerned with assimilation. The *improvisational* stream performs an alternative to the world of white America and celebrates the vital connection between the Spirit and African-American saints, both living and dead. I will discuss the development of these two streams in turn, but, first, I describe key characteristics of the seed-bed of all African-American Protestant worship: slave religion.

Slave Religion: The Seedbed of African-American Protestant Worship

Africans sold into the slave system of the "New World" colonies confronted a spiritual crisis. Torn violently from home, family, country and continent, destined if not for an early death then for a life of perpetual servitude, captured Africans stood face to face with the terror of non-personhood.[6] The journey across the sea as a jumbled mass of humanity packed so as to discourage bonds of family and language added to the disorientation.[7] North American slavery ensnared members of many different tribes and nations. West Africans practiced their own versions of slavery in the seventeenth and eighteenth centuries.[8] But the rupture of being taken forcibly off the continent of one's birth, the lack of legal rights accorded slaves in the Americas, and, especially, the lack of any hope of freedom for oneself or one's descendants made entry into this web of horror categorically different.

Men and women were thrust into the holds of ships, united only in dread and hatred of those who dared to buy and sell them as livestock. Slavery not only tore its victims from their homes and families, but also from their familiar religious cultus. Captivity prevented slaves from full participation in traditional religious practices, but slaveholders also suppressed even those modest rites that could be continued in the new context of bondage.[9] In the face of this crisis, the Africans began the construction of a new worldview. The slaves slowly accepted and transformed the symbols of the only religious system available to them, the Christianity of their owners.[10] The slaves embroidered the stories and rites of the religion of their masters according to their own designs. James Cone writes: "[Black religion] ... is a spiritual vision about the reconstruction of a new humanity wherein people are no longer defined by oppression but by freedom".[11]

Cone makes the further claim that this reconstruction is ritually based. Through ritual actions such as preaching, singing, praying, undergoing conversion, and shouting, black people experience "liberation no longer [as] a future event, but as a present happening in the worship itself".[12] The slaves combined African traditions, European Christianity and the insights of living in bondage to construct worship traditions that celebrate freedom and thereby empower the people to resist oppression.

Five periods are evident in the history of slave religion. From 1619–1725, North American slavocracy took shape; African practices were suppressed; and missionaries made initial but ultimately unsuccessful attempts to attract slaves to Christianity. From 1725–1760, the First Great Awakening swept down from New England and through the South. While affecting mostly white colonists, slaves heard egalitarian strains in revival preaching. After the American Revolution, the Methodist and Baptist missionaries of the Second Great Awakening attracted large numbers of slaves to Christianity, independent congregations formed, and the rhetoric of inalienable rights offered a vision of emancipation that would not be fulfilled. After 1800, the repression of independent black worship and the accommodation of the gospel to slavery among southern whites, and many northerners, too, made necessary the secret practice of slave religion in what Raboteau has named the "invisible institution".[13] Finally, slave worship in the "invisible institution" reached mature form as the Civil War approached.

Africans to Slaves

Africans came to the so-called New World with Spanish explorers in the sixteenth century. The first Africans recorded as being sold as slaves in North America were a group of 40 men and women brought to Jamestown, Virginia in 1619.[14] The North American slave trade affected vast numbers of Africans. Berry and Blassingame write:

> The first Africans arrived in the New World in 1502; by the time the slave trade ended in the 1860's, more than 100 million blacks had either been killed or transported from their

homeland. Although statistics on the trade are imprecise, it appears that from 400,000 to 1 million of the 10 to 50 million Africans forcibly transported to the Americas came to North America between 1619 and 1808, when the legal slave trade ended.[15]

In the first century of British settlement, settlers throughout the colonies owned slaves. Vermont, the first free state, did not pass its emancipation laws until 1770. Richard Allen, the founder of the African Methodist Episcopal Church, was born a slave in Philadelphia before the Pennsylvania laws of 1780 began a gradual process of weaning its white citizens from the luxury of slave labor. 90 per cent of African peoples resided in the South until after the Civil War, and the plantation system was unique in the efficiency of its exploitation.

In North and South, at the very inception of the slave trade, slaveholders recognized the connection between African religious practices and revolts and so suppressed the African rites.[16] Henry Mitchell argues that slaves may have considered the Christian God worthy of attention because their own Gods did not protect them from capture.[17] In any case, the slaves' traditional practices did quickly lose recognizable shape.[18] Yet scholars such as Peter Paris believe it is possible to trace continuities in African-American spirituality to Mother Africa. He writes:

> … the traditions of African people both on the continent and in the diaspora are diverse in cultural form yet united in their underlying spirituality. The former is evidenced mostly by the differences of language and other cultural mores. The latter is seen in the broad consensus among African peoples that the three forms of life, namely, nature, history, and spirit are ontologically united and hence interdependent.[19]

Africans could not continue their familiar ways of life in the American colonies. Their owners destroyed their kinship structures, outlawed their rituals, and threatened their very identities. Yet, the slave system could not put an end to the slaves' desire for freedom, nor could it steal their memories of Africa, their conception of the unity of all life, their storytelling techniques, aphorisms, folk wisdom, or music.[20] The African slaves reshaped the religion of their masters as it was offered to them. They adopted the stories of the Bible actively and creatively. They discovered points of continuity between African cosmology and Christian doctrine, such as the existence of a High God, multiple forms of divinity, and the importance of worship to religious observance.[21] Slaves not only found familiar ground in the Christian mythos but brought from their own traditions an emphasis on the liberative themes of Christian teachings. Cone writes: "When Christianity was introduced to slaves, Africans converted it to their religious heritage, by refusing to accept any version of the gospel that did not harmonize with the African spirit of freedom".[22]

The conversion of slaves to Christianity was neither quick nor simple. The first record of the baptism of Africans in the British colonies dates to 1623.[23] But few Africans accepted Christianity as their own religion during the first century of American slavery. The early missionaries were Anglicans whose polity placed significant restrictions on the worship of converts. In 1701, the Church of England established the Society for the Propagation of the Gospel in Foreign Parts to bring the gospel to Africans and Native Americans in North America.[24] Anglican missionaries emphasized an educational approach to conversion and required potential converts to spend a good deal of time in classes which slaveholders were reluctant to allow. They also expected converts to have facility in English, which the Africans were slowly acquiring.[25] In addition, slave-owners did not permit extensive mission work until laws clearly established that baptism did not qualify slaves for manumission.[26]

Slaves who did convert were discouraged if not explicitly prohibited from worshiping separately from whites, or at least without some white supervision.[27] Not until 1693 is there record of a separate worship service of an African-American congregation.[28] Mechal Sobel has shown the extensive interdependence of white and black religious practice in seventeenth-century Virginia due to the intimacy of masters and slaves in plantation life and the shared experience of biracial worship.[29] The whites who hosted the first African-American converts controlled the worship of the community but African influences began to permeate the Euro-centric environment. African-American Protestant worship in the first century of slavery hinted at the extent of subsequent independent adaptations.

African Spirituality and Methodist Egalitarian Enthusiasm

George Whitefield arrived in North America in 1738.[30] Through Whitefield, slaves received their first exposure to Christianity's liberative potential. His egalitarian impulses attracted slaves. He writes to his white audience:

> Think you, your children are in any way better by nature than the poor negroes? No! In no wise! Blacks are just as much, and no more, conceived and born in sin, as white men are; and both, if born and bred up here, I am persuaded, are naturally capable of the same achievement.[31]

Whitefield preached in New England and the South. Early on, he opposed slavery and actively said so. He preached to and baptized some slaves but most blacks had neither the desire nor the option to convert during this period. And, then, as we shall see repeated again and again, Whitefield modified his anti-slavery stance in the face of white opposition.[32]

The First Great Awakening introduced sweeping changes to European-American Protestant worship. American Evangelical Christianity emerged out of the highly popular innovations of Whitefield and his missionary colleagues. Among African Americans, the First Great Awakening opened a door. Few entered the churches as converts, but many took a second look at the religion of their masters. Whitefield's dramatic style of preaching, his expectation of embodied response among his listeners, and his message of the radical equality of all people before God became mainstays of African-American Christianity. Slaves converted to Christianity not only because of the ecstatic ritual of the revivals, which reflected ritual practices of their African heritage, but also their perception of Christianity's liberative themes in sermons of the revival preachers.

The Birth of Independent African-American Christianity

During the Revolutionary Period, 1760–1800, African slaves detected a scent of freedom pervading the land and desired a portion of its perfume. They reasoned that the desire for freedom from royal authority might spread to freedom for all from tyranny. They were, of course, disappointed. Revolutionary leaders bought unified resistance to the crown at the price of silence on the issue of slavery. At the very time of the country's birth, the founders betrayed their so-called inalienable values of equality and liberty.[33]

Yet, another round of evangelization among the slaves, this time successful, commenced in this period as well. Methodists and Baptists led The Second Great Awakening (1790–1860). The Methodists were able to convert large numbers of slaves to Christianity because they approached them with zeal, encouraged them to contribute in worship, and utilized the accessible language of experience and ritual in catechesis. John and Charles Wesley had begun their movement in England as a renewal of mission efforts to the poor and working class. In North America, they sought out the same type of convert, and so not surprisingly approached African Americans. Wesley recorded his first baptism of slaves in 1758.[34] Francis Asbury, the leader of American Methodism, condemned slavery in the constitutional documents of American Methodism in 1743.[35] Asbury also traveled extensively with "Black Harry" Hoosier, renowned as an exemplar of the preaching talents of uneducated African slaves.[36] The encouragement of black preachers was a second important reason for the attraction of slaves to Christianity during the Second Great Awakening. A third was the more accessible language of faith employed by these more experientially oriented groups. Asbury encouraged preachers and ordinary believers to share personal testimony of their faith experience rather than utilize formal dogmatic formulae. Methodists also allowed for the Eucharist to serve as a means to conversion rather than a reward for proven faithfulness or doctrinal orthodoxy. Slaves, whose traditional religions were similarly expectant, welcomed the ritual-based spirituality of Methodism.

The Baptists, schismatic off-shoots of New England Puritanism, followed a congregational church structure offering slave converts local autonomy. Slaves, given the hypocrisy of their masters' religion, considered the freedom to determine the content and form of their religious practice crucial. In addition, baptism by immersion by which Baptists marked the moment of conversion stirred memories of African water rites. The rite of baptism also allowed slaves to experience the movement from oppression to freedom, at least in the religious sphere. Washington writes:

> Out of a determination to overcome the legacy of social invisibility fostered by white racism, [Black Baptists] used the liturgical power of baptism by immersion to transform "a bastard people" into a new social creation with its own cosmology.[37]

Among the Baptists, slaves and free blacks found some measure of hospitality and a larger measure of freedom to worship separately. The first African-American congregations to govern their own religious lives were Baptist communities.

During the Second Great Awakening, Methodist and Baptist evangelists, black and white, convinced large numbers of slaves to be baptized and join churches through the medium of revival worship. Revivals developed out of variety of European Protestant traditions. Evangelists refined John Wesley's innovations to suit the American terrain, elaborated on Reformed teachings requiring a period of introspective preparation before reception of the sacraments, and intensified the Puritan principles of subsidiarity and biblicism. But the coincidence of African conversions and the institution of exuberant and embodied rituals on the American scene raises questions about the contributions of slaves to these new Christian worship forms. James White admits: "Much of the vigorous active participation of the frontier worship and revivals had African precedents".[38] Mechal Sobel is bolder: "[revivals] came when and where whites were in extensive contact with blacks".[39] Slaves converted to Christianity during the Second Great Awakening because they heard in the sermons of circuit riders a message of spiritual power and because revivalists accepted and even imitated their active responses to that power.

The Repression of Black Autonomy and Biracial Worship

With the legal separation of baptism and manumission, slave-owners began to accept slave conversion.[40] Some owners supported the work of missionaries and allowed separate worship opportunities. Others used Christianity solely as an instrument of social control. White preachers notoriously misused scripture to teach slaves to renounce aspirations for freedom. Raboteau quotes from the catechism of Charles Colcock Jones: "[slaves must] … count their Masters 'worthy of all honour,' as those whom God has placed over them in the world; 'with all fear,' they are to be 'subject to them' and obey them in all things …".[41] Worship controlled by European Americans reinforced exploitative social relations. As a result, slaves worshiped independently whenever possible.

As the number of black converts grew, however, whites, even those who had formerly encouraged slaves to become Christians became fearful of separate meetings. They interfered with meetings that had formerly been allowed and inflicted severe punishments if secret meetings were discovered. Nat Turner's rebellion in 1831 provoked immediate and harsh reprisals on the free exercise of religion among slaves. Turner, inspired by the prophets of the Hebrew Bible and Christian apocalypticism, led a small group of slaves in the slaughter of fifty-seven whites in Southampton County, Virginia. In response, legislators throughout the South forbade slaves to assemble for worship and made it illegal for any black person, slave or free, to preach.[42]

Because of the increased repression after the Turner rebellion, biracial worship, common in the seventeenth century albeit before large numbers of slaves converted, again became the norm in southern churches. At the same time, the racist overtones of southern white worship became more pronounced. In opposition to increasingly strident northern abolitionists, southern Christians argued that slavery was God's means to bring the gospel to the heathens of Africa.[43]

Biracial worship in the antebellum South demonstrated forcefully the inequality between white and black people. In Anglican and Presbyterian churches the starkness of this inequality was most pronounced. Seating was most often segregated with whites in positions of prominence. Most of the service was directed exclusively at the white members with only a short reflection for the slaves on the theme, inevitably, of obedience.[44] The Eucharist was served separately to reinforce distinctions between blacks and whites. As an example, in a Presbyterian Church in Charleston, S.C., in 1814, according to the traditions of the Church of Scotland, tokens were given to members who completed the required penitential preparations for participating in communion. White members received silver coins; slaves were given pewter.[45]

White Methodists and Baptists offered greater hospitality to African-American members. John Boles writes:

> ... the lower class structure of the early Baptist and Methodist churches, most of whose members did not own slaves and felt estranged from the wealthier whites who did, enabled them to see blacks as potential fellow believers in a way that white worshipers in more elite churches seldom could. From the moment of their organization, typical Baptist or Methodist churches included black members.[46]

White Methodists and Baptists, being working class folk themselves, treated African Americans with a greater sense of equality than the wealthy members of the Anglican and Presbyterian churches. Baptists especially fostered the African-American desire for autonomous institutions and frequently allowed blacks to hold separate services, if not organize independent congregations. Poor whites and slaves shared similarly limited levels of literacy and Methodist and Baptist ministers responded by using a popular vocabulary and concrete imagery in worship. Slaves showed their appreciation for the egalitarian spirit of the Methodist and Baptist communities, but, even in mixed revivals, biracial worship could not satisfy the need for slaves to pray for their own freedom. The deepest yearnings of Christian slaves acquired full expression only beyond the ears of whites.

Worship in the "Invisible Institution"

In reaction to the restrictions on independent "visible" worship and the subordination of the gospel to white supremacist ideology in biracial services, slaves devised other venues of religious expression. Raboteau records the frustration of slaves with white preachers in a quote from Lucretia Alexander:

> The preacher came and ... [h]e'd just say, "Serve your masters. Don't steal your master's turkey. Don't steal your master's chickens. Don't steal your master's hawgs. Don't steal your master's meat. Do whatsomever your master tells you to do." Same old thing all the time. My father would have church in the dwelling houses and they had to whisper ... Sometimes they would have church at his house. That would be when they would want a real meetin' with some real preachin'... They used to sing their songs in a whisper and pray in a whisper. That was a prayer-meeting from house to house once or twice—once or twice a week.[47]

As an alternative to the self-serving worship of whites, slaves, at great risk, met together in secret, out in the brush, or down by the water, to worship in their own way. Costen writes:

> The Invisible Institution was not an accident of a few rebellious people. It was a divine necessity for a people for whom religion was integrally related to all of life. The hypocrisy of a distorted gospel, heard under the influence of slave masters who desired to keep slaves in check, forced the slaves to identify time and space where they could freely be in communion with God and each other. Hearing the words of the Bible interpreted in the light of their oppression freed the slave worshipers to pour out their sufferings and needs and express their joys in their own sacred space. Separate and apart from those who denied their freedom on earth, slaves were free in worship to hear and respond to the Word of God.[48]

In the "hush harbors", the slaves created distinct Christian rituals, ones that drew on their collective memories of Africa, the hardship and joys of their lives in the New World, and the stories of Israel and Jesus. Costen lists the following elements of slave worship: call to worship, prayer, singing, preaching, and shouting.[49] Her enumeration includes standard elements in most Protestant worship traditions but her analysis indicates the adaptation which these familiar items underwent in response to the circumstances of slave existence. For instance, "call to worship" refers not to a scriptural sentence that opens a service but to an elaborate system through which slaves announced a service and facilitated the gathering of the community.

Slaves announced meetings in code through their work songs since these meetings were punishable offenses.[50] They prepared the appointed place since slaveholders did not permit the establishment of a permanent sanctuary.[51] The crowd gathered slowly, allowing time for conversation about hardships, concerns and joys. Risk, fear and commitment accompany illicit worship, encouraging ritual forms of heightened expectation and strong community boundaries. Raboteau writes:

> ... at the core of the slaves' religion was a private place, represented by the cabin room, the overturned pot, the prayin' ground, and the "hush harbor". This place the slave kept his own. For no matter how religious the master might be, the slave knew the master's religion did not countenance prayers for his slaves' freedom in this world.[52]

In similar ways to their elaboration of the call to worship, slaves fashioned elements of worship such as prayers, songs, and sermons in distinctive ways. Each was participatory, rhythmic, and embodied. In prayer, slaves shared leadership, welcoming petitions from anyone present. During the sermon, the preacher expected, even required, responses from the congregation. Slaves utilized rhythmic, even metered, patterns of speech and silence,[53] lending the entire service a musical quality.[54] Activities were not cerebral, emotive or physical by turn, but all of these at once and always. Slaves, subject as they were to masters who could strike at their minds, hearts and bodies at whim, responded with their entire being in the freedom of the ritual time and space.

The slaves not only adapted standard elements of European-American Protestant worship but also invented new ones. On the Sea Islands of North Carolina, because of the density of recent African arrivals and the opportunity for independent worship, slaves created a new ritual form, "the ring shout".[55] This rite of spiritual possession has clear African antecedents clothed in Christian language. An oft-quoted account by a visiting northerner describes a "shout":

> ... a true shout takes place on Sundays or on "praise" nights through the week, and either in the praise-house or in some cabin in which a regular religious meeting has been held. Very likely more than half the population of the plantation is gathered together ... But the benches are pushed back to the wall when the formal meeting is over, and old and young, men and women, sprucely dressed young men, grotesquely half-clad field hands, the women generally with gay handkerchiefs twisted about their heads and with short skirts, boys with tattered shirts and men's trousers, young girls barefooted, all stand up in the middle of the floor, and when the "sperichil" is struck up, begin first walking and by-and-by shuffling around, one after the other, in a ring. The foot is hardly taken from the floor, and the progression is mainly due to a jerking, hitching motion, which agitates the entire shouter, and soon brings out streams of perspiration. Sometimes they dance silently, sometimes as they shuffle they sing the chorus of the spiritual, and sometimes the song itself is also sung by the dancers. But most frequently a band, composed of some of the best singers and tired shouters, stand at the side of the room to "base" the others, singing the body of the song and clapping their hands together on their knees. Song and dance alike are extremely energetic, and often, when a shout lasts into the middle of the night, the monotonous thud, thud of the feet prevents sleep within half a mile of the praise-house.[56]

The ring shout is still practiced today; but, even in sanctuaries where fixed pews do not accommodate movement on this scale, some physical manifestation of the spiritual forces which enliven the community is common in African-American churches.[57]

Slaves, and free African Americans in later years as well, integrated the shout into the larger traditions of Protestant worship. Walter Pitts notes that southern black Baptists paired the shout with a period of contemplative prayer to form the "binary structure" of Afro-Baptist ritual.[58] He names the first part "Devotion" and the second "Service", emphasizing the way in which African-American worship first moves its participants out of the structures of everyday life and then offers them a transformative experience that lets them return renewed and refreshed into their daily routines. Pitts finds this twofold structure common to a variety of African and African-American ritual forms. The development of the ring shout demonstrates how African Americans continued to interweave their African heritage with their American experience as they transformed the religion of the slaveholders.[59]

In addition to its importance as a unique development in the history of Christian worship, the shout illustrates the class divisions that arise between African Americans in the nineteenth century. On a visit to the South in 1878, Bishop Payne, of the AME church, stopped a shout in progress before him. He writes:

> After the sermon they formed a ring, and, with coats off sang, clapped their hands, and stamped their feet in a most ridiculous and heathenish way. I requested the pastor to go and stop their dancing ... I have been strongly censored because of my effort to change the mode of worship, or modify the extravagances indulged in by the people ... To the most

thoughtful and intelligent I usually succeeded in making the "Band" disgusting; but by the ignorant masses, ... it was regarded as the essence of religion ... Among some of the songs of these "Rings" or "Fist and Heel Worshipers" [were what I would call] "corn-field ditties" ... Some one has even called it a "Voodoo dance".[60]

Ecstatic worship offended Payne's sensibilities and to him would continue to justify the "civilization" of African Americans. Payne sought forms of worship that would encourage African Americans to seek education and acceptance, however partial, in the mainstream. Many argue that Payne had simply internalized white values, while others accept his attempt, however naive, to leave all vestiges of slavery behind for the chance to forge a new identity for former slaves as a free people.[61]

Worship in the invisible institution incorporated and encouraged reinterpretation of Christian doctrines. Experiencing freedom in the fragile and temporary world of their secret gatherings, slaves rejected the call to obedience of white missionaries and preachers. Among themselves, slaves encouraged each other to survive and resist; they affirmed their humanity in opposition to the denial of whites, expressed their often cloaked understandings of their plight, passed on their motherwit and other survival strategies, and kept alive their memories of Africa and their hopes for freedom. In contrast to slaveholders, who legitimized their right to own other human beings in worship, slaves in the "Invisible Institution" expressed their desire to be free.[62]

In sum, slaves combined remnants of African Traditional Religion which survived the dislocation and active suppression of the slave trade with the evangelical Christianity of the Second Great Awakening in the context of bondage in the American colonies into a unique ritual tradition. Slave worship "competes" with slaveholder worship.[63] Slaves performed an alternative worldview to that of the slaveholders, emphasizing themes of freedom, self-determination, and eschatological hope. Slave worship is not uniform but reflects various combinations of African survivals, the personalities and denominational emphases of evangelists, and the identity and context of those converted. Finally, slave religion expresses a unitary cosmology and anthropology in which all forms of life both human and extra-human are intimately and interdependently related. Slaves perform their worldview in a mode that is holistic—participatory, communal, embodied, emotional, and intellectual at once. Slave worship constitutes an inescapable primary source of all subsequent styles of African-American ritualizing, albeit a source that some heirs treated with contempt and others embraced.

Visibility, Separation, and the Solidification of *Classical* African-American Liturgies

As southern slaves constructed and performed the ring shout, a second movement of African-American liturgy began to take shape in the North. The aims of free blacks in worship differ from those of slaves. Free blacks had attained some measure of freedom but not full citizenship. As W.E.B. DuBois writes:

It is a peculiar sensation, this double-consciousness, this sense of always looking at oneself through the eyes of others, of measuring one's soul by the tape of a world that looks on in amused contempt and pity. One ever feels his twoness,—an American, a Negro; two souls, two thoughts, two unreconciled strivings; two warring ideals in one dark body, whose dogged strength alone keeps it from being torn asunder.[64]

The worship of free blacks in the North reflects this experience of "twoness". I employ the history of the African Methodist Episcopal Church as the primary example of *classical* African-American liturgical traditions.

Four periods comprise the history of liturgical development among free blacks and their descendants. Northern free blacks established the first autonomous African-American denominations between 1794 and 1863. Between 1863 and 1919, *classical* worship patterns solidified as mission efforts flowered and the promises of Emancipation evaporated. From 1920 to 1956, class distinctions resulted in the alienation of the migrating masses, bourgeois quietism, and the growth of social welfare efforts. Finally, the civil rights era offered an opportunity to demonstrate again the power of African-American religion to instigate social change, but established worship patterns prevail, even to the present day.

The Birth of the Historic Black Churches

Richard Allen and Absalom Jones organized the Free African Society in 1787.[65] Out of this organization of free blacks, Allen founded the African Methodist Episcopal Church (AME), formally constituted in 1816. The AME and other African-American Methodist churches emerged from the white Methodist Episcopal Church not because of doctrinal disputes like those which caused many other Protestant schisms, but because Allen and his compatriots felt keenly the hypocrisy of those who purported to be their brothers and sisters in Christ but who did not treat them as equals.[66] Allen and Jones originally envisioned the Free African Society as a secular organization that people would join in addition to, rather than instead of, church membership. They did not intend to leave the congregation of St. George's Methodist Church until the day they were pulled from their knees during prayer.

In November of 1787, the congregation of St. George's gathered for the first time in a newly renovated sanctuary, a project to which both black and white members had contributed. During the construction phase of the project, the elders, without informing Allen and Jones and other blacks, instituted segregated seating patterns for the expanded space. When Jones and Allen took their customary seats, an elder confronted them and tried to pull them from their knees despite their request to wait simply until the end of the prayer.[67]

Even after this insult, Jones and Allen sought permission for separate worship opportunities only. When the northern white Methodists rejected their request for autonomy in matters of worship and the choosing of leaders, they felt it necessary to convene new churches. Jones and Allen came to different conclusions about which denomination would make the best sponsor. Jones became an Anglican priest, and with the majority of early members of the Society founded St. Thomas African Episcopal Church.[68] Allen, who broke with the Society over prayer styles when

Quaker-like practices were used to frame meetings, remained loyal to the worship of evangelical Methodism and founded the Mother Bethel African Methodist Episcopal Church.[69]

Carolyn Stickney Beck, in her study of Mother Bethel in the present day, describes a typical Sunday service.[70] The order is highly structured. After a lengthy time of arriving and gathering, the service begins and includes the following actions: the entrance of worship leaders, a Prelude, a responsive Call to Worship, the Doxology, a Hymn of Dedication, the Morning Prayer by an assisting evangelist, an Anthem, a responsive reading, the recitation of the Decalogue, a choral response, the Gloria Patri, a Gospel choir selection, announcements, a Cathedral choir selection, a time to welcome visitors and receive greetings, announcements by the Pastor, the Pastoral Prayer, a time of shout, the Offertory and its Dedication, a Hymn of Preparation, the recognition of the officers of the church, the Sermon, a choral response, an Invitational Hymn, and another Offering. On First Sundays, the ordinance of the Lord's Supper is celebrated and occurs at this juncture.[71] The service closes with an exchange of greetings, the corporate recitation of the Apostle's Creed, a Recessional Hymn, the Doxology and a Benediction. The order is full. Services are lengthy. Faithfulness to Wesleyan liturgical practices is evident. And yet, Beck assures us, there remains room for spontaneous participation as well. She writes:

> ... while the official program and the established liturgy are important, indeed essential, they provide only the framework. The most significant activity, with respect to the members' feeling of participation in a vibrant community, occurs in the interstices, in those areas that are not prescribed. The feeling of community, that intangible sensation which the anthropologist experiences and recognizes as validation of his or her interpretation but is not translatable to a non-participant, is present most intensely when interstitial, rather than structural activity predominates. When contagious shouting erupts, or when everybody expresses amusement as the pastor good-naturedly chides the president of the Corporation for overstating the male point of view, at the expense of the female point of view, the observer senses community. By comparison, this sense does not emanate as noticeably from the choir's processional or recessional or from the reading of the Decalogue.[72]

Jones and Allen exemplify the predicament of many free blacks who attempted to participate in northern churches but in frustration formed autonomous institutions. Berry and Blassingame write: "Despairing of reforming white churches, believing they were the only real Christians in the land, they withdrew from white congregations and formed their own religious organizations".[73]

The AME and its sister organizations retained the creeds, polity and discipline of the denominations from which they sprang. The African-American dispute with European-American churches was not about doctrine. The African-American churches considered themselves completely orthodox, and, in fact, more faithful than whites whose treatment of African Americans demonstrated loyalty to white supremacy rather than to equality within the Body of Christ. The AME introduced its constitutional documents with a preface declaring a commitment to racial solidarity and abolitionism. It also limited membership to people of African descent. Because of these actions, some commentators characterize African Americans as separatist.[74] However, these measures serve only to cultivate racial solidarity in the face of white hypocrisy. By all accounts, Allen intended to reunite with white Christians as soon as they repented of their racism.

Emancipation and the Establishment of Classical Worship

After Emancipation, the "Invisible Institution" became a visible church. AME missionaries followed the Union Army south during the Civil War and reaped the harvest of newly emancipated slaves seeking to express their religious views openly. The denomination grew quickly. As noted above, not until 1758 were the first African-American Methodists baptized. Mother Bethel opened its doors in 1794. In 1861, the AME had 20,000 members, and, in 1896, 450,000.[75] African Americans celebrated openly their long-awaited freedom in Christian churches, joining churches in large numbers.

In this time of expansion, the worship of AME communities assumes patterns to which it remains loyal today. I designate these patterns, shared throughout the African-American churches founded by northern free blacks, *classical* African-American Protestant worship. Through the term *classical,* I intend to convey not only that these traditions are central in African-American religious history, but also that their representatives claim them as normative at the expense of the legitimacy of the folk-based practices of the slave legacy and the *improvisational* stream. *Classical* African-American worship is the liturgical stream of what came to be called "The New Negro"—those who with some access to education and economic stability sought to blend into the larger society but encountered such frequent rejection that at least temporary separation into segregated institutions proved necessary. *Classical* African-American worship, while dependent on the innovations of slave religion, rejects as unhelpful to the struggle for equality the more extreme ecstatic practices of the "Invisible Institution" such as the shout, employing instead worship styles of the European-American frontier revival movement.

Classical worship draws upon but moves away from the norms of worship in the "Invisible Institution". Richard Allen was born a slave. He worked in the home of one master and the fields of another. He bought his freedom and struggled to transform himself and his followers into free American citizens but not by forgetting the experience of slavery nor those who remained in bondage. Most other leaders in the early generations of the AME and the other independent churches also were from the South or had relatives in bondage. But, on the whole, these churches based their worship patterns on those of their white counterparts with the caveat that among every class of African Americans the communal praise of the God known in Jesus remains a primary means of healing from the daily strife of racism. In the North, free blacks attempted to join white society, gain education, and earn a living. For some, like Bishop Payne, assimilation required a more intellectual, rational, and less emotional worship style. In contrast, those who lived in the South and had to wait for emancipation until 1863, who had struggled to keep some sense of identity through African ways of thinking and doing, and who had worshiped in secret away from the eyes of whites, cultivated more radical therapeutic methods to heal their discontent.

Classical African-American worship utilizes the principles and norms of American revivalism, the branch of Christian liturgy through which African

Americans became Christians. Dramatic shifts in the norm, structure, and content of Christian worship occurred on the American frontier.[76] As one of the offspring of the missionary impulse that caused these shifts, the African-American churches inherited and integrated these new features and, at least in the *classical* stream, have remained faithful to frontier tenets.

On the frontier, missionaries used worship as the primary means to convert non-believers. Evangelists developed services to accomplish their pragmatic aims. They abandoned service books, the restriction of congregational song texts to psalmody, and the restraint of New England propriety. They adopted new rhetorical styles, sang non-biblical hymn texts, and provoked demonstrative responses. African Americans followed the lead of frontier evangelists in establishing pragmatic goals for worship. However, African Americans required worship that not only attracted converts but also invoked an alternative reality beyond the social order of white supremacy. Even when Blacks were free from bondage, they still needed a haven from the deprivation and disrespect of the racist society in which they lived. Worship expressed the solidarity of the community in its commitment to survival as a people.

In the independent black churches, believers accomplished these goals by expressing the full complexity of their lives before God. They brought both joy and sorrow, mind and heart, poverty and riches to the table and shared them together. They gathered with prayer and song (interwoven and/or simultaneous) to acknowledge one another's presence, to leave behind the burdens of the week, to lift up concerns, and to give thanks and praise. Worshipers sang, chanted, or moaned their prayers. Their petitions were spontaneous, situational, and practical. Similarly, sermons were relevant to the people, expressed in images more than concepts, and responsive to the needs and concerns of those present.

Following the norm of pragmatism, revival preachers proposed a new structure to worship. On the frontier, among the unchurched, worship was no longer the communal prayer of the gathered faithful but an effort to call outsiders to conversion. Instead of an occasion to share ancient and formative stories and symbolic actions for the sake of community renewal and nurture, worship became a single act of persuasion. In this context, the ancient structure of sharing the Word and table fellowship gave way to a structure of warm-up, preaching, and harvest.[77] This three-part structure reduced the opening activities to "preliminaries" and sacraments to concluding acts of the revival week or "season" and not integral parts of regular worship. The three-part revival structure remains the most common form of worship in independent black churches today. The prominence of the sermon and the weekly altar call (or, "opening of the doors of the church") that follows remain as two highly visible examples of frontier origins.

Frontier traditions also revised the content of worship services. Frontier worship introduced new gestures and rites to encourage the full, embodied participation of worshipers, new styles of preaching, and new types of music. African Americans contributed to and benefited from these changes.

First, Frontier revivals introduced new techniques for involving participants. Revivals brought people out of isolation on small farms for a period of concentrated social activity. Preachers whooped and hollered and the people hollered back. White writes:

New techniques were introduced: a mourner's bench for those who desired prayer for their conversion, the sawdust trail for converts to come forward, and a series of bizarre physical expressions, which some leaders opposed and others relished as signs of true conversion. Camp-meeting leaders agreed that in order to move people spiritually it was also necessary to move them physically.[78]

The techniques of the revivalists may have attracted African Americans not because they were bizarre but because they were familiar, if only in the fading memories of now distant lands. African worldviews do not separate the spiritual realm from the material, the emotional from the rational, or the body from the soul. As White notes: "Most of the vigorous active participation of the frontier worship and revivals had African antecedents".[79] African Americans had already developed the "shout" and other forms of worship that were equally participatory, ecstatic, and embodied. One might say the revivals were the "Africanization" of European-American religious expression. In any case, the new emotional and demonstrative expressions of the frontier period fit easily with African-American styles and were accepted, and even extended, in much of the worship of the independent black churches.

From whatever combination of cultures the ecstatic demonstrations derived, it is at least clear that they meant different things to white and blacks. Rhys Isaac writes:

> Preoccupation with sin and the control of the body in a war of the spirit against the flesh were not central features of the Afro-American value system. Hence, the crying out, falling down, and ecstatic release that appeared both in slave worship and in white evangelical meetings had different connotations for participants drawn from different cultures.[80]

Isaac elaborates with a few examples. White behavior was more individualized while blacks sought collective redemption. Whites were preoccupied with controlling their own sin while blacks sought healing. Blacks refused distinctions between sacred and secular realities.

Camp Meeting planners regularly accommodated African-American participants.[81] Peter Cartwright, a revival preacher, felt strongly about engaging in mission to slaves.[82] He encouraged owners to allow slaves to attend revivals. He also made sure to schedule his Camp Meetings to include Sunday, the day when slaves were traditionally freed from their normal duties. Eventually, Cartwright moved from Kentucky to the free territory of Illinois when his frustration with slavery grew overwhelming.

Second, frontier worship introduced new styles of preaching to the Christian repertoire. Sermons that occurred within the context of worship, from the time of the establishment of Christendom in the fourth century until the time of the Wesley brothers, were primarily addressed to baptized Christians for the purpose of interpreting the scriptures, exhorting believers to higher ethical conduct, or giving doctrinal instruction.[83] Facing missionary challenges on a scale not experienced since the days of the early church, the evangelists on the American frontier presided at rites that emphasized preaching to the unconverted. They developed a rhetorical style that could catch the attention of those who were not otherwise interested in

Christianity and then prick their consciences so that they might repent and convert. The sermon was the central event of these protracted meetings so its performance also had to hold the crowd's attention. White writes:

> In the usual service shaped by revivalism, the sermon as the second and dominant part of the service could invite fervent response through shouts of "Amen" and other positive exclamations. Thus the level of participation was not confined to hearing but included a limited amount of dialogue. The preliminaries produced a feeling of expectancy, and the sermon was the climax of the service. Such a situation could encourage exhibitionism and a tendency to do the spectacular. Despite this temptation, great "princes of the pulpit" flourished and were emulated by countless others. The results could be measured concretely by the number of converts who presented themselves during the singing of the hymn of invitation.[84]

African Americans accepted and expanded the preeminence of the sermon above all other liturgical activities and its role as a call to conversion. Of "black preaching", White observes: "The whole congregation is pulled into this performance and it is essentially dialogic with a competent minister listening as well as speaking and listeners speaking in dialogic form".[85]

Frontier evangelists recognized that revival sermons could also contribute to social reform. They used the same techniques that caused people to repent of their former lifestyles to recruit them for various causes. The Temperance Movement, abolition, and women's suffrage are causes that European-American revivalists promoted at their meetings. African Americans spoke out on slavery and some were involved with women's rights and other issues, but, most importantly, discovered that sermons could prick the consciences of whites on the issue of racial equality. African-American revival preachers encouraged both whites and blacks to challenge racist structures.

Third, frontier preachers introduced innovations in the area of liturgical music. Frontier preachers used music to create moods of expectancy before the sermon and of celebration of the converted afterwards. In addition, revivalists accepted and promoted new compositions. The musical repertoire of the frontier included simple choruses and the emotion-laden hymns of Isaac Watts. African-American churches used much of this repertoire while also tapping the resources of their own song tradition, the spirituals. These latter, made renowned in the late nineteenth century by the Fisk Jubilee singers, presented, in a new time and with innovative arrangements, the heritage of slave religion.[86]

Classical African-American Protestant churches emphasize experiential rather than educational preparation for ordained ministry, are suspicious of fixed prayers and service books, and prefer the free choice of texts by preachers rather than a lectionary. They vest substantial power in the presider, encourage emotional involvement and demonstrative participation in song and in the sermon through oral and gestural responses, rely on improvised prayers, and emphasize the experience of conversion and subsequent sanctification. These characteristics are based upon frontier, and older European-American, precedents but are lived out in a distinctly African-American style.

The *classical* stream of African-American worship has followed the trajectory of other enthusiastic off-shoots of Christian worship.[87] Beginning with the Free African Society, African Americans organized institutions that helped them attain some measure of security in the American socio-economic order, transforming themselves from chattel to oppressed but participating members of the larger society. *Classical* African-American worship evolved out of slave religion into a means for assimilation, even while serving as a haven from continuing discrimination.

The Deradicalization of Classical Worship

Despite the continuing existence of racist barriers, members of the independent black churches eventually experienced some measure of economic and social acceptance in the wider culture. Entrance into the American middle class brought with it a new possibility of assimilation into the mainstream and a subsequent desire to follow worship patterns of the majority culture. A decrease in emotional expression seems a common attribute of those who are upwardly mobile.[88] Wilmore entitles this process the "deradicalization" of black churches. In his view, early- to mid-twentieth century developments in the African-American churches shifted concern from the survival and liberation of the community to institutional politics.[89] This trajectory allowed African ritual patterns to recede in favor of more "American" ones.

It is clear that *classical* churches also contributed, and continue to contribute, to the welfare of African-American people, indeed to American culture generally. Abyssinian Baptist Church in New York City is one example of a large, wealthy congregation that developed social welfare programs in response to the needs of those in its vicinity.[90] Northern churches, both Methodist and Baptist in affiliation, not only initiated the newly emancipated slaves into formal Christian institutions, aiding in their adjustment to freedom, but also provided a haven for the migrants who moved north to find economic opportunity when Reconstruction ended. Congregations, such as Abyssinian, became more conservative liturgically as pastors such as Adam Clayton Powell, Sr., and his son, Adam Clayton Powell, Jr., chose political rather than ritual channels to promote social change. Many other churches pursued quietism in both the political and social realms. Cone writes:

> Too much confidence in what God is going to do often creates an other worldly perspective which encourages passivity in the face of injustice. That happened to the great majority of blacks from the time of the Civil War to the coming of Martin Luther King, Jr.[91]

The Civil Rights Era: The Reawakening of Classical Worship

The crisis of race relations in the mid-twentieth century precipitated a re-emergence of the social protest dimensions of African-American religious practices. As a participant in this collective re-awakening, Martin Luther King, Jr. responded to the challenge which the arrest of Rosa Parks represented in Montgomery in 1955.[92] He, the son of a prominent Afro-Baptist preacher with a northern education, demonstrated in his preaching and leadership the vital connection between African-

American religion and social activism. King accepted a leading role in a movement that sought to weave together once more the prophetic and activist resources of African-American Christianity. King found texts, themes, and songs that encouraged resistance to structures of oppression in the worship patterns of his southern Baptist tradition. He used worship, along with training in the philosophy and techniques of non-violent resistance, to empower his followers for direct protest of legalized discrimination. He demonstrated that Christianity could again spark progressive social change. While he led worship in the *classical* style, he emphasized themes of resistance, returning to an African worldview that holds together political and spiritual concerns. The content of his messages and his choice of texts and music moved people to participate actively in the struggle for racial reconciliation, placing their bodies in harm's way. Wilmore writes: "The real power of his southern campaign lay in his ability to combine dexterously a simple but profound philosophy with the folk religion and revival techniques of the black Baptist preacher".[93]

King's integrationist movement provided a substantial challenge to the established churches, black as well as white. He criticized the political passivity that resulted from the wedding of African-American worship traditions to a naive theory of progress in the area of American racial relations. While seeking reconciliation with the nation as a whole through moral suasion, although in the form of the active provocation of white hypocrisy and violence rather than mere rhetoric, King reasserted prophetic themes in African-American Protestant traditions.

After the Civil Rights movement, the initial successes of the black middle class multiplied. The professionalization of the black elite and their relocation from "ghetto" to "sub-division" followed the legal gains. Many of those who escaped the confines of their former neighborhoods sought new forms of religious expression that were consciously in contrast to the styles of their childhoods. Some established churches in their new neighborhoods, churches that were often less expressive than those they had left, whether affiliated with the same denomination or not. Others joined the established churches of their new locations. These churches, usually belonging to *mainline* denominations, shifted in demographics like the suburbs in which they were located—from white to mixed to black—as black migrations to the suburbs spurred a second "white flight" even further from the cities. Some middle-class blacks remained affiliated with the churches of their youth, driving into the cities each Sunday. On the whole, these commuting congregations tend to draw few members from those who actually now live in the surrounding neighborhood, as their worship assumes a style more comfortable for suburban dwellers. Worshiping "decently and in order", it seems, is a sign of achievement of some measure of the American dream. Traditional "folk religion" practices were left to those who could not, or would not, follow the "successful" to outlying areas. The chasm between the middle class and the poor—"two nations within a nation"—continues to widen in both its geographical and social dimensions.[94]

In response to the Civil Rights movement, African-American Christians adopted active, political modes of ritual performance. They participated in rituals of the street in addition to their worship in the pew. As ethical and confessional performances, the marches, freedom rides and lunch-counter confrontations demonstrated the power of African-American religion to sustain the struggle for liberation. The sermons and songs sung in black churches empowered people to take the risks of exposure, arrest and violence. But the services themselves remained stable. *Classical* African-American Protestant worship remained loyal to frontier liturgical norms. Wealthier and more highly educated blacks developed a taste for *mainline* European-American forms while poorer blacks adopted more *improvisational* practices—in the end, however, no new liturgical tradition emerged from the turbulence of the Civil Rights Era.

The *classical* stream of Protestant worship serves both black autonomy and the ideal of an integrated society, exhibits variety in local expressions, cultivates racial solidarity, and remains closely tied to its roots in frontier revival forms. The historic black churches are justly proud of their continuing independence from *mainline* European-American denominations, and the worship they practice rebuts white racism. *Classical* liturgies vary because of class status, denominational affiliation, and personal performance style of preachers. *Classical* liturgies reflect the newly-won freedom to form churches that could declare openly the need for African-American racial solidarity in the face of white supremacy. *Classical* worship follows the norm, structure, and content of frontier revivals. *Classical* African-American liturgies remain stable in form and content, perhaps because, for their adherents, they address satisfactorily the experience of twoness, the reality of being both and neither African and American, the tension between freedom and frustration.

African-American Folk Religion and *Improvisational* Worship

Alongside the development of the *classical* liturgical movement, folk practice continued as well. The "Invisible Institution" was the primary arena for the development of African-American folk religion. However, when slaves and free blacks obtained permission to worship by themselves, they created visible institutions to foster their independent liturgies as well. Even before Richard Allen and Absalom Jones formed the Free African Society in 1787, independent congregations took shape in the South. For example, David George and Jesse Galphin founded The Baptist Church of Silver Bluff, South Carolina sometime between 1773 and 1775.[95]

Independent African-American churches in the antebellum South conserved slave practices with less dilution than the missionary churches of the AME and other northern denominations. These rituals are the basis of what I will call the *improvisational* African-American liturgical traditions. The *improvisational* movement includes those churches that relinquished not only the ritual forms of the frontier, on which the *classical* liturgies are based, but ritual scripts of any kind. *Improvisational* worship unlike white Pentecostal worship that derives from the Methodist-Holiness tradition is a visible form of slave religion.[96] *Improvisational* worship is African-American folk religion among, primarily, those descendants of slaves who received official freedom but remained confined to the laboring classes.

The development of *improvisational* African-American worship subdivides into three historical periods. *Improvisational* worship originates in southern Afro-Baptist churches in the late eighteenth century. Between 1877 and 1919, a period of widespread racially-motivated violence, the Pentecostal revival began, giving new institutional form to African-American folk religion. Finally, since 1919, *improvisational* African-American liturgies have developed alongside, and as an alternative to, *classical* traditions.

The Origin and Formation of Improvisational *Worship*

Improvisational African-American Protestant liturgical traditions are the visible legacy of slave Christianity. Slave practices forged in secret in the "Invisible Institution" were practiced openly in independent black congregations. Independent African-American churches in the antebellum South were most often Baptist. Baptists not only practiced the egalitarian evangelical version of Christianity that attracted slaves to their masters' religion, but held individual autonomy sacred.[97] Baptist missionaries, more than the representatives of any other denomination, showed a willingness to license black preachers whether slave or free, to welcome black exhorters into the pulpit, and to allow for independent worship and parish governance. Methodists, too, preached the equality of all people before God, but their hierarchical polity limited the opportunities for blacks to participate in institutional decision-making.[98] Raboteau writes:

> Aided by the impulse to respect the independence of the individual relationship between man and God's will, and especially by the Baptist articulation of the autonomy of each congregation, black preachers and black churches were able to exercise a degree of authority, power, and self-government denied them in other areas of life by the system of slave control. In the middle of the conflict between two social values—the practical necessity of slave control and the ideal of religious freedom—slaves sometimes discovered they could take advantage of the confusion and act as if the Gospel of Christian fellowship included them after all.[99]

The independent black churches were not fully autonomous, of course. To ensure the stability of slavocracy, European-Americans reserved the right to scrutinize all African-American activities. Often a white pastor would oversee African-American worship insuring that it remained compatible with the theology of slaveholders.[100] In addition, after a slave rebellion, vengeful crowds and hostile legislators restricted the free exercise of religion in African-American churches. Still, these churches allowed African-Americans to form and oversee social institutions, experience that would prove valuable after Emancipation.

Worship in the "visible" churches of the antebellum south included a variety of combinations of African survivals and frontier revival elements. In rural areas, where slaves could worship alone, they created "praise houses" and practiced the ring shout, expressing their joy and hope openly. Costen writes: "… slaves in praise houses had the freedom to sing, pray, shout, read Scriptures, exhort, and experience conversion".[101] Most independent congregations were established in cities, however. Afro-Baptist churches in southern cities included a mix of free blacks and slaves, and followed more formal worship patterns. Charles Lyell, a visitor from Britain, published his travel notes from a service at the First African Church in Savannah, Georgia. He writes:

To see a body of African origin, who had joined one of the denominations of Christians, and built a church for themselves—who had elected a pastor of their own race, and secured him an annual salary, from whom they were listening to a good sermon scarcely, if at all, below the average standard of compositions of white ministers—to hear the whole service respectably, and the singing admirably performed [makes one reconsider the ability of negroes to make progress in civilization].[102]

Andrew Marshall, pastor of First African, led three services each Sunday, presided over the Eucharist quarterly, and attracted a large number of members and curious tourists. The preaching service included the basic elements of a frontier liturgy: songs to warm-up the congregation, lengthy extemporaneous prayers, and a sermon delivered without the aid of notes. Lyell remarked upon the vivid imagery, accessible language and harmonious singing that he encountered in the Savannah service. While Marshall possessed singular talent as preacher and liturgist, the service Lyell describes follows patterns of the frontier traditions closely.

First African Church in Savannah was well established and worship there reflects the tension of visible African-American churches which must balance larger cultural norms against the unique needs of their constituents. First African adopted a "respectable" style as it gained status in Savannah. Although unlike white Baptist churches, First African's status remained precarious and could be swept away if it raised any alarms among white slaveholders. Independent African-American congregations in the antebellum south, adapted their worship to the exigencies of the moment. Where they could find some measure of freedom and security, they followed European-American revival patterns closely. Where whites imposed more restrictions, they turned back to folk ritual forms and employed stronger ritual responses to their situation. *Improvisational* African-American liturgical traditions are the techniques of politically and socially weaker communities. *Improvisational* worship allows more room to express the pain of bondage and, after emancipation, continued repression.

Tears, Migrations, and the Pentecostal Revival[103]

The late nineteenth and early twentieth century brought a surge of black migration from South to North and from country to city. African-Americans moved in order to acquire greater economic and social opportunity and to escape the new reign of terror in the South after Reconstruction. With the end of Reconstruction, freedom from bondage became primarily freedom for whites to rape, lynch, disenfranchise, and intimidate. Some blacks escaped to the North and found relief; others found only further alienation. In the rural South and in the unfamiliar surroundings of northern cities, many African Americans found comfort in the Holiness and Pentecostal movements, to which we will turn in a moment. Others opted to serve the country that despised them, offering their lives on the battlefields of the First World War. Upon their return, African-American soldiers found their generosity rejected as they were greeted by lynch mobs.[104]

All this being said, it is also true that earlier, at the turn of the century, a new and interracial spiritual revival erupted. Afro-Baptists, African-American Holiness preachers and European-American Methodist and Holiness adherents experienced anew the gifts of the Spirit promised to the first apostles. They called themselves Pentecostals, recalling the pouring out of the Spirit among the diverse gathering of Jews in the marketplace of Jerusalem following Jesus' death and resurrection.

Like the first Pentecost, this twentieth-century revival rested on the reception of the gift of tongues. On 1 January 1901, a Bethel Bible College student, Agnes Ozman, while contemplating an assignment on the gifts of the spirit, began to speak in tongues. Her teacher, Charles Parham, a white Holiness revivalist, believed that Agnes, and subsequently a number of other students, had inaugurated the dawn of the predicted age in which the Spirit would be directly available to all. Parham formulated the doctrine that speaking in tongues is the necessary and sufficient sign that one has been baptized by the Spirit. The linking of sanctification and *glossolalia* distinguished Parham's followers from the larger Holiness movement and served as the doctrinal foundation for modern Pentecostalism. Unfortunately, the utterances did not persist. Parham was forced to close his school in Kansas. A few years later, he set up a new school in Houston, Texas.

William Seymour, an African-American Holiness preacher, enrolled in Parham's Houston program. After completing his training, Seymour accepted a job as associate pastor of a Holiness church in Los Angeles in 1905. He chose Acts 2:4, "anyone who does not speak in tongues is not baptized by the Holy Spirit" as the text of his first sermon. He insisted, following Parham's doctrine, that all who were fully sanctified would speak in tongues. Offended because she had not received the gift of tongues, the pastor, Neely Terry, promptly fired Seymour. Undaunted, he began preaching in an abandoned church on Azusa Street in 1906. His services drew people from all over the world and culminated in a three year revival. Most Pentecostal denominations trace their origins to Seymour's preaching on Azusa Street. The Azusa revival caused quite a stir. An article in the Los Angeles Times states:

> Breathing strange utterances and mouthing a creed which it would seem no sane mortal could understand, the newest religious sect has started in Los Angeles. Meetings are held in a tumble-down shack on Azusa Street, near San Pedro Street, and devotees of the weird doctrine practice the most fanatical rites, preach the wildest theories and work themselves into a state of mad excitement in their peculiar zeal. Colored people and a sprinkling of whites comprise the congregation, and night is made hideous in the neighborhood by the howlings of worshipers who spend hours swaying forth and back in a nerve-racking attitude of prayer and supplication. They claim to have "the gift of tongues," and to be able to comprehend the babel.[105]

To this reporter and to other witnesses, Pentecostal worship was bizarre and frightening. Within the history of African-American Protestant liturgical traditions, however, the ecstatic displays at Azusa Street are not surprising at all. Hollenweger writes:

> The "Pentecostal experience of Los Angeles" was neither the leading astray of the church by demons (as the German Evangelical Movement claimed), nor the eschatological pouring out of the Holy Spirit (as the Pentecostal movement itself claims) but an outburst of enthusiastic religion of a kind well-known and frequent in the history of Negro churches

in America which derived its specifically Pentecostal features from Parham's theory that speaking with tongues is a necessary concomitant of the baptism of the Spirit.[106]

Pentecostal worship draws upon the legacy of slave practices that lie beneath all African-American worship traditions. In his work on Holiness figures in Mississippi, David Daniels identifies links between slave congregations and their worship practices with the Holiness communities of the late nineteenth and early twentieth centuries.[107] Daniels finds that Holiness leaders and congregations in Mississippi are as likely to emerge from local churches of Baptist affiliation as from Methodist ones. He identifies a significant portion of Mississippi Holiness adherents who come to this allegiance as one of three branches of a Baptist reform movement. The triumphant group, the progressives, establish a Baptist orthodoxy of systematic theology, racial uplift, politically active evangelicalism, and orderly (or, in my terms, *classical*) worship. The conservatives remained tied to European-American Baptist principles of local autonomy, suspicions of the legitimacy of spiritually-based political activism, and the worship of the slave legacy. The third branch, led by Charles Price Jones, combined the message of racial solidarity and progress with re-structured slave practices to create *improvisational* forms of worship to serve the needs of African Americans in the post-Reconstruction era. After being expelled from Baptist connections, Jones founded, along with Charles Harrison Mason and others, Holiness churches and, in 1897, a new denomination, The Church of God in Christ (COGIC).[108] The autonomy of local churches in Baptist polity had allowed ex-slaves and their descendants to preserve the folk practices of their past until the Holiness movement provided a new legitimization of ecstatic practices. Spirit possession became central to worship once more, affirming African ritual forms. Hurston writes:

> The Sanctified Church is a protest against the high-brow tendency in Negro Protestant congregations as the Negroes gain more education and wealth. It is understandable that they take on the religious attitudes of the white man which are as a rule so staid and restrained that it seems unbearably dull to the more primitive Negro who associates the rhythm of sound and motion with religion. In fact, the Negro has not been christianized as extensively as is generally believed. The great masses are still standing before their pagan altars and calling old gods by a new name.[109]

In *glossolalia*, in the holy dance and other kinesthetic responses, Pentecostal worship incorporates the participation of the whole self in its performance.

Mason spent five weeks at the Azusa Street revival with Seymour, received the gift of tongues, and returned to Mississippi to spread the message of Pentecostalism among the Holiness churches.[110] Jones and Mason split over the issue of tongues. Mason retained control of COGIC and reincorporated it as the first Pentecostal denomination in the US. As an example of his liturgical innovations, Mason developed the rite of "tarrying". Tarrying, like the shout, follows the regular worship service, employs rhythmic speech and music, extends over hours, tests physical endurance, serves as a means to encounter the Spirit, engages the whole self in worship and supplication, and requires the community to yearn together for both individual and corporate healing.[111] Worship in COGIC embodies the flow of the *improvisational* stream from slave religion to an Afro-Baptist autonomous congregation to Holiness perfectionism and, finally, to Pentecostal *glossolalia*.

Members of African-American Pentecostal churches tend to be less established than members of *classical* churches and therefore are less prone to insist upon decorous *mainline* values, such as emotional and expressive restraint. At the same time, the political dimension of community life is often less obvious in *improvisational* churches than in *classical* ones which were created as alternatives to white structures. Pentecostals, like members of *classical* churches, resist racism but employ strategies of transcendence rather than separation, as they welcome all who desire to encounter the spirit. The Church of the Living God (Christian Workers for Fellowship), a Holiness church founded by William Christian in 1889, teaches that Jesus was black, but this important symbolic protest to white hegemony is unusual.[112] In the clash of rural roots and unfulfilled promises, as African Americans sought opportunity and independence in cities, Pentecostal worship offered solace, community, and a place to vent frustrations and cultivate hope.

In general, Pentecostal worship is more fluid than *classical* African-American Protestant worship. The primary emphasis is not on preaching or even on biblical texts but on direct experience of the presence of the Spirit among the gathered community. Pentecostals claim their worship reconstitutes the "pure" practices of the early church. Pentecostals reject the historical development of Christian liturgy into a formal rite that can be written down in a book and repeated. They seek an encounter with the Spirit in the present, not adherence to traditional rubrics.

In addition, Pentecostal worship diffuses the heightened attention normally focused on preacher and choir by allowing anyone present the freedom to express her/his apprehension of the Spirit at any time.[113] For example, while the sermon is a channel for the Spirit to speak through the preacher to the needs of the people, a spontaneous prayer or song may, and sometimes does, interrupt the preaching, which may or may not resume later. Here, the minister acts more as the lead performer of a jazz ensemble where improvisation is, somewhat ironically, institutionalized than as a conductor of a symphony that is played with great artistry but "as written".

While free of mandated orders, Pentecostal services do regularly contain songs, prayers, a sermon, and ecstatic behavior in predictable patterns.[114] Local congregations craft their own services without denominational control. However, the common experience of adapting rural worldviews to the poverty, overcrowding, and unfulfilled expectations of turn-of-the-century cities narrows the range of worship formats from the diversity of the larger and more heterogeneous *classical* denominations. Pentecostal liturgies are not written down in prayer books or hymnals like those *mainline* Protestants publish. Instead, as in many black churches, but to a heightened degree, the pastor, in relation to other worship leaders and especially the musician(s), is responsible for maintaining the flow of any particular service and must have the skill to respond to outbreaks of praise while molding a coherent event.

One consequence of allowing interruptions is a very different conception of time than will be found in most other worship traditions. While revivals accustomed white and black Americans to lengthy and emotional sermons which Pentecostal preachers often emulate, Pentecostals wait on the Spirit to initiate songs, prayers and praise as well. A song that is moving the people into unity and joy may continue for half an hour. A prayer chanted by one of the deacons may take even longer. Pentecostals, black and white, expect to "tarry" on Sunday.[115]

The Pentecostal movement, as the Great Awakenings before it, appealed first and foremost to poor and marginalized people. Pentecostal worship encourages participation of the whole person rather than just one's mind and allows for emotional and kinesthetic expression. African Americans resonated, again, with the holistic understanding of the human self and the lack of distinction between music and dance, music and religion.[116] In fact, the Pentecostal tradition might be considered the culmination of the "Africanization" of Christianity in the North American context. In White's understanding: "The Pentecostal tradition is the only tradition that blacks have helped to shape from its very beginnings".[117]

At the same time, the Pentecostal tradition has attracted not just African-American and not just poor adherents. European Americans participated in the earliest days of the Pentecostal revivals. While Seymour and Mason were both African Americans, the Azusa Street revival and the denomination included both black and white members. Charles Mason ordained many of the preachers of the movement, both white and black. Mason's interracial assemblies raised more than eyebrows:

> Mason's activities did not go unnoticed. During the World War I era Mason was jailed a number of times for his pacifist views, despite his explicit support of the law and of the war bond drive. The FBI placed him under official but secret surveillance nationwide, working closely with the War Department, the Justice Department, and the local police in many cities. Not least among the FBI's concerns was the fact of Mason's interracial following.[118]

By 1924, however, whites withdrew to form their own churches, segregating themselves from their black brothers and sisters.[119]

Pentecostalism split into white and black institutions with distinct styles of worship, but, at its roots and in its vitality, all Pentecostal worship remains indebted to African-American liturgical traditions. African-American Pentecostals continue to practice a visible form of slave religion. While adapting to new circumstances in modern, urban America, Pentecostal worship reflects the participatory, ecstatic, and holistic performance styles of the "Invisible Institution".

Recent Developments

Improvisational African-American Protestant worship continues to evolve. While worship in many Afro-Baptist churches and some Pentecostal communities resembles *classical* styles as a result of members rising in socio-economic status and education, many African Americans continue to practice the "old-time religion" of their slave forebears. *Improvisational* worship remains resilient, retaining its spontaneous and ecstatic qualities in the face of challenges. *Improvisational* worship continues to serve as strong medicine to combat the nihilism of American culture, and more specifically of African-American existence in the ghettoes of contemporary US cities.[120]

Since 1920, *improvisational* worship has transformed itself from a rural to an urban tradition. Mason sent missionaries to follow the migrants to the industrial cities of the North following World War I. COGIC missions were astoundingly successful and the denomination grew from 50,000 members in 1920 to over 400,000 by 1970.[121] Most contemporary *improvisational* worship occurs in storefronts along city streets rather than in praise houses in the southern countryside. Storefront churches reduce the distance between street and sanctuary, appearing similar to places of regular commerce, where the curious can stop and inquire without intimidation.[122] Pentecostal worship welcomes marginalized urban dwellers, offering a taste of home for those who miss the intimacy of small town living and lowering the barriers to the those down on their luck.

A second shift among *improvisational* churches is the growth of political involvement. COGIC contributed to the civil rights struggle of the 1960s and has continued to promote activism in the cause of racial justice. With the departure of white members and the boom of urban churches, *improvisational* African-American churches accepted responsibility to serve the needs of black people through housing, educational, and food programs and through political activism. *Classical* churches, and the secular organizations they created such as the NAACP and The National Urban League, remain the most potent African-American political institutions, but Pentecostal churches have also made contributions.

Third, although the early revivals involved people of many races, Pentecostalism in the US is now developing primarily among homogenous groups (e.g., the membership of COGIC is almost entirely black and that of The Assemblies of God is almost entirely white). In general, African-American Pentecostals, in contrast to European-American ones, have bishops, are less likely to ordain women, encourage pastors to found their own churches and serve them for life, subordinate doctrinal legalism to faith experience, and demonstrate their commitments to social concerns.[123] In worship, black Pentecostals experience ecstasy with more frequency and vigor. Most African-American Pentecostal churches establish a formal liturgical role known as the nurse or nurse's aide, women trained to keep members undergoing possession safe from harm.

Finally, Pentecostal Christians are moving into the mainstream economically and religiously. They are entering the middle and upper-middle classes. They are joining ecumenical groups such as the World Council of Churches. Exposure to new sets of social and theological norms will inevitably influence worship patterns as well.

In the *improvisational* stream, African survivals regain prominence within a recognizably Christian symbolic language system and rural roots are blended with urban realities. *Improvisational* traditions recapture a fully participatory performance style. European-American frontier revival patterns are modified to emphasize fluid structures, spontaneous expression, and ecstatic experiences. Spirit possession becomes prominent in the revival of African sensibilities and slave realities. Like *classical* traditions, *improvisational* worship is a visible manifestation of practices born in the "Invisible Institution". Slave practices become subject to scrutiny from the larger culture, to disruptive visits from the curious, and to European Americans who find it compelling enough to seek membership. Pentecostal worship, especially, displays an openness to interracial communion, albeit one regularly rejected by whites. In the "Invisible Institution" and in the independent black churches of the antebellum South, slaves and former slaves practiced their strong therapy for healing in the midst of oppression. Ironically, these drastic methods of healing have proven the most attractive African-American worship forms to people of other racial/ethnic backgrounds, as evidenced by both the Pentecostal and Neo-Pentecostal revivals of this century.

Conclusion

African-American Protestant liturgical traditions demonstrate the creative adaptation of Christianity to the specific history of Africans brought forcibly to the British colonies of North America during the legal slave trade between 1619 and 1808 and their descendants. American slavery forced Africans to forge a religious interpretation of their circumstances out of the faith traditions of their "owners". In the "Invisible Institution" slaves crafted practices that inspired hope and formed African Americans into a distinct racial group united in a desire for freedom. After Emancipation, two liturgical streams flowed from the combined sources of African survivals and European evangelical Christianity. Enumeration of some distinctions between *classical* and *improvisational* worship follows in the first section of these concluding remarks. At the same time, *classical* and *improvisational* styles remain interrelated and both are identifiably African-American. A brief reflection on African-American liturgical music illustrates the continuing dynamism in African-American liturgical history within the still identifiable streams of *classical* and *improvisational*. A few final thoughts on the character of African-American Protestant worship close the chapter.

Distinctions Between the Classical and the Improvisational Streams

The two living streams of African-American Protestant liturgical traditions respond to the particular needs of sub-groups within the African-American people. Joseph Murphy has taken pains to point out the similarities of the worship of the many groups which comprise the African diaspora. He finds an emphasis on the manifestation of the Spirit in the bodies of those gathered common to them all. I concur with his thesis but find the identification of distinctions between *classical* and *improvisational* worship styles to be necessary as well. In response to their different circumstances, such as their proximity to, or distance from, slavery; their access to education and mainstream political allies, or lack thereof; and their relative success in the national economy—free blacks in the north and independent congregations in the antebellum south developed, respectively, the *classical* and *improvisational* styles. Both *classical* and *improvisational* styles are rooted in the merging of African and American experiences and memories but in different ways.

Especially important is the difference in attitudes toward European-American Christians. The *classical* churches were born when African Americans found they could not practice Christianity free of white supremacy in white-controlled denominations. In contrast, the Pentecostal churches cultivated a fragile and short-lived but bold mixing of races, even as white supremacist violence reigned around them. In the early Pentecostal period, whites and blacks joined together in spontaneous praise and community—under primarily African-American leadership. Together worshipers of African and European descent celebrated the arrival of the gift of tongues, even as their unfortunate separation quickly followed.

A second difference between *classical* and *improvisational* worship is their contrasting resolutions of the tension between spontaneity and order. The *classical* patterns are wed to the revival order of warm-up, sermon, and harvest, if not to published rubrics such as those employed in the AME. The flow and feeling of most *classical* services is predictable. There is room for spontaneous responses, which sometimes extend the service, but the order itself remains stable. In contrast, *improvisational* services have a Spirit-based order. There is a list of events that are likely to occur, such as prayers, songs, and a sermon, but the timing of each depends on the Spirit's lead. While there are predictable patterns in these liturgies as they are, in fact, highly structured ritual events, a central aspect of the structure is that the order depends on the adaptation of the action to the emotional and spiritual leanings of the gathered community. All African-American traditions include some measure of spontaneity but in general the *improvisational* services are more open to "riffs" than *classical* services.[124]

A third difference is the understanding of the role of the presider. Tom Driver employs the terms "priestly" and "shamanic" to describe the distinctions that I want to highlight.[125] He compares a Roman Catholic ordination service with its bestowal of authority that resides in institutional hierarchy to a *voudoun* initiation ceremony where authority lies in the ability to be possessed, to convey healing, and to bestow an identity in relation to the local community.[126] A pastor in an *improvisational* congregation leans toward the shamanic side of this duality and a pastor in a *classical* church to the priestly side. *Classical* services encourage and even depend on the active participation of the gathered community, but the authority and prominence of the pastor is unquestioned. The pastor is a shamanic priest, a person endowed with institutional power to lead the ritual performance with high, but variable, levels of participation. In *improvisational* traditions the phrasing is reversed; the minister is a priestly shaman. Pentecostal churches are concerned with the ability of the ritual leader to channel the Spirit, identify its presence in the midst of the congregation, and interpret its message for the community. *Classical* pastors function as models, as someone whose relation with the Spirit is vital and disciplined into discourse and praxis acceptable not only among the beloved community but also out in the larger society. *Improvisational* pastors function as present-day apostles, speaking the words of the Spirit, acting in the name of God to heal, rebuke and save.

Pluralism Within Stable Categories: The Case of African-American Liturgical Music

Through the upheavals of recent decades, worship in most African-American churches has remained strikingly constant. Perhaps because of the apprentice-like system of clergy preparation, perhaps as a conscious resistance to cultural change, the black churches have maintained their liturgical forms. Some congregations, both *classical* and *improvisational*, have circumscribed the range of acceptable behavior during services. Others offer greater freedom as neo-Pentecostal influences are felt.

While critics such as womanist scholars[127] occasionally arise to propose alternative liturgical patterns, the two streams remain coherent.

Below this placid surface, one element of worship, music, has undergone significant development since the turn of the century. The history of black church music illustrates the interdependence of the *classical* and *improvisational* streams on each other and their common ties to the slave legacy. While music is central to all African-American worship and so a change in musical styles affects the entire service, the innovations that have occurred do not constitute a creation of a new type of liturgy. Musical developments are, instead, a part of the general trend in African-American liturgical traditions toward diversification within the two streams.

Music—along with preaching, prayer, the conversion experience and testimony about it, and the shout—is central to African-American Protestant worship.[128] Music, along with the other elements, derives much of its characteristic style from the African heritage of the slaves. The spirituals were composed collectively in the call and response of early African-American preaching and then honed in subsequent celebrations—much as the work songs developed in the fields. African rhythms undergird both the improvisations of musicians and the cadence of preachers. Lincoln and Mamiya write: "A study of black singing, then, is in essence a study of how black people 'Africanized' Christianity in America".[129]

But this process of Africanization is neither simple nor unidirectional. African-American musical performances quickly split into two parallel traditions—never separate but always in tension. On the one hand, African Americans were pulled toward European aesthetics, replicating the ideology, style, repertoire, and practice of white Protestant churches. On the other hand, they attempted to conserve the uniqueness of African-American experience and an African aesthetic. Portia Maultsby writes:

> The parallel evolution of these traditions reflects the duality of the black experience in America. At the core of this experience was the struggle to maintain an African cultural identity, while meeting the expectations of American society at large. Black people responded to the struggle by developing a repertoire of folk spirituals and gospel music, which now make up the foremost musical idiom of autonomous Black churches.[130]

The divergent approaches of Richard Allen and Daniel Payne, both AME bishops, exemplify the tension between these two impulses. Allen published several collections of spirituals and African-American adaptations of European hymns for the denomination. Payne wanted "to drive out this heathenish mode of worship".[131] While most African-American churches remain loyal to Allen's suggested repertoire, Payne's position also has enjoyed lasting influence. Payne substituted choral performances of anthems and spirituals for hymns with congregational participation.[132] In one of the ironies of liturgical history, Payne employed the choir, an institution utilized by European-American revivalists to whip up the emotion of potential converts, to calm worshipers down. Most African-American churches today have choirs and one can see them employed both to encourage and to restrain congregational responses.

With the advent of Pentecostalism, a new musical form emerged. Portia Maultsby writes:

> At the turn of the twentieth century, the music of the earliest autonomous Black churches consisted of spirituals and lined-out hymns, sung to the accompaniment of handclapping and footstomping. The addition of tambourines, drums, piano, horns, and (later) guitar and Hammond organ, created an original body of Black religious music known as gospel.[133]

The invention of the musical forms now known as "gospel" took place mainly among urban, Pentecostal congregations. Pentecostal musicians experimented with previously untried instruments, musical technology (such as microphones) and secular idioms to create the new sound. Since that time, gospel has itself gone through several stages of development. Albert Tindley brought the original gospel sound into the *classical* churches. Thomas Dorsey added blues idioms from his secular career to create what is now called "Traditional Gospel". More recently, gospel artists began concert tours and recording careers, initiating "Commercial Gospel". On the whole, the earlier genres emphasized congregational participation and were based in the churches, while the newer styles tend to be performed in more concert-like modes and employ a wider variety of secular, pop music idioms. Improvisation, the interdependence of sound and movement, complex rhythmic patterns, and a layering of parts are characteristics of Gospel music. All forms of Gospel continue to be performed in churches today.

One other historic genre of African-American music deserves note—the freedom song. Originating with the compositions of white abolitionists, songs of protest sustained the Civil Rights movement of the 1950s and 1960s. Many of the modern songs were adaptations of much older ones. For instance, "We Shall Overcome" is a politicized version of Albert Tindley's "I'll Overcome Someday". Lincoln and Mamiya write:

> The freedom songs did not passively lament the black condition; they made God active in human history day by day with social agitation. African Americans were not just singing about freedom, they were systematically seeking it, and their songs were deliberate instruments tactically utilized in the effort ... As the spirituals provide an authentic window for religion in the life of the slave, so do the freedom songs offer a documentary on what the lives of black people were like in America one hundred years after slavery had ended.[134]

While the repertoire of African-American churches consists almost entirely of the traditional European hymns of Watts and Wesley, spirituals, freedom songs and gospel music, two new contributions, one practical and one academic, deserve comment. Anthony Lucas, a pastor and musician in New York City, employs "rap" throughout one of his church's weekly services.[135] What are now called "hip hop" musical idioms have attracted not only formerly disinterested young people in the neighborhood, but senior members of the congregation as well. The use of secular musical forms has been as central to the development of church music as it has been controversial. Lucas's use of rap parallels Thomas Dorsey's infusion of gospel with blues idioms and exemplifies how African-American liturgists and artists continue to adapt Christian traditions to new circumstances.

Jon Michael Spencer provides a radical critique of the current repertoire of black church music. He writes: "... black hymnody is by and large captive of Eurocentric biblical analysis, interpretation, and doctrinal guardianship that support the subordinationist traditions of sexism, racism, and classism".[136] In his opinion, both the creation of new compositions and the revision of traditional music are necessary for the cultivation of more faithful, committed and just congregations. The use of rap and Spencer's "ethnohymnology" are both marginal trends in African-American religious circles, yet the popularity of Lucas's innovations and the strength of Spencer's passion may help them gain a larger following. As Lincoln and Mamiya state: "... change does not come readily to religion in any case, for religion is the prime custodian of what tradition has sanctified".[137]

Be that as it may, the history of African-American liturgies reveals the ability of these traditions to adapt to the various circumstances of those who perform them. Through slavery, emancipation, continued oppression, and urban flux, African Americans developed ritual traditions that have served as one component in their struggle for survival and liberation. While the *classical* and *improvisational* streams have remained recognizable despite sustained criticism from within and without, they have done so by adapting and diversifying within their boundaries. In the relatively short span of 300 years, African-American liturgical traditions have evolved to meet the spiritual needs of their community and will no doubt continue to do so.

Final Thoughts

Both *classical* and *improvisational* liturgies interweave "African" and "American" cultural strands in order to resolve the tension characteristic of African-American experience, the tension between maintaining a unique identity and adapting to the expectations of the larger culture. African-American Christian worship combines African survivals, Western Christian traditions, and the embodied memory of oppression with, its corollary, the continuing struggle for liberation. Cornel West characterizes African-American life as a "cultural hybrid". He writes:

> ... the cultural hybrid character of black life leads us to highlight a metaphor alien to Malcolm X's perspective—yet consonant with his performances to audiences—namely, the metaphor of jazz. I use the term "jazz" here not so much as a term for a musical art form, as for a mode of being in the world, an improvisational mode of protean, fluid, and flexible dispositions toward reality suspicious of "either/or" viewpoints, dogmatic pronouncements, or supremacist ideologies.[138]

African-American Christian worship has, throughout its history, proved itself able to contain and nurture an improvisational disposition to the ever-changing situation of the community to which it belongs and in which it functions to instill hope and sustain struggle.

In addition, African-American Christian worship conjures an ethos of "participatory celebration". In discussing the African-American preaching tradition, Evans Crawford connects the experience of duality—being both and neither African and American—with the technique of "call and response". He writes: "Certain ways of using pause and silence ... represent the strenuous forces of the preacher's soul claiming a people's heritage, in a society that has often tried to suppress their expression and communication".[139] The whole congregation is called on to participate in the ritual sphere in reaction to the denial of full participation in the larger society. And, in this sense of ownership, in this affirmation of one's importance as an active agent in history, in this performance of a transformed social order in which one is "Somebody", there is joy. At their best, African-American worship traditions overturn the racist hierarchy of larger society by demonstrating the wisdom and worth of their communities in the doing of liturgical activities.

As there is no African music without dance, there is no African-American ritual without embodied expression.[140] African-American worship engages the entire being of participants. Evans Crawford reminds us that some African-American congregations move more than others, respond more or less expressively to sermon and song. Yet, he claims that even where the response is more "felt back" than "talked back" response can still be detected.[141] The language of African-American worship emphasizes not only the body but also the spirit. There is, in fact, only a semantic distinction between the two. The body allows the spirit to be sensibly expressed. The bizarre physical expression of the frontier revivals are not at all alien to African conceptions of ritual. It is characteristic of African-American worship to give deference to the presence of the spirit in the midst of the gathered community rather than to any particular written text, whether canonical or otherwise. It is the Word performed that is authoritative, not the dead letter.

Finally, African-American worship serves the community of which it is a part in cultivating resources, spiritual, material, psychic, for the struggle to carry on amidst a white supremacist culture. African-American worship has functioned most often as an alternative to the structures of society that threatened, both collectively and individually, the members of the community. African-American worship, as a competing ritual system of Christianity in American society, has by its very presence declared the hypocrisy of Christian racism. While not without faults of their own, black churches embody a prophetic critique of a crucial failing in European-American Christianity while sheltering their members from its worst effects and on occasion forcing some measure of remedy. African-American Protestant liturgical traditions are the ritual legacy of a captive people who transformed an alien tradition into a ritual system that made survival possible and liberation destiny. African-American Protestant worship is an implicit critique of European-American worship and a paradigm for the inculturation of the Christian story in the US.

CHAPTER 3

"Cities on Hills":
An Analytical Narrative of the Construction of European-American Protestant Liturgical Traditions

European-American Protestant liturgical traditions sprang to life as self-conscious alternatives to the medieval Roman Mass. Beginning in the sixteenth century, reform-minded Europeans asserted their right to create modes of Christian practice independent of Roman, and, later, of various imperial and national, authorities. Luther, Zwingli, Calvin and their followers crafted liturgies that reflected local realities, humanist insights, and newly rediscovered documents from the era of the early church. As African-American worship facilitated the formation of African Americans as a distinct people, early Protestant worship accompanied the emergence of pre-modern Europeans, a people with a new sense of identity as individuals (as opposed to being a member of an immutable class category) and citizens (as opposed to being a subject of one's king or queen).

European-American Protestant liturgical traditions span nearly four hundred years, from the settlement of Jamestown in 1607, which occasioned the establishment of the Church of England in the colony of Virginia, to the present day. This span of time has included the emergence of new denominations with particular liturgical emphases and the adaptation of older families of rites to new historical circumstances. Members of these traditions continue to adopt new forms of liturgy and modify existing ones.

As in the previous chapter, characterization of the worship practices of numerous groups of people over a significant span of time is fraught with risk and difficulty. Europeans, like Africans, arrived on the shores of this New World from many different countries.[1] They were English, Dutch, French, Spanish, Irish, German and Scottish. European immigrants followed a variety of dreams across the Atlantic. Some sought adventure or profit. Others desired land, honor and fortune for their king or queen. Still others desired freedom to worship without interference. They were Catholic, Lutheran, Anglican, Presbyterian, Congregational, Deists, humanist, unchurched, Puritan, Quaker. They were preachers, explorers, soldiers, missionaries, farmers, hunters, landholders, governors. They were loyalists, democrats, apolitical. Nevertheless, in the course of time, some identifiable traits of the worship of Protestants of European descent arose out of these disparate beginnings.

Although I will identify common traits of European-American Protestant liturgical traditions in the course of this chapter, my conclusions rest upon reading between the lines of historical and liturgical scholarship. Because European Americans define their own beliefs and institutions as the norms of American society, they do not characterize them as "white" but rather as "American". In the same way, European-

American scholars of European-American subjects do not identify themselves as "white" but as, for instance, a historian of American churches. In addition, whereas scholars write explicitly of African survivals in the worship of Black churches, they do not use a comparable term for cultural adaptations that took place in Europe. In fact, culturally-conditioned aspects of European traditions are more prevalent in US Protestant liturgical traditions, since they were not subject to the same forces of annihilation as the traditional practices of enslaved Africans. Identification of these modifications is especially crucial for multicultural congregations, since the assumption that the practice of European Americans is the norm while African-American styles are challenges to that norm creates an unequal basis for negotiation.

In Chapter 2, I identified central characteristics of African-American Protestant liturgical traditions. The worship styles of African-American communities arise out of the creativity of a people confronted with the crisis of being defined as less than human because of the color of their skin. European-American Christians created that crisis of faith for African Americans even as we exploited the toil of their hands and their contributions to US culture. Therefore, despite the fact that (or, perhaps, because) these traditions are my home, I approach European-American Protestant liturgical traditions with a hermeneutic of suspicion, seeking the elements of creativity that are evident in the historical record but concerned also with the links between these rites and oppressive social power.

The narrative that follows emphasizes two contrasting claims. On the one hand, European-American Protestant liturgical traditions tend to equate European-American civilization with the coming Kingdom of God, confusing the flawed and temporal with the ideal and ultimate. On the other hand, European-American Protestant liturgical traditions facilitate the encounter of God and God's people, forming local communities of faithful and self-critical Christians. European-American Protestant liturgical traditions reflect the temptation of those with social power to adjust their rites in ways that support their privilege. Those who benefit from established social arrangements almost inevitably, and often unconsciously, seek to reinforce them. Systems of rites that display the social order as derivative of the divinely created order are crucial elements in this effort. At the same time, Christian traditions call social arrangements into question. In Christianity, the rites intend to preserve and re-present the salvific and liberating experiences of people of faith past and present, sacred texts preserve stories of God's intervention in history on the side of the downtrodden, and prophetic voices relate visions of an ultimate future of peace and justice.[2] European-American Protestants continue to create new, authentic styles of worship, while also displaying their captivity to their biases.

I detect two streams within the history of European-American worship. First, there are what are now called the *mainline* traditions: The Episcopal Church (USA); The Presbyterian Church (USA); The United Methodist Church; The Evangelical Lutheran Church of America; The United Church of Christ and related denominations. This branch of churches developed out of the Protestant Reformation, adapted to the cultural shifts of the Enlightenment, and became the churches of the (relatively) privileged classes of European Americans. The *mainline* churches emphasize rationality, morality, and decorum.

The second stream, the *enthusiast,* took shape in reaction to the rationality and liberalism of the first. Rooted in the liturgical innovations of the Great Awakenings, *enthusiast* traditions are now most clearly represented in The Southern Baptist Convention, The Assemblies of God, and related independent Baptist, Holiness, and Pentecostal denominations. *Enthusiast* worship seeks to engage believers and convert unbelievers. The freedom to respond demonstratively in worship tends to attract those with relatively little economic security or social privilege, and enthusiasm often wanes as adherents climb the socio-economic ladder. While the streams of liturgical style cut across denominations—often splitting denominations in two. For instance, while the Baptist and Methodist traditions contributed most significantly to the development of European-American "enthusiasm", many churches in these denominational families now worship in *mainline* style. To make matters more complicated, Baptists in New England have roots in the *mainline* Puritan stream but, swept up in the First Great Awakening, came to accept the "new measures" and utilized revival techniques in their mission efforts. These "new measures" soon became standard liturgical fare, and, thus, the style employed throughout The Southern Baptist Convention. Following a different path to a similar destination, while Methodists inherited a dual tradition of sacramentalism and revivalism, the tension between branches of the denomination that seek to restore prayer based upon early church forms and those who embrace the norms of popular culture remains to this day.

I organize the discussion of the characteristics of European-American Protestant liturgical traditions in this chapter around these two streams. They are sibling traditions within the family of European-American rites. While sharing much in common, they are also markedly different. They develop as distinct responses by European-American Protestants to various historical circumstances. I will address each in turn.

I conclude the chapter by identifying central themes of European-American Protestant liturgical traditions, in order to facilitate comparison with my observations about African-American Protestant liturgical styles in Chapter 2. I seek, again, not to box in the variety of worship styles of white people in this country but to propose language that portrays the central characteristics of the worship of this racial group. The purpose, once more, is to provide a historical perspective for, among others, multicultural congregations that desire to create authentic local liturgies in which all members may participate equally and fully.

Mainline worship: from Margin to Center

The British were the dominant colonial presence in what is now the United States, by the mid-seventeenth century.[3] While the British took longer to launch their imperial conquests than the Spanish and French, British colonists settled thickly upon the "new world" when the necessary developments had occurred. One set of historians describe it:

> By the early 17th century conditions in England were conducive to colonial venture. A capitalist class was rising with funds to invest in such projects. There were many

discontented who would be ready to emigrate—religious minorities who desired toleration or the chance to impose their own kind of religious uniformity and those who suffered economically from the enclosure movement and rising prices.[4]

The early British colonies exhibited the diversity of worship styles for which US churches are still known. While Virginia's charter established the Church of England, the English dissenters, and especially those known as Puritans, molded the dominant religious sensibilities of the colonies. Ahlstrom writes:

> By the most remarkable happenstance almost the entire spectrum into which Christian life and thought were refracted by the tumultuous English Reformation was recapitulated in the American colonies. Sometimes the circumstances were strangely reversed, with Quakers dominant in Pennsylvania, Roman Catholics in Maryland, and Congregationalists in New England—while Anglicans often found themselves an unprivileged minority … In one colony or another each major reformatory tradition would gain full expression; and because of the principle of toleration, other non-English traditions would in due course make their contribution. Persecution and harassment of minority groups would also erupt in the New World, but ultimately all churches would flourish in a degree of freedom unknown elsewhere. Puritanism, above all, would leave a legacy no less significant than the impact of Luther upon the German nation.[5]

The details of Puritan worship will be taken up below. Here, I simply note that the Puritans equate America (or at least their own settlements) with Christian civilization itself, hold a rational understanding of the faith (albeit combined with emotional commitment as well), and emphasize simplicity and order in worship. Each of these are themes central to the history of *mainline* European-American Protestant liturgical traditions.

I note within the history of the *mainline* stream of European-American Protestant liturgies six periods that highlight central developments. First, *mainline* liturgies originate in the Protestant Reformation, more specifically in the break with Rome by the Swiss churches in the sixteenth century and the break with Canterbury by the English Separatists in the seventeenth. Second, the early history of Puritans in New England, 1620–1725, is the period in which *mainline* patterns are introduced to, and begin to be shaped by, the North American environment. Third, the First Great Awakening and the American Revolution, 1725–1790, reveal competing understandings of the relationship of rationality and emotion in worship. Fourth, between 1790–1890, *mainline* worship encounters the frontier, the Second Great Awakening, the split of North and South, and the Civil War. Fifth, since the Civil War, *mainline* worship has experienced a welcome stability, even as it has undergone significant reform based primarily on the restoration of service book traditions. Finally, from the mid-twentieth century until today, in the face of the Holocaust and the social revolutions of the 1960s, liturgical experimentation parallels a movement towards convergence in *mainline* worship patterns.

Geneva: Birthplace of Reformed worship

Several of the oldest and most dominant branches of European-American Protestant worship grew out of the liturgical principles of sixteenth century Geneva. John Calvin (1509–1564), the chief Reformer of Geneva from 1541–1564, viewed his city as a model for Reformed communities throughout Europe. A Scot, John Knox (ca. 1505–1572), seeking refuge from Queen Mary's counter-reforms in England, and experience in a community more open to Reformed principles than the exiles in Frankfurt, arrived in Geneva in the late 1550s. Knox translated Calvin's liturgy for the parishioners of the exile church in which he served and returned home with it in 1558. In 1564, the Church of Scotland adopted Knox's liturgy as its standard order of worship and published it as *The Book of Common Order*. Reformed principles also served as the basis for *The Westminster Directory,* promulgated in 1645. The Puritans and other British separatists in England, and in New England, based their liturgies on Calvinist principles as well.

John Calvin studied first law and then theology in the humanist atmosphere of the University of Paris. He brought a keen intellect and great philological skills to the ranks of the Reformation. He joined the Reformed cause under duress as King Francis I, to whom the first edition of his magnum opus, *The Institutes of the Christian Religion,* is addressed, persecuted his friends.[6] In response, Francis forced Calvin into exile. Calvin never returned to his native land. He also never pursued the life of peaceful study that he desired.[7] He began contributing to debates about worship early on, as this was an area in which he differed significantly from Martin Luther (1483–1546) on the "right" and Ulrich Zwingli (1484–1531) on the "left".[8] His liturgical proposals were published as *The Form of Prayers* in 1542.

Calvin based his liturgy upon the work of two mentors: Martin Bucer (1491–1551) crafted the worship of Reformed churches in Strasbourg. Calvin spent three years with him while forced from Geneva during disputes over the amount of control he could exercise in the city, specifically over his right to deny the sacraments to congregants.[9] William Farel (1489–1565) swept away the Roman Mass in the churches of Geneva, reducing the liturgy to bare essentials: confessional rites, the reading of scripture, the sermon and a prayer. Farel's housekeeping allowed Calvin to construct a fuller service without contending with the Mass itself.[10]

I summarize Calvin's teachings about worship in three principles. First, worship is necessary for the assurance of God's elect. According to Calvin, people encounter the divine presence in Word and sacrament, respond to God's initiating grace with thanks and praise, and move first into unity with each other and then outward to perform ethical action in the world.[11] Calvin believed human beings need assurance because, once we are attuned to the glory of God's righteousness, the demands of God's law, and the impossibility of our faithfulness, we do not see evidence of our election but only our continuing depravity. In recognition of our self-doubt, God provides the church as a means to supply us with nourishment as a child is nourished by her mother. This nourishment takes two primary forms—the preached word and the sacraments. But acknowledging the fragility of our ability to perceive grace from the spoken word, Calvin emphasizes the importance of the sacraments. He writes:

> For seeing we are so weak that we cannot receive him with true heartfelt trust, when he
> is presented to us by simple doctrine and preaching, the Father of mercy, disdaining not
> to condescend in this matter to our infirmity, has been pleased to add to his word a visible
> sign, by which he might represent the substance of his promises, to confirm and fortify us
> by delivering us from all doubt and uncertainty.[12]

In contrast to the Scholastics who emphasized the action of the priest in making Christ
present in the sacraments, Calvin asserts that God is the initiating and central actor
in worship. In describing the genius of the Reformed liturgy, Nicholas Wolterstorff
writes: "... God acts here and now, affirming that his promises are for real".[13] To
emphasize the active presence of God, Calvin provides strong prayers of invocation
before the sermon and before the Supper. Both word and sacrament are experiences
in which God confronts human beings in forms that we can grasp through our senses
in order to assure us of God's abiding love.

Calvin's second principle subjugates all matters of Christian life to the Word of
God, eschewing all human inventions, no matter how ancient or assumed. Calvin
attacks any ceremony that confuses the distinct roles of God and humanity in the
economy of salvation. However, while affirming the Word of God as the supreme
authority in all matters, he understood the Word as a living word, not restricted to the
actual received texts of the Bible. His commitment to biblical standards is subject to
pastoral flexibility. He writes:

> ...the Lord in his sacred oracles faithfully embraced and clearly expressed both the whole
> sum of true righteousness, and all aspects of the worship of his majesty, and whatever was
> necessary to salvation; therefore, in these the Master alone is to be heard. But because he
> did not will in outward discipline and ceremonies to prescribe in detail what we ought to
> do (because he foresaw that this depended upon the state of the times, and he did not deem
> one form suitable for all ages), here we must take refuge in those general rules which he
> has given, that whatever the necessity of the church shall require for order and decorum
> should be tested against these. Lastly, because he has taught nothing specifically, and
> because these things are not necessary to salvation, and for the upbuilding of the church
> ought to be variously accommodated to the customs of each nation and age, it will be
> fitting (as the advantage of the church will require) to change and abrogate traditional
> practices and to establish new ones. Indeed, I admit that we ought not to charge into
> innovation rashly, suddenly, for insufficient cause. But love will best judge what may hurt
> or edify; and if we let love be our guide, all will be safe.[14]

Calvin structured his service on the patterns of the New Testament (while
admitting the references were few and obscure) and those of the early church made
newly available through the work of Humanist scholars such as Erasmus.[15] Even
so, he was not shy about making modifications to established traditions, whether
biblical, Roman or Reformed. For instance, while he believed the Lord's prayer
to be the norm of all exchanges between Christians and their God, he insisted that
people need only pray according to its spirit and not feel limited to its actual words.[16]
This same freedom can be seen in his position in the Reformation debates about
the Lord's Supper. He was not wed to the literal meaning of the words: "This is
my body". Instead he thought metaphorically—when we eat bread together, we are
feeding on Christ. Interestingly, his liberalism in regard to The Words of Institution

contrasts with literalism elsewhere. He held inviolable the creedal formula that Christ had been bodily resurrected "and sits at the right hand of God the Father". This being the case, the congregation cannot eat Christ on earth around a table, but instead, occasioning a heightened emphasis on the participation of the Spirit, the congregation is lifted up to the heavenly banquet table to receive "the body" directly from Christ on high.[17]

Calvin's third principle is that worship should edify. He created his liturgy among residents of a relatively prosperous and independent city. The people of Geneva were among the pioneers in experiments with communal structures free of king and pope. They were making their own decisions in social, religious and economic spheres. They were able to read and wanted to understand the content of the prayers, which they had heard previously only in Latin, a language they no longer spoke. Calvin gave his parishioners a vernacular liturgy. He offered them long portions of scripture with the best interpretation of the day at every service. He supplied fresh translations of the psalms and new tunes with which to sing them.[18] He also insisted that "all should be done decently and in order" so that nothing obscured the worshipers' understanding of what was being done. Just as Paul encouraged early Christians to pray for the gifts of interpretation and prophecy rather than the ability to speak in tongues (I Corinthians 14:26–40), so Calvin wanted everything in worship to illumine rather than to obscure or divide. Calvin explained every symbol employed in worship. He insisted that no sacrament could be performed without having a sermon precede it. He also brought the font to the front of the room and baptized only during regular Sunday services so that all could see and hear what baptism meant.

Calvin contributed significantly to the richness of Christian liturgical thought and practice. Yet, his own principles define not only the strengths but also the primary weaknesses of Reformed liturgies. For instance, while Calvin insisted that worship provide needed assurance to believers, he created substantial barriers to that assurance. Calvin assumed the church would include both saints and sinners. He welcomed any and all to listen to the preaching and to participate in the prayers, but, in the course of the eucharistic rite, he excommunicates sinners, a practice known as "fencing the table". He also invented a custom of a time of preparation before each celebration of the eucharist.[19] Calvin uses the meal as an opportunity not only to acknowledge publicly the election of those whose proper conduct is beyond doubt, but also as an opportunity to humiliate those who are known and unrepentant sinners. While elsewhere insisting that human beings need to apprehend God's promises through their senses, Calvin structures the encounter with God at table as the reception, not of assurance, but of reward.

Similarly, while Calvin desired worship to edify, he bequeathed prayers that are "prolix and verbose".[20] The tone of the Geneva liturgy is penitential and didactic. Calvin felt compelled to explain everything. Even prayers addressed to God contain lessons and reprimands for human ears. He writes:

> Grant...that we might rightly perceive our lost estate by nature, and the condemnation we have deserved and heaped up to ourselves by disobedient lives. So that *conscious that in*

ourselves there is no good thing ... we may give ourselves up in firm trust to thy beloved Son.[21]

In addition, Calvin exerted a high level of control over the citizens of Geneva. Through legions of elders and deacons, he scrutinized their private lives. In worship, he emphasized acts of introspection, confession, and a rigorous fencing of the table.[22] He encouraged understanding, but at the same time reserved for himself final authority in areas of doctrine. The style of his liturgical leadership, and even of his pastoral prayers, indicates his self-understanding as the central teaching authority within the congregation. White writes: "So great was the imperative to teach that each service contains a condensed course in theology and ethics".[23]

Calvin's liturgy contains a dynamic of hospitality and repulsion. The people are welcomed to the table and yet significant obstacles are placed in the way. They are repeatedly assured both of their election by God and their depravity. They are called to participate in their own redemption but are constantly excoriated by the clergy. They are given access to the scriptures through rigorous humanist scholarship but reminded of their slight capacity for true understanding. They are called to give authority and attention to God alone and yet hear constant moral didacticism in the place of divine address. This tension between human striving and divine providence evident in many aspects of the liturgy increases in the subsequent development of the Reformed tradition. Pioneers in the movement from subject to citizen, from laborer to entrepreneur, from superstition to scientific investigation, the sixteenth-century Swiss embody the tensions of later generations of Europeans, who will answer in various ways the question of how to enjoy responsibly the expanded opportunity for self-determination that they experience when they are freed of the shackles of ignorance, poverty, and, even, geographical confines in the context of divine Providence.

After Calvin, Reformed theology became more focused on "predestination". His understanding that the church was both visible and invisible, so that Christians could not know, but had to assume that they, and others, were of the elect, receded before a new emphasis on proving one's regeneration. McGrath writes:

> The idea of a covenant between God and his elect, paralleling the covenant between God and Israel in the Old Testament, began to become of major importance to the rapidly expanding Reformed Church. The "covenant of grace" laid down God's obligations to his people, and his people's obligations (religious, social and political) to him. It defined the framework within which individuals and societies functioned. The form which this theology took in England—Puritanism—is of particular interest. This sense of being the "elect people of God" was heightened as the new people of God entered the new promised land—America.[24]

Puritan worship in New England

The Puritans were disciples of Calvin in England. They contended that, while Henry VIII's ecclesial reforms were substantial, they had stopped short of the ideal. For instance, while Henry won freedom from Roman authority, the Puritans wanted to be freed of royal control and episcopal polity as well. While Henry dismantled the monastic orders and claimed their property as his own, the Puritans wanted further emphasis on the priesthood of all believers, going so far as to equate professional and family life in the secular world with Christian vocation. While Cranmer's texts appeared after Henry had died, the Puritans agreed, in principle, that vernacular liturgies should be published in affordable formats like the 1549 *Book of Common Prayer*.[25] Still, they desired liturgies with less ceremony and more flexibility for local adaptation. The Puritans even acknowledged substantial agreement with Anglican theology, especially as it drew heavily on Calvin in its doctrinal constitutions. Yet, they could not be satisfied without further democratization of the church (through either a Presbyterian or Congregational, rather than an Episcopal, system of governance) and strict adherence to the bible in all matters of faith and church life. Royal and Anglican authorities considered the Puritans a threat and actively persecuted them until the Toleration Act of 1689.[26]

Among the Puritans, factions arose over questions of strategy. Some exhibited willingness to continue the reform effort within the Anglican communion. Others desired to establish an alternative sect. Some of these latter left not only the Anglican communion but also England. One of these groups, the Pilgrims, went first to Holland and then to Plymouth beginning what would become a steady migration to North America. Life in the "new" world enabled the Puritans to establish themselves as "pure" communities. Beyond the reach of crown and miter, they were now the ruling party of church and state, able to order their life as they saw fit.

The Puritans desired to live a fully reformed Anglican lifestyle as a model for the church they had left behind. White writes: "... the Boston Puritans considered themselves Anglicans worshiping as Anglicans should but were legally prevented from doing in the homeland".[27] In the wilderness of New England, they pieced together housing, a meeting house, an economy, a way of life.[28] A part of their effort to form a new society was to establish their own ritual system. They worshiped at home each day with prayer and bible study, attended a lecture once a week, and services twice on Sunday.[29] They imitated the Scottish practice of abstinence from all secular activity on the Sabbath, while eschewing most of the traditional church year, with its seasons and feast days that they felt risked obscuring the primacy of Sunday.[30] The morning and evening Sunday services were slightly different, but both emphasized preaching.[31] The morning service highlighted the role of the pastor who offered a lengthy sermon and an equally lengthy pastoral prayer. The evening service had more space for congregational participation and response.

The Puritans held four central liturgical principles. First, everything in worship must have biblical warrant. The Puritans departed from Calvin's contention that God did not decree specific practices but allowed customs to change according to the needs of the church in various circumstances. To the contrary, the Puritans held that God would not leave matters as important as worship to human invention. Their primary concern differed from Calvin's. They sought to eliminate the human tendency towards idolatry, rather than on giving assurance to self-doubting humans. They saw in every human ceremony the possibility of creating false gods, "creaturely self-assertions against God's will".[32] While they found few concrete descriptions of Christian worship in the biblical texts and spent considerable energy interpreting the references that do exist, they would allow no other method to determine their liturgical practice. Davies writes: "[their] enduring aim in worship was to maintain only Christ's pure ordinances as authorized by the Word of God rather than determined by the conventions of ecclesiastical tradition or the willfulness of human invention or fancy".[33]

Second, worship signifies and maintains a covenant relationship between God and God's people. The Puritans understood their communities to be composed of visible saints; they were God's elect. All members were required to make a public profession of faith and signed a formal community covenant. Covenant documents provided a structure for the whole of life. Davies writes:

> Their interest was not in the historic drama of the past, but in the spiritual civil war of the present, in which Christ fought Satan for the possession of souls. Puritans in their type of spirituality, did not, like Roman Catholics or Anglicans, aim directly at the imitation of Christ. Rather they recapitulated in themselves the story of Everyman Adam, from temptation and fall, through reconciliation, restoration, and renewal.[34]

Worship provided guidance for daily living as the Puritans sought to fulfill their covenant obligations and, thereby, to be worthy of "all God's benefits". Scripture, and its interpretation by the minister in preaching, served as a source of inspiration and moral lessons. The preacher delivered the sermons, often over an hour in length, in "the plain style".[35] Congregations expected a preacher to explain the scriptures so that all could understand the "doctrine, reason and use" of a given passage.[36] Congregants took notes and the head of the house customarily questioned family members on the themes of the sermon over dinner.[37] The Puritan covenant structure ensured that the moral and theological lessons that the pastor conveyed in worship were attended to and influenced the whole of one's life.

The third principle of Puritan worship is simplicity. Puritan worship created an experience of stark encounter. Nothing stood between the worshipers and their God. The Reformation shifted the primary locus of participation from the medieval dependence on sight to hearing, reflecting a shift from image (Christ embodied in the host) to text (Christ represented in the Word preached). The Puritans took this trend to an extreme. The austerity of these iconoclasts was evident in their homes, their churches, and their lives. Decoration was minimal and practical. Puritan "worldly asceticism" considered simplicity and rationality beautiful.[38]

Finally, worship practices, while based strictly on biblical warrant, are in fact locally defined, a principle also known as *subsidiarity*.[39] Each covenant community determined its own specific order of service, although standard patterns quickly developed. Among Puritans, every person took responsibility for his or her own spiritual life, and, similarly, each community worshiped according to its particular, collective interpretation of biblical mandates. Local decisions also determined the content of each service. Pastors crafted sermon and prayers, but the congregation often responded to the sermon with their own interpretations and could make prayer requests known.[40] Lay people also sang. Early on, the Puritans maintained Calvin's restriction of hymn texts to the psalter, but, beginning in the late eighteenth century, they sang original compositions as well. The remainder of the service was left to the pastor, who had special responsibility among the saints. A seventeenth- or eighteenth-century Puritan preacher was to be a model saint, a biblical scholar, a practical theologian, and a liturgical presider. He (they were all male) developed an original sermon of about one hour in length for each service and offered extemporaneous prayers of similar duration.

As was the case in Geneva, the principles of Puritan worship also determined the primary weaknesses of their tradition. Their emphasis on biblical warrant for all practices cut them off from the riches of Christian spirituality throughout the ages.[41] The requirements of articulating one's faith publicly and living in accord with the community covenant intimidated some and turned off other members of succeeding generations.[42] Their emphasis on simplicity meant that senses other than ear and eye were simply not addressed.[43]

Puritans were people who continually had to balance self-confidence and anxiety.[44] They were valiant in their struggle for survival in the harshness of what was to them a New England wilderness and yet continually prayed for forgiveness of unknown wrongs in the face of tragedies that they interpreted as divine judgment. They declared their righteousness as a community of the elect and yet sought ever clearer ways to manifest evidence of their election. They asserted their possession of the keys to the kingdom as they sat in judgment over their neighbors, determining who deserved access to the privileges and responsibilities of the covenant, while continually confessing their own unworthiness and failings.

The Puritans believed they were living out their own struggle with temptation under the complete control of God, who was both Judge and Savior. They believed they were among those chosen to reach such perfection as life-in-the-flesh might allow and yet could not dismiss their doubts. Their worship continually called them to be better, with the threat of destruction always at hand and the promise of eternal bliss beyond. They wedded the divine plan with their own individual struggles and the fate of their vulnerable settlements. Their primary legacy, still potent in European-American culture, consists of an interweaving of national fortune and divine pleasure. Davies writes:

> ... the Puritan concept of sacred time ... presupposes a covenanted people in New England, an elect and holy nation, a new Israel. This covenant conception provided the transforming myth by which successive generations felt their country to be unique, their spiritual fortune assured, their way of life hallowed, and their values approved by God. If it lacked flexibility, this firm conviction was the strength and support of the Puritan soul.[45]

Even as their counterparts in England gained political ascendancy and imposed national reform, albeit temporarily, through the Westminster Conventions of 1642–1645, the Puritan ethos in New England was breaking down. The initial fervor dissipated as the seventeenth century wore on. The *jeremiads,* a special genre of excoriating sermons, did not result in widespread repentance and renewal. The prosperous economy of Boston demanded attention. The security of land ownership alleviated anxiety about physical survival and, perhaps, lessened the need for an all-pervasive religious system to govern life. The demise of the indigenous people shifted down to the lowest levels of the collective unconscious, no longer a daily threat, nor a reminder of the ambiguous roots of colonization. Meeting houses became, simply, churches, reserved only for sacred purposes and no longer the center of all civic and ecclesial activity. Worship became the obsession of a few and conversion more an exception than a rule. The covenant community became a minority in the midst of the growing pluralism and secularity of society rather than the backbone of the social order.

The Enlightenment, Jonathan Edwards and the First Great Awakening

Not every New England colonist professed a Puritan version of Christianity, nor, for that matter, any faith at all. In addition, many who did attend church did so without becoming full members. Yet, Puritan communities remained vibrant into the seventeenth century and their religiosity pervaded their communities. As time passed, however, public profession of faith among the children of Puritans became less frequent. Members of the second and third generations did not know the context of persecution from which their forebears had fled, and their commitment to a Puritan identity held less vigor. In 1662, desperate to keep their communities viable, the New England Puritans invented a Half-way Covenant, whereby children of community members might be baptized even if their parents had not publicly professed their faith.[46] The Half-way Covenant encouraged another generation to remain affiliated with the churches, but also weakened the identification of Puritan churches as pure communities of visible saints.

The decline in Puritan piety was related to other trends in European culture. Among these, the Enlightenment was the most important. In medieval Europe, religion explained and regulated the whole of life. Enlightenment thinkers discovered rational laws that governed the natural order, challenging the power of religious authority. The Reformers demonstrated how the intellectual tools and technologies of Renaissance humanism could be used to challenge the authority of medieval Catholicism, as one contribution to this profound shift in European self-understanding.[47] Scientific and philosophical advances of the seventeenth century served this transition as well. In science, Galileo and Newton, among others, established the method of scientific proof through experimental testing which undermined explanations based solely upon tradition. At the same time, philosophers such as Descartes and Locke suggested that people ought to believe only what could be rationally, or, even more specifically, mathematically, proven. Walker, et al., write:

> These developments in science and philosophy provided the foundations for that movement which characterized the atmosphere of the eighteenth century, the Enlightenment. The Enlightenment was the conscious effort to apply the rule of reason to the various aspects of individual and corporate life. Its fundamental principles—autonomy, reason, pre-established harmony—deeply influenced the thought and action of the modern world and conditioned the atmosphere into which Christianity moved.[48]

The Magisterial churches, namely the Lutheran and Reformed branches of Protestant traditions, accepted Renaissance humanism and emphasized the centrality of human understanding to faith. These churches embraced Enlightenment insights without recognizing the potential threat they held to the place and function of worship. White, describing eighteenth century Lutheranism, writes:

> The Enlightenment attempted to understand Christianity exclusively in rational terms. God's work was portrayed as that of a watchmaker who contemplates a well-made universe without interfering with its operation. It is natural, given such a disposition, to look at the sacraments as unlikely intrusions of divinity into human life. As a result the Enlightenment tended to suppress what sacramental piety still survived, although without eliminating the practice of sacraments. Curiously, the Enlightenment kept sacraments as biblical commands, and therefore obligatory, but celebrated them infrequently and with little enthusiasm.[49]

In colonial America, Enlightenment teachings shaped a new religious movement, Deism, which attracted a significant portion of the intellectual class with its rational and democratic philosophy. Worship among the Deists and a growing number of sophisticated East Coast Christians took on a strong moralistic caste. "The message of the Eucharist became 'be good' rather than 'God is good'".[50] Deists, and other "enlightened" Christians, symbolized their emphasis on preaching by allowing the pulpit to dominate the table architecturally. They intended worship to teach people how to live within the natural harmony around them. "For deism ... the end of worship was not communion with God but social harmony. Ceremonial was dismissed as useless and became minimal".[51] This did not mean that worship was abandoned. The Unitarians, an eighteenth century Congregational off-shoot, de-emphasized the sacraments (so much so that, in 1832, Ralph Waldo Emerson refused to celebrate the Lord's Supper at all), but at the same time introduced several important innovations in worship. They shifted the pulpit from a long wall to one of the short ones, added organs and choirs, and employed new architectural styles.[52] Deism and Unitarianism both drew former Puritans to their ranks, attracting converts with their aesthetic and rational emphasis in matters of faith.

In response to the decline of piety and the rise of new alternatives, Puritan conservatives clung stubbornly to the notion of a holy community and its strict membership requirements, while enlightenment adherents envisioned a secular moral community. Between them, Jonathan Edwards (1703–1758) emerged. Edwards combined strict Puritan values and Enlightenment philosophy.[53] On the one hand, he was the grandson of Solomon Stoddard, who supported the Half-way Covenant and an "open table" approach to the sacraments in order to preserve the Puritan ethos. On the other, Edwards was a graduate of Yale, where he developed a theological philosophy based on the approach of Enlightenment pioneer, John Locke.

In 1726, Edwards accepted a position as associate pastor in Northampton, Massachusetts, under his grandfather. He became full pastor at the time of his grandfather's death in 1729. His preaching brought him renown, revitalized the faith of many, and attracted a large number of new converts. Edwards found this "awakening" to be a "surprising act of God"[54] in response to the general decline in commitment of the descendants of Puritans and a hopeful alternative to the compromises of his grandfather.[55] He wrote in 1735:

Our public assemblies were then beautiful; the congregation was alive in God's service, every one earnestly intent on the public worship, every hearer eager to drink in the words of the minister as they came from his mouth; the assembly in general were, from time to time, in tears while the word was preached; some weeping with sorrow and distress, others with joy and love, others with pity and concern for the souls of their neighbors.[56]

Edwards defended the demonstrative responses to his preaching from conservatives and liberals alike, forging a new Reformed synthesis for a battered theological and liturgical tradition. He rediscovered a connection between a rational faith and the human affections like the one which had moved the first Puritans to leave their homeland in order to create a model Christian community in the wilderness of North America. The responses of his congregation showed that heart, mind, and body could all play a part in the response of a believer to God. Edwards interpreted the revivals for the world through his prolific writings, while testing the new measures for faithfulness to the Spirit of God at home.[57] Other churches experienced a similar movement of the spirit, and the series of revivals that occurred throughout the colonies became known as the First Great Awakening.

In the Great Awakening, a new worship style, the revival, took shape. Inspired by Edwards' theological contributions, his fellow evangelists structured services primarily to convert nonbelievers rather than primarily to nurture the faith of believers. Fiery preaching, and the responses it generated, were, literally, center stage. The emotional and gestural responses these "new measures" aroused appeared on the American frontier in succeeding generations. Ahlstrom writes:

Flamboyant and highly emotional preaching made its first and widespread appearance in the Puritan churches (though by no means in all), and under its impact there was a great increase in the number and intensity of bodily effects of conversion—fainting, weeping, shrieking, etc. But we capture the meaning of the revival only if we remember that many congregations in New England were stirred from a staid and routine formalism in which experiential faith had been reality to only a scattered few.[58]

Under Edwards, Puritan (now known more commonly as Congregational) worship placed less emphasis on restraint of body and emotion. Eighteenth-century Puritan communities needed not so much to purge the converted of stubborn sin, but to excite the religious affections of the lukewarm and to call the unchurched into full communion. Edwards cultivated an encounter between worshipers and their God that demanded immediate bodily expression and not simply intellectual assent. He writes: "... the mind can have no lively or vigorous exercise, without some effect upon the body".[59]

While emphasizing that one can only demonstrate that one's conversion was true and spiritual through one's Christian practice, Edwards owned slaves. At the end of his life, he advocated on behalf of Native Americans, and his son and many of his students would contribute to the abolition movement. However, Edwards accepted and even supported the "the traditional social hierarchy of eighteenth century Anglo-America ... [and was] loath to see the radical theological implications of his support for revivals issue in correspondingly radical social applications".[60] Edwards assumed the superiority of the white over the black race: "Edwards himself never evidenced any sense of contradiction between his own disinterested ethic of freedom and the fact of slavery".[61]

In another of the great eighteenth-century cultural shifts, the American Revolution against the English monarchy turned attention from religion to politics. The war devastated European-American Protestant churches. Ministers were called away to fight or serve as chaplains; many were killed. Church buildings were destroyed. Church membership fell along with the commitment of those who remained affiliated. Deist principles gained increasing popularity. By 1800, only five percent of the population belonged to a church. Walker, et al., write:

> The churches that spread in America were clearly transplanted churches. But in the new environment, and especially for churches that had been established in Europe but not in the colonies, there was confusion and hesitation, because familiar practices and procedures often did not work well. Many church members who had been faithful in the Old World did not (or for reasons of distance could not) retain their religious ties in the New. The established bodies were also troubled, both by the decline in fervor of their own members and by the spread of dissidents in their midst. Furthermore, the effects of the rationalism and Deism of the Age of Reason were beginning to be felt in the churches, and many outside of them were indifferent or even hostile to religion. Despite the growth of churches through immigration, a situation in which a steadily increasing segment of the population had no religious connections was developing.[62]

Beginning in 1725 with the Great Awakening, two conflicting trends are evident in the history of *mainline* traditions. On the one hand, American evangelical religion and its revival worship form was taking shape. *Enthusiast* traditions are the topic of the next section, but they influenced *mainline* worship as well. The Great Awakening introduced innovations such as greater congregational participation, increased bodily movement, and poetic forms of theological discourse to European-American Protestant liturgical traditions as a whole. On the other hand, in response to these trends, Deists, Unitarians, and other liberal Christians further emphasized decorum, rationality and morality.

I note three observations regarding this period of contradictions. First, both trends are European-American trends; both enthusiasm and rationalism are liturgical styles of white people in America. Second, both the liberal and the revival traditions accept Enlightenment principles about the world, although in different ways. The liberal traditions reject any notion of supernatural intervention in the world of nature. There is no expectation of divine presence, much less activity, among the worshipers. In contrast, although the revival traditions retain a sense that the divine spirit is active in worship and moves people to conversion, these traditions accept the Enlightenment emphasis on the individual. They supplant the Pauline image of the church as "the Body of Christ" with an ecclesiology based upon the notion that "Jesus is *my* personal Lord and Savior", and they treat the sacraments as membership rites, which recognize rather than facilitate one's conversion and sanctification. Third, the Great Awakening involved members of established New England Congregationalist Churches, the landowners and professionals, whereas the contemporaneous Methodist movement in Britain appealed mainly to members of the working class. The relation of ecstatic worship forms and class location is important, and yet there is no absolute correspondence of high ecstasy to low economic security.

As the nineteenth century begins, the Puritan legacy remains, but the life and worship of New England fades into the shadows. European-American communities understand themselves as pioneers under divine mandate to establish a holy nation. This mandate justifies the violence of the conquest of the new world. Further, the prosperity, both material and spiritual, that they acquire as a result of the conquest is seen as a sign of divine favor. Subsequent generations inherit this sense of national destiny, but now in secular and imperialistic vocabulary. They pursue the freedom to establish their own civic order, but disregard those not a part of the community covenant—the indigenous, the African, the newcomer. They are endowed with equal measures of self-reliance, self-confidence, anxiety, and self-doubt. The Puritan legacy moves some, mostly those with some means, toward the cerebral and moralistic tendencies of Puritanism and drives others, mostly the less fortunate, westward to the opportunity and chaos of the frontier.

Revivalism and Schism in the Nineteenth Century

After the colonies gained independence from England, their new Constitution created new and unprecedented relations between church and state. In the young nation, not only would there be no established church, but all churches received the right to exist without interference. Churches were free of the privilege, but also the burden, of defending themselves as the one true church. Instead, the churches existed as equals, both to compete for members and to cooperate in projects of mutual interest. The separation of church and state prepared the stage for the emergence of new and substantial revival, mission, and social reform efforts in the nineteenth century, a cultural movement known as The Second Great Awakening.

Discussion of the liturgical innovations of the Second Great Awakening can be found in the next section on *enthusiast* traditions. Here, I mention only those aspects of the revival movement that influenced the *mainline* churches. The Methodist, Baptist, and Presbyterian churches promoted the Second Great Awakening most forcefully. The first two groups figure prominently below in my discussion of the *enthusiast* stream. I take up the Presbyterians here.

In the mid-eighteenth century, a rift emerged among Presbyterians, among other denominations, because of contrasting responses to the emergence of revivalism. In Congregationalism, the two sides were known as Old Lights and New Lights; Presbyterians used the terms Old School and New School.[63] The Old School endeavored to maintain the Reformed traditions of Calvin and Westminster, such as the doctrine of predestination and an orderly worship style. The New School adapted willingly to the challenges of the frontier, moving to less formal expressions of the faith and more emotional styles of worship. Many able revival preachers were Presbyterians, but Charles G. Finney (1792–1875) stands out as one who successfully instituted revival techniques in the established churches of the east.

Finney proposed a pragmatic approach to Christianity. He understood the function of the church to be the conversion of sinners. He wanted the church to convert as many as possible as efficiently as possible without being confined to traditional doctrine and forms of worship. He writes: "… under the gospel dispensation, God has established no particular system of measures to be employed and invariably adhered to in promoting religion …".[64] Instead, each generation must determine the style of worship that best fits its circumstances. Based on his experience, Finney was certain that revivals were the best vehicles for this promotion of religion. And, for him, a revival is no mysterious work of God but a system of techniques that when properly performed will consistently bring results.[65] A revival confronts backsliders and unregenerate sinners with their own sin and its consequences so they might accept their need for grace. He continues:

> God has found it necessary to take advantage of the excitability there is in mankind, to produce powerful excitements among them, before he can lead them to obey … Not that the excited feeling is religion, for it is not; but it is excited desire that prevents religion. The will is, in a sense, enslaved by the carnal and worldly desires. Hence it is necessary to awaken men to a sense of guilt and danger, and thus produce an excitement of counter feeling and desire which will break the power of carnal and worldly desire and leave the will free to obey God.[66]

Finney experimented extensively and identified several techniques that led reliably to the conversion of numerous participants.[67] First, he employed a popular, even coarse vocabulary, speaking to common people in their own manner. Second, he treated all persons equally; all were sinners and all potential saints. He made no distinction between black, white, rich, or poor. He campaigned vigorously on behalf of the abolition movement and allowed women to speak in "promiscuous assemblies", rejecting interpretations of biblical texts such as I Corinthians 14:34–35 that many said required women to be "seen but not heard". Third, Finney disregarded the traditions of set times for worship. Seeking to disrupt the routines of potential converts, he would preach at irregular hours and hold protracted meetings, lasting up to a week. Fourth, he singled out those who wavered before repentance, seating them in front on an "anxious bench" and focusing his prayers and exhortations directly upon them. Finally, he drew crowds to his revivals by advertising. Finney's techniques met his own criteria for success by bringing thousands into the church.

Finney's reliance on the participation of sinners in their own conversion, not to mention his assumptions about the clerical (as opposed to divine) role in promoting religion—positions that contribute to a theological stance known as Arminianism—led to controversy in the predestination-oriented Presbyterian Church.[68] Finney did not flinch from criticism and continued to promote revivalism over gradualism[69] and perfectionism over depravity.[70] Conservatives eventually forced him from his position at The Second Free Presbyterian Church in New York City. He accepted instead the pulpit of an independent Congregationalist church, the Broadway Tabernacle, and from there went on to the Presidency of Oberlin College.[71]

Finney's opponents in the Old School were proponents not simply of another style of worship, but, in fact, a different religious system. For Finney and his allies in the New School, religion consisted of human acts of obedience. For the orthodox, religion was God's work of saving humanity and only secondarily the response of gratitude by believers. Members of the Old School understood worship as an encounter initiated by God. In their view, Finney's techniques, however "successful" they might appear, denied the proper relation of sinner and Savior because they stressed the role of the preacher in bringing sinners to conversion. The Old School defended the principles of Westminster, allowing only those worship practices with scriptural warrant and emphasizing growth in understanding of scripture and doctrine over emotional responses to sermons.

Recent immigrants from Scotland and Ireland were the largest group which defended Reformed orthodoxy among Presbyterians. The greatest concentration of Old School adherents was in the South. The presence of Scotch and Scotch-Irish adherents of Old School approaches on the southern frontiers may help explain the relatively low record of success of Presbyterian revival efforts there.[72] In any case, the geographical division of southern Old School and northern New School quickly took on added significance.

In 1801, the New School joined a "Plan for Union" that combined missionary efforts with the Congregational churches.[73] The doctrinal compromise inherent in ecumenical efforts enraged the Old School. In 1837, finding themselves in power at the General Assembly, the Old School threw out the Plan and its supporters.[74] The split of the Presbyterian Church into Old and New, for all intents and purposes, split the denomination north and south as well. The Presbyterian schism anticipated the more general division of churches by the abolition movement and the Civil War.

In the final decades of the antebellum period, the revival movement fueled a number of social reform movements. Finney and other evangelists found their conversion techniques suitable to recruit supporters of various social causes as well. Finney pursued abolition most strenuously but also championed the temperance and women's suffrage causes. The revivals promoted a sense of urgency and empowered participants to organize and act on their convictions. They were a part of the great democratic movements of their day, showing the power of committed people to make concrete reforms.

On the opposite side of the spectrum, the liberal churches, such as the Unitarians, also engaged in social reform. The Unitarians and other enlightened Christians emphasized ethical action as the result of religion. They rallied behind rational argument rather than emotional commitment. Their greatest contribution was in the arena of education: the promotion of public schools and the funding of many private ones. These liberals shared the Arminian perspective with revivalists, emphasizing human responsibility in matters of faith. Both groups contrasted sharply with the orthodox position of reliance on God's Providence.

In the North, liberal and evangelical reformers combined forces to address the issue of slavery. First, the liberals, including some secular humanists such as William Lloyd Garrison, organized formal protests and published anti-slavery tracts.[75] Garrison himself proved too radical for most, but his outrages kindled responses in others and allowed more moderate activists to gain acceptance. By 1840, the churches of the North, both liberal and New School, took up the cause, decrying the "peculiar institution".[76]

In the South, the reaction was equally strident. While southern Presbyterians were conservative in terms of worship, other denominations, specifically the Methodists and Baptists, had brought revivalism below the Mason–Dixon line. Churches of all stripes in the South accommodated to slavery or died. For example, although

Wesley rejected slavery in the documents instituting the American Methodist Church at the Christmas Conference of 1784, nineteenth-century southern Methodists accommodated slavery and allowed slaveholders full membership. In reaction to northern criticism, the southern position became increasingly defensive and strident. White southerners felt unable to consider democratic reform because they were completely outnumbered by their slaves. Ahlstrom writes:

> Slavery was, to be sure, a labor system, but more fundamentally, it was considered an essential means of social control over a race which at the time was considered by almost everyone (including most abolitionists) as an inferior branch of the human species … Western ideals of equality and freedom simply could not be accepted.[77]

European-American Protestant worship contributed to the impasse over slavery that resulted in the Civil War. First, as the Second Great Awakening gained momentum, revivals became more common in both North and South. Revivals depend on emotional appeals which tend to place strict alternatives before potential converts. Revival preachers use stark and contrasting images: sinner and saint, heaven and hell, salvation and damnation. Of the South, Ahlstrom writes: "Revivalism also contributed its emotionalism and anti-intellectual mood to the politics of the era, and in so doing probably contributed to the expression of extremist views, just as it had in the North".[78]

Second, the churches, both enthusiast and mainline, wrapped the positions of their own side in divine rhetoric.[79] In worship, both northern and southern European-American Protestants, celebrated the justice of their cause and rehearsed the evil of their enemies. In sermon, prayer and song, preachers invoked God to aid their own side. Abraham Lincoln interpreted this strange symmetry of faith at the end of the conflict in his Second Inaugural Address:

> Both read the same bible, and pray to the same God; and each invokes His aid against the other. It may seem strange that any man should dare to ask a just God's assistance in wringing their bread from the sweat of other men's faces; but let us judge not that we may not be judged. The prayers of both could not be answered; that of neither has been answered fully. The Almighty has his own purposes … If we shall suppose that American slavery is one of those offenses which, in the Providence of God, must needs come forth, but which having continued through His appointed time, He now wills to remove, and that He gives both North and South, this terrible war, as the woe due to those by whom the offense came, shall we discern therein any departure from those divine attributes which the believers in a Living God always ascribe to Him?[80]

The Civil War, then, highlights both the divisions and the commonalities of European-American Protestant worship in the nineteenth century. Revivalism predominates, but both orthodox and liberal styles remain viable. Revival preachers employ nearly identical liturgical forms in North and South, but in the cause of vastly different worldviews. Forgetting, if not denying, their own complicity in the slave trade and the fears of white southerners who live as a racial minority, albeit in structures of their own devising, northern whites speak easily of the evil of slavery. In the South, worshipers learn the Bible verses that "prove" the inferiority of the black race and the obedience slaves owe their masters, cultivating nostalgia for "the Lost Cause". Even as the denominational structures of European-American Protestantism split, worship remains fairly constant with a mixture of *mainline* and *enthusiast* strains in both North and South.

Worship, specifically revivalism, played a role throughout the war as chaplains and other missionaries preached to the troops on both sides. Testimonies of soldiers and officers alike attest to the importance of their faith in helping them endure the hardships of war. Wartime revivalism with its propensity to divide the world into good and evil may have contributed to the tenacity of the fighting and, ultimately, to the length of the conflict.[81] In any case, the Great Awakening persisted through the Civil War in a more visible manner than the modest frontier missionary work pursued during the Revolution.

After the war, peace and Reconstruction did not repair the schism in European-American churches. Northern missionaries poured into the South, seeking primarily to convert the newly freed slaves. But these efforts only enhanced the alienation of northern and southern branches of the large European-American denominations. The Methodists remained divided until 1939;[82] Presbyterians, until 1983;[83] and Baptists, still. In separation, worship in northern and southern bodies becomes increasingly distinct. The northern European-American Protestant churches, responding to continued industrialization and scientific advancement, move further toward liberal models of worship. The South, rejecting modern discourse as northern and therefore alienating, clings to its "old time religion".

Liberalism and Restoration

Nineteenth-century revivalism influenced European-American Protestant worship forms in nearly all denominations. The majority of local services in many denominations shifted from the shapes instituted by Calvin and other founders and to what has been called the frontier "hymn sandwich". In this form, worship is divided into three parts: preliminaries, sermon, and harvest, with hymns serving as brackets between these.[84]

The great exception to the nineteenth-century convergence of *mainline* worship around the frontier "hymn sandwich" was the Anglican communion. The *Book of Common Prayer* protected Anglicans from revival tendencies. Instead, the Church of England and the Protestant Episcopal Church in America experienced restoration movements. The Anglo-Catholic Revival encouraged a return to frequent communion, attention to preaching, more elaborate ceremony, and more formal architectural styles including divided chancels. The "higher" (read, closer to medieval Roman Catholic) liturgical principles accompanied a renewed interest in social justice concerns among many Anglo-Catholic priests.

Anglican worship of this era held great appeal for many middle-class Americans, reflecting their own aspirations for leisure and beauty. The Presbyterian Church was one denomination that struggled to retain members who came to be attracted to Anglican worship.[85] Presbyterian church leaders responded to this Anglican "threat" by re-examining and re-incorporating the riches of their own Reformed worship traditions. Whereas in the seventeenth century, Presbyterians, along with other British nonconformists, had abandoned service book traditions at the Westminster Assembly, now interest in a service book reappeared. Many Presbyterians became disillusioned with the meager fare provided by those not gifted in liturgical composition, especially when they experienced the rich prose of the *BCP*. As Anglican forms enticed people away from their churches, Presbyterian restorationists proposed that the denomination balance the principle of local relevance with a renewed awareness of the rich history of Christian prayer. Charles Baird, a strong voice for Reformed restoration, wrote in 1855: "Do ecclesiastical rules exclude us from the use of the best liturgical compositions, and force us to rely on our individual resources of conception, however crude and meager, and immature, we find them?".[86] Baird pointed Presbyterians back to Geneva. Other denominations looked to their own roots in order to counter the loss of distinct liturgical identity amid the revivals.

Pulled along by the same rising class-consciousness that encouraged *mainline* restoration efforts, older *enthusiast* churches, especially the Methodists, modified their worship practices as well:

> As Methodist people become more affluent and educated, they become more middle-class and self-conscious. Emotional displays were discouraged and spontaneity was relegated to the prayer meeting … The substitute for emotionalism and spontaneity came to be aestheticism and new types of social activism.[87]

A concern to manifest divine creativity through human artistic creations is a central theme of turn-of-the-century *mainline* worship. The churches of northern whites, followed later by middle-class southerners, began to build gothic churches, utilize robed choirs and install art.[88] A prominent advocate of the pursuit of aesthetic values in worship, Von Ogden Vogt, writes: "To perceive beauty is to be moved by something of the same emotional course as attends on the perception of Divinity. And to create beauty is in some sense to participate in the character of Divinity".[89]

In such restorationist worship, the sermon remained central, but as a teaching opportunity and not a call for conversion as revival sermons provided. In addition, most worship leaders did not spontaneously compose prayers during Sunday morning worship. Instead, prayers were prepared in advance and printed in the bulletin. As a result, congregations were able to participate in the act of praying, but that participation was scripted. As worship became more formal and "beautiful", it also became dedicated to liberal ideals. Moral interpretation of the scriptures and sacraments were highlighted as pastors encouraged their people to contribute to the coming of God's reign through good works. A progressive optimism emerged even as analysis of social problems deepened through, for example, the work of Walter Rauschenbusch and the Social Gospel movement. Rauschenbusch acknowledged the contribution of liturgical forms to concerns for justice and offered his own collection of prayers to the churches. He writes:

> [In public prayer], if ever, we feel the vanity and shamefulness of much that society calls proper and necessary. If we had more prayer in common on the sins of modern society, there would be more social repentance and less angry resistance to the demands of justice and mercy.[90]

Both Rauschenbusch and Ogden Vogt expected their age, the early modern era, through the humanizing influences of their own insights, to contribute to progressive social change and the increase of justice in the land. Ogden Vogt even linked aesthetic and social reforms:

> There is something about the experience, whether of art or of worship, to be enjoyed for its own sake, an end in itself, but also something essentially untrue and wrong in any claim of mystic communion which does not result in new values seen in the common world, cleansing of sin, and isolation, and the definite dedication to some service of that enlarged vitality engendered in that experience.[91]

The Depression and the two "Great" Wars broke the liberal consensus among *mainline* European-American Protestants. The experience of widespread poverty and radical human evil necessitated abandonment of facile notions of social progress. Neo-orthodoxy emerged as the theological response to the tragedies of the early twentieth century, with Reinhold Niebuhr as its leading voice. He writes:

> ... moralists, both religious and secular, ... imagine that the egoism of individuals is being progressively checked by the development of rationality or the growth of religiously inspired good will and that nothing but the continuance of this process is necessary to establish social harmony between all human societies and collectives ... They completely disregard the political necessities in the struggle for justice in human society by failing to recognize those elements in man's collective behavior which belong to the order of nature and can never be brought completely under the dominance of reason or conscience. They do not recognize that when collective power whether in the form of imperialism or class domination, exploits weakness, it can never be dislodged unless power is raised against it.[92]

As its name suggests, neo-orthodoxy sought to restore traditions older than modern liberalism to prominence in European-American religious thought.

In liturgy, restorationism gained wider support as the neo-orthodox found a corrective to liberal rationality in the penitential piety of Reformation-era liturgies. Twentieth century restoration also reached beyond the Reformation to the ancient churches through dialogue with participants in the Roman Catholic liturgical reform movement. Ecumenical dialogue and the shared resources of ancient prayers created a second and larger movement towards convergence among European-American Protestant *mainline* worship traditions in the twentieth century.

Homogenization and Experimentation

The convergence of *mainline* European-American liturgical traditions begins with nineteenth century restorationism. As we have seen above, the initial call for restoration of the Reformation era liturgies was a reaction, on the one hand, to the encroachment of revival forms and, on the other, to the popularity of high church Anglicanism. In response, liturgists such as Charles Baird supplied texts—in his case, historical examples from Geneva, Edinburgh and Westminster—to aid the less gifted and recall for Presbyterians the richness of their own tradition. *Mainline* European-American Protestants reached back to their own sixteenth-century (or, for

Methodists, eighteenth-century) documents first. What I am calling convergence began, therefore, as a movement toward denominational distinction. However, the methods of historical investigation, which made possible the recovery of the original liturgical principles of each separate tradition, led scholars to the common liturgical forms of the early church and fueled twentieth-century ecumenical efforts.

The insights of nineteenth-century restorationists led, first, to the recovery of service book traditions. Although Baird himself had little hope that a Presbyterian worship book would be published any time soon, his work inspired consideration of the idea. In 1865, the Church Service Society was formed to study the matter.[93] The first Reformed service book in America, *The Book of Common Worship* was published 41 years later, in 1906. Methodists argued across the divide of "formalism" and "enthusiasm," and under protest published an order of service in the 1880 *New Hymnal*. Not until 75 years later, in 1945, could the Methodist Church publish its first full-fledged service book in the US.

While nineteenth-century efforts were limited to recovery of denomination-specific, founding patterns, they sparked interest in the subject of the history of Christian worship and inspired a new generation of scholarship. Twentieth-century efforts, because of newly rediscovered ancient documents, were able to reach back beyond all the western, denominational schisms to a more ancient, common era. New archeological discoveries raised the prospect of reconstructing early Christian worship and allowing them to reshape present-day practices.[94]

Twentieth-century liturgical reform has also been ecumenical in character. Even the Roman Catholic / Protestant divide has been bridged as Protestant scholars supported, learned from, and contributed to the work of Catholic liturgists. As the Second Vatican Council (1962–1965) changed the face of Roman Catholic worship, Protestants transformed their own worship practices. Presbyterian books were published in 1932, 1946, 1970, and 1993;[95] Methodist, in 1945, 1965–6 and 1989;[96] Protestant Episcopal, in 1979[97] and Lutheran in 1958 and 1978.[98] Even the United Church of Christ, with its congregational polity, printed books in 1948 and 1986.[99] All of these books were either reviewed, or included contributions from, representatives of a variety of denominations. In addition, ecumenical organizations, such as *Societas Liturgica*, founded in 1969, and The North American Academy of Liturgy (1974), bring together scholars and liturgical leaders from a variety of Christian bodies to share insights on the liturgy. Scholarly exchange continues to result in revisions of numerous rites and denominational overlap.

The publication of ecumenical prayer books, however, has created what Paul Bradshaw calls a "homogenization" of worship.[100] Ecumenical exchange has created an unprecedented ecumenical convergence. Against this trend, James White argues that diversity is itself a good that should not be lost in efforts to reunify the churches. He writes:

> It is the peculiar vocation of Protestant worship to adapt Christian worship in terms of peoples as their social contexts and very beings change. Protestant worship has reflected these shifts with notable success in the past; it is best equipped to do so in the future. That is its special historical responsibility in the totality of Christian worship.[101]

The liturgical renewal movement consists of a variety of strategies to increase the meaning and efficacy of Christian rituals. The movement has scholarly, pastoral, legislative, experimental, and radical branches. Virgil Funk contends that the reform phase of the liturgical movement ended with the publication of *The Constitution on the Sacred Liturgy* (or, in its Latin original, *Sacrosanctum Concilium*) on 4 December 1963.[102] Funk argues that by incorporating into institutional practice most of the insights of historians and reformers, Vatican II diffused the momentum for change. A similar dispersal of energy occurred among Protestants as new service books were published. Ultimately, though not without exceptions, liturgists within denominational bureaucracies have shifted modes from protest to implementation.

Implementation of the reforms continues and further revisions arise, but the movement towards ecumenical convergence among the major bodies involved in liturgical reform appears to be slowing, as if it has run its course. While documents such as the World Council of Churches' *Baptism, Eucharist and Ministry* stand as testimony to the substantial areas of agreement in liturgical thought and practice among Christian churches, substantial areas of disagreement remain and may be irreconcilable.[103]

Alongside the movement towards convergence, *mainline* European-American Protestant liturgical traditions are also experiencing a new era of experimentation and diversification. Beside the movement to fixed forms, ancient texts and ecumenical dialogue, a movement towards less rigid orders, which are able to be revised easily to respond to the particular needs of community members, can also be identified. The first phase of experimentation drew on the folk movements of the 1960s. Influenced by the flower children even while resisting the excesses of 60s youth culture, formerly restrained members of the American mainstream worshiped informally. Folk services emphasized bonding among community members through a spirit of playfulness. Most aspects of these experiments have been abandoned. As song leaders put down their guitars and returned to their organs, and the felt banners faded and were taken down, other movements arose among both academics and practitioners on the margins of *mainline* traditions. I simply provide one example here, the critical perspectives of feminist liturgical traditions.

Feminist liturgical work challenges Christian worship to attend to the realities of the lives of women.[104] Janet Walton calls for a re-evaluation not only of the tangible elements of current liturgies that carry patriarchal overtones, such as texts, architectural design, movements and models of leadership, but also some of the fundamental assumptions of liturgists.[105] She encourages re-thinking three ideas regarding liturgical preparation and presidency: the exercise of authority in decisions about how to worship, the place of the body, and definitions of community. Marjorie Procter-Smith revises the very notion of Christian prayer in both its private and public manifestations based upon the alienation and abuse experienced by women in the supposedly bias-free arena of Christian liturgy.[106] Feminist liturgies offer an alternative to traditional liturgical principles, proposing, among other things: that worship should be planned by the group worshiping and not by denominational committees or any one designated leader, and that traditional boundaries of denomination and even religious traditions should be negotiated anew based upon the common experience of being a woman in American culture.[107]

While feminist perspectives on worship remain marginal among *mainline* European-American Protestants, their existence illustrates how members of *mainline* churches continue to adapt their rites to varying circumstances based upon the experience of marginalized voices and new theological insights. All denominational worship books published in the last three decades contain services and service music from all branches of Christianity and emphasize similar liturgical principles based upon the thought and style of known ancient liturgies. Convergence is the major trend among *mainline* liturgical traditions. Yet innovation continues as well and, as the loss of pluralism—a fundamental trait of European-American Protestant liturgical traditions—attracts notice, may gain momentum once again.

In sum, *mainline* liturgical traditions are characterized by their emphasis on the centrality of scriptural authority in establishing faithful practices, in their commitment to turn from the principle of pragmatism and restore the richness of the received tradition especially the rediscovered prayers of the early church, and their recent ecumenical convergence with its consequence of encouraging reliance on printed liturgical texts. While *mainline* denominations are currently declining in numbers and influence, members of these churches remain disproportionately powerful in US society. The Puritans were a dissenting and marginal tradition in Europe but, in North America, they, and their descendants, took on central roles in religious, social, and political spheres. The commitment to shape liturgical practices based solely upon scriptural warrant, a counter-cultural claim in the context of the Anglican communion, became linked with social power in the New World and served to justify rather than criticize worship practices that perform a view of the cosmos as orderly and static. The aggressive responses towards dissenters demonstrates the fear generated in *mainline* Christians when their rites are threatened. The revival movements influenced all US Protestant worship traditions and substituted pragmatism over biblical warrant as the justification for worship practices. *Mainline* traditions followed this trend along with most other European-American Protestants, but, since the mid-nineteenth century, have reversed course and begun to restore earlier traditions. They turned first to their respective roots in the writings of their sixteenth-century founders and later to early church texts. The shared interest in the practices of the first four centuries resulted in ecumenical dialogue. These shared conversations (and shared prayers) resulted in a convergence of texts that is especially notable in the current generation of service books. *Mainline* liturgies rely heavily on published texts—whether local and idiosyncratic or ecumenical and ancient—leaving little room for spontaneous expression by the gathered community. While important examples of new, alternatives models arise on the margins of this stream, such as feminist innovations, in general these traditions are quite stable. The commitment to perform published texts rather than allowing extemporaneous participation and the loss of alternative orders reduce the expectations among gathered communities for an encounter with an active and transforming divine presence within the time and space of the liturgy. *Mainline* liturgies tend to rehearse familiar social relationships rather than provide an experience of counter-cultural equality and care that motivates participants to establish justice and peace in the world.

The *Enthusiast* stream: The Democratization of American Christianity

European-American Protestants are not a monolithic group and have followed more than one stream of liturgical forms. I name the second European-American stream the *enthusiast*. While exhibiting considerable variety and dynamism, the worship patterns of *enthusiast* churches share three common characteristics. First, *enthusiast* churches understand themselves to be "mission driven" and so exhibit a willingness to change worship patterns in order to attract new members.[108]Second, *enthusiast* churches draw their members, at least at first, from groups on the margins of society.[109] Members of society's mainstream, such as today's Neo-Pentecostals, may participate in *enthusiast* forms of worship, but they are not the originators of ecstatic worship forms nor do they constitute the majority of members in such churches.[110] Third, *enthusiast* traditions involve embodied participation by worshipers. Without the constraints of middle-class propriety, worshipers in *enthusiast* traditions express their religious convictions in spontaneous vocal responses, demonstrative gestures, and full emotional participation in worship.[111]

I divide the history of European-American Protestant *enthusiast* worship into five historical periods. First, *enthusiast* traditions emerged among European-American Protestants during the First Great Awakening, 1725–1790. Second, Methodist polity and pragmatism, and the opening of the American frontier, allowed European-American Protestant enthusiasm to blossom fully in the Second Great Awakening (1790–1860). Third, American evangelical Protestantism, the designation by which European-American *enthusiast* churches came to be known, took mature form between 1806–1906. Fourth, in 1906, the Pentecostal revivals began, commencing a new era in *enthusiast* worship. Finally, in recent decades, *enthusiast* churches have experienced a movement towards homogeneity in worship.

In these periods, four patterns of *enthusiast* worship are prominent: the worship of the Puritan revivals, the worship of the frontier, the worship of the defeated South, and the worship of Pentecostalism. Each of these has already been introduced above. The goal here is to highlight aspects of each that illumine the uniqueness of European-American *enthusiast* worship in relation to the *mainline* stream.

Early American Enthusiasm: Edwards and Whitefield

In the First Great Awakening, Jonathan Edwards defined the theology of the revival. He was practitioner and critic but, above all, philosopher. George Whitefield was the model revival preacher. His talents in the pulpit and the number of converts who responded to his tours throughout the colonies were both without equal.[112] Known as the Grand Itinerant, Whitefield reached thousands, stirring them to new levels of Christian commitment, and then moving on to the next crowd.[113] Whitefield begins the great tradition of European-American preachers, who confront the listener with the Word of God so as to create a crisis that is understood to be a opportunity for transformation, rather than offering a doctrinal argument to which the listener might assent.[114]

In addition, Whitefield differed from Edwards on the issue of slavery, exhibiting greater ambiguity. Edwards owned slaves, unwilling or unable to challenge the basic social structures of his time. When Whitefield arrived in North America in 1738, he opposed slavery and actively said so. Later, he shifted his position from abolition to compromise. He asserted it was better to preach to slaves and deny them freedom than not to preach to them at all. In 1745, he accepted ownership of a plantation and became a slaveholder himself. He rationalized his actions by arguing that since slavery was unlikely to be dismantled in his lifetime he should ensure the fair treatment of those entrusted to his care.[115]

Both Whitefield and Edwards stand with one foot in each of my categories of *mainline* and *enthusiast*. Whitefield was an Anglican priest, yet was sympathetic to many Wesleyan reforms, and, in consequence of his constant criticism of Anglican practice, ended his life as a non-denominational evangelical preacher.[116] Edwards defended revivals within New England Congregationalism as continuous with the Puritan legacy and Enlightenment philosophy. They both challenged *mainline* churches to worship in such a way that people were not simply assured of their goodness, but were also convinced of the truth of the gospel and its claims upon their lives. They developed and led liturgies that confronted participants, stimulating them to respond. They also challenged the *enthusiast* churches, which their legacy would help shape. Edwards, especially, called for worship that was sound, both intellectually and theologically. He also emphasized that true conversion would give rise to fruits of righteous living. Both Whitefield and Edwards accepted definitions of their own day regarding the fruit in which worship might issue, notably that it would not lead to the dismantling of slavery. Yet, these two early *mainline* European-American Protestants were intent on demonstrating the transformative potential of the Christian message "rightly preached".

Worship on the American Frontier

Edwards and Whitefield were influential but their innovations did not long effect the established churches of the eastern seaboard. The *mainline* churches returned to, or remained in, a state of comfortable order. Instead, American revivalism followed the movement of settlers west. Out in the wilderness, *enthusiast* worship blossomed. New evangelical innovations contributed to its rapid expansion. The most important of these were the Methodist missionary structures. In this section, I will discuss, first, the Wesleyan legacy and, second, the most important liturgical invention of the frontier preachers, the Camp Meeting.

The Legacy of Wesleyan Reforms in England John Wesley (1703–1791), with his brother, Charles (1707–1788), supplemented Anglican worship forms of their time to appeal to the poor and industrial laborers of urban areas.[117] They preached out-of-doors to reach those intimidated by ecclesial architecture. They employed poetic forms rather than rational discourse, expressing much of their theology through their many hymns. They welcomed emotionally-based responses to the gospel, not limiting their hearers to intellectual assent. White writes:

> New forms of mission had to be found in worship as well as new systems for health, education, and public welfare to minister to a largely unchurched population. The

inhibitions that restrained educated and affluent people could be ignored. People could sing and shout with uninhibited joy. The level of active participation could be raised by encouraging people to sing with fervor, give personal testimonies, and pray spontaneously in class meetings. Although Wesley was careful not to confuse genuine religious affections with mere boisterous behavior, Methodist worship invited vigorous and loud participation. Scant wonder, then, that it was labeled "enthusiasm" for there was an abundance of outward signs of the Spirit's inward working.[118]

While accused of enthusiasm, John Wesley was, by all accounts, a liturgical conservative. He based many of his so-called innovations on early church precedent. Critics dubbed the movement "methodism" because of its renewed emphasis on the sacraments and daily office of regularized prayer. Methodist worship in England followed the *Book of Common Prayer* closely. Wesley employed his "new measures" chiefly in evangelization and in small group devotions.

E.P. Thompson interprets Methodist worship as not only liturgically but also politically conservative. He claims Methodist worship served to mold an obedient and submissive industrial working class in nineteenth-century England. Parallel to Max Weber's observations of the interdependence of Calvinist theology and the ideology of capitalism among the bourgeois, Methodism appealed to and helped transform agricultural and artisan piece workers into efficient contributors to the emerging industrial economy. Middle-class Protestantism identified proof of election with dedication to and success in one's secular vocation.[119] Methodism, in contrast, created a community in which the poor felt welcome. Once members of a close-knit and hospitable small group or class, Methodists were threatened with expulsion if they did not submit to a strict moral code. The experience of acceptance became an enforcement mechanism for behavior that, not surprisingly, fitted the needs of factory owners. Thompson writes: "The factory system demands a transformation of human nature, the working 'paroxysms' of the artisan and out-worker must be methodised until the man is adapted to the discipline of the machine".[120]

After Wesley, leaders of British Methodism sought to stem the tide of enthusiasm and, after 1800, campaigned to end the extended gatherings for revivalistic preaching and prayer known as camp meetings in England because of their more radical democratic implications. While Methodist Christianity served some of the needs of working people, it also functioned to dissipate energy that might have fomented revolt against the de-humanizing aspects of industrial capitalism. Wesleyan liturgical principles encouraged ecstatic release in specific worship settings while enforcing strict discipline in all other areas of life. Thompson writes:

> Nothing was more often remarked by contemporaries of the workaday Methodist character, or of Methodist home-life, than its methodical, disciplined, and repressed disposition. It is the paradox of a "religion of the heart" that it should be notorious for the inhibition of all spontaneity. Methodism sanctioned "workings of the heart" only upon the occasions of church; Methodists wrote hymns but no secular poetry of note; the idea of a passionate Methodist lover in these times is ludicrous … it is difficult not to see Methodism in these years as a ritualized form of psychic masturbation. Energies and emotions which were dangerous to the social order, or which were merely unproductive…were released

in the harmless form of sporadic love-feasts, watch-nights, band meetings or revivalist campaigns ...

The Sabbath orgasms of feeling made more possible the single-minded workday direction of these energies to the consummation of productive labor. Moreover, since salvation was never assured [due to Wesleyan perfectionism], and temptations lurked on every side, there was a constant inner goading to "sober and industrious" behavior—the visible sign of grace—every hour of the day and every day of the year.[121]

The Birth of the Camp Meeting   Wesleyan methods were modified quite drastically in late eighteenth-century America. The missionaries found fertile ground for evangelical preaching on the frontier. But they found British enthusiasm too constraining in this challenging context. They soon dropped the "traditional" in Wesley's "traditional pragmatism" approach. The frontier populace, illiterate and unchurched, rugged and independent, required new methods. The Camp Meeting form evolved in response. The Camp Meeting combined several older traditions from Scotch Presbyterian, Puritan, and Methodist precedents. While it was not the only form of worship employed on the frontier, the Camp Meeting displays the primary characteristics of worship in this era.

The Methodists in America celebrated Wesley's enthusiasm with more abandon than their Britain counterparts. Francis Asbury (1745–1816), the first American Methodist bishop, emphasized Wesley's pragmatism.[122] Asbury set aside Wesley's adaptation of the *Book of Common Prayer*, entitled *Sunday Services for the Methodists in North America*, in 1792, only a year after John Wesley died. For Asbury, freedom to adapt worship in ways that fostered mission among Americans, especially the unchurched on the frontier, was paramount. While his English counterparts railed against the Camp Meeting, Asbury promoted it.[123] Hatch writes: "Americans continued to champion the Camp Meeting, turbulence and all, for a simple reason: it was a phenomenally successful instrument for popular recruitment".[124]

After the 13 American colonies gained independence from England, expansion to the West began in earnest. The settlers lived without the restraints of familiar social structures. Johnson writes:

The population was comprised primarily of young men, rough, driving, and bumptious. A tendency toward drunkenness, immorality, quarrelsomeness, gambling, and an exalted sense of personal importance were common faults. Yet other frontier characteristics were possessed as well: generosity, neighborliness, independent-mindedness, frankness, incurable optimism, and a resentment against all government.[125]

The frontier contained a largely unchurched population of illiterate, isolated, independent settlers. Frontier missionaries drew upon a variety of traditions to create a new style of worship that was accessible and effective among frontier settlers. Reformed, Puritan, and Methodist traditions all contribute to the development of the Camp Meeting. I address each in turn.

From the Scottish branch of the Reformed Church came the tradition of the sacramental season and a large number of important missionaries and worship innovators. The sacramental season was a twist on Calvin's requirement of a period for introspection before receiving the sacraments. In Scotland, ministers announced the quarterly celebration of the eucharist at least a week ahead of time so that people could spend time in preparation. On the American frontier, the sacramental season inspired evangelists to call people together for an occasional period of intense religiosity. The protracted meeting, large gatherings over four or five days, grew out of this precedent.[126] Important preachers and liturgical innovators such as James McGready, Alexander Campbell, and Barton Stone also arose from Reformed communions.

From the Puritan heritage, frontier missionaries took the principles of biblicism and subsidiarity. Evangelical preachers held scripture to be inviolable and desired to follow its guidelines in structuring worship as in all other things. At the same time, they desired to adapt worship to the challenges of the frontier in order to attract new converts who were not biblically literate, if they were literate at all. The principle that all liturgical decisions should be made at the lowest possible level balanced the confines of biblical warrant. Frontier evangelists based their innovations on the teachings of Edwards, among others, who justified a sense of freedom in relation to worship forms within broad biblical boundaries. While resting at first on general claims to biblical warrant, as time went on, Frontier revivalists, emboldened by their own success, dropped pretensions that their practices were biblically based and shifted to purely pragmatic principles.

Reformed and Puritan contributions should not be forgotten, but it would fall to Asbury and his circuit riders to fully exploit the possibilities of American frontier missions. Methodist polity provided a structured system of mobile preachers, fixed parishes, district ministers, and bishops.[127] Asbury respected the spirit of independence that reigned over the frontier, utilizing overlapping levels of clergy to respond quickly to the needs of the constantly shifting population. Outdoor preaching was another Wesleyan innovation that was copied on the frontier. Finally, the Methodists tradition of sung theology proved popular among frontier settlers.

Frontier religion employed a variety of forms of public prayer, including regular Sunday worship in more densely populated areas (although, at first, in homes rather than specially designed buildings), family prayers, and bible study (both lay and clergy led).[128] But the quintessential frontier institution was the Camp Meeting. The Camp Meeting drew people from long distances as one of the few forms of social interaction available to settlers.[129] Many claim credit for inventing the form and the debate over its origins continues.[130] What is clear is that beginning in 1790, a variety of extended outdoor meetings were held in the Appalachian region in a variety of settings and under the direction of a variety of clergy with Baptist, Methodist and Presbyterian affiliations. These forerunners culminated in the gathering of approximately 25,000 people at Cane Ridge, Kentucky in August 1801 and "catapulted the camp meeting onto the national stage".[131]

The Camp Meeting developed a structure of preaching, praying, and conversion. Preparation for the gathering of large crowds necessitated the clearing of land near fresh water, and the building of preaching stands, pews, a table, and "mourners'" benches or tents for those struggling towards conversion.[132] Worshipers would normally arrive on Thursday and the revival would culminate on Sunday with the baptism of new Christians and a celebration of the Eucharist. A typical day would begin with a wake-up call, breakfast and family prayers. Services would then be held at 8 am, 11 am, and 3 pm, with breaks for meals, socializing, and attendance to those who were "struck" by the preaching. A final evening service with an extended altar call would be held in the eerie glow of firelight.[133]

Each service would differ slightly, but most began with a short prayer and singing, followed by a lengthy sermon and culminating with demonstrative exhortations to repentance by various clergy. Variations included the addition of extra songs, special activities such as a group march around the grounds, "the handshake ceremony", or a Love Feast; community business such as announcements or fund-raising appeals; and time for responses to the sermon.[134] The sermon was clearly central and was delivered without notes by mainly self-educated, robust circuit riders, who knew well the hardships of the frontier themselves. These "sons of thunder" engaged their listeners at their own level and excited dramatic responses. While seeking to convert the unregenerate, preachers also addressed many of the practical temptations of frontier life and forged links between evangelical religion and social reform movements such as those involving women's suffrage, temperance, and abolition.

The Camp Meeting fulfilled non-religious functions in frontier society in addition to its missionary role. As one of the few gatherings of large numbers of settlers, the meetings also hosted the curious, merchants (most often purveyors of foodstuffs, but liquor sales were not unknown), politicians, barbers, bootblacks, dentists, publishers, prostitutes, doctors, and a variety of hecklers and critics.[135] The Camp Meeting was a holiday, most often held in the fall, either just before or just after the main harvest. It was a time of rare leisure, good food, hospitality, old and new friends, and match-making. There were scandals of illicit sexual behavior and drunkenness.[136] Many conversions proved insincere and short-lived as well. Still, the Camp Meeting served to remind those who attended that, even in the isolation of frontier settlements, they were citizens of a larger society. Johnson concludes:

> Men in the privations of pioneer life reverted to primitive traits in habits and customs of daily living. The backwoods revival tamed these anarchistic tendencies of the unchurched settler at the same time that it furnished him with an arena of social expression ... In the absence of an established church the word of God was brought to many who might otherwise have remained untouched.[137]

Hatch contends, however, that camp meetings did more than simply institutionalize some order on the frontier. In fact, frontier revival worship represents a new development in American Christianity, namely the rise of a popular religiosity.[138] He writes:

> It seems appropriate to term this time of social ferment the Second Great Awakening. Christendom had probably not witnessed a comparable period of religious upheaval since the Reformation—and never such an explosion of entrepreneurial energy ... [The Second Great Awakening] splintered American Christianity and magnified the diversity of institutions claiming to be the church. It sprang from a populist upsurge rather than from changing mores of established parishes. The movement captured the aspirations of society's outsiders. It was only secondarily the response of clergy nervous about

eroding deference and competing churches. The heart of the movement was a revolution in communications, preaching, print, and song; and these measures were instrumental in building mass popular movements.[139]

Frontier worship established the *enthusiast* stream as a clear alternative to *mainline* traditions. The central contrast between the two streams involved factors of social class. Frontier preachers were chosen not based upon traditional Protestant criteria of education but on the basis of their own conversion and the conviction with which they shared their testimony with others. Circuit riders were ordinary frontier people who shared the life experience of that trying context with their parishioners. The frontier movement involved lay people in worship, in the process of conversion and in church founding and administration. Frontier worship encouraged the embrace of an ecstatic worship form among European-American Protestants.

American Evangelical Protestantism

The northern and southern branches of the Methodist Church separated in 1844. The Southern Baptist Convention was formed in 1845. The New School Presbyterians divided itself into northern and southern bodies in 1857. The Old School of the Presbyterian Church and the Lutheran denomination split in 1861.[140] The issue of slavery and the hardening of both northern abolitionism and southern defensiveness rent European-American Protestant churches in two. Revivalism encouraged the extremists on both sides of the Mason–Dixon line, and may have contributed to the length and destructiveness of the war.[141]

The South suffered physically and psychically in the fighting, and in defeat. The destructiveness of the war left southern religious institutions in shambles. The desire to re-establish the gentility of southern life grew even as defeat became inevitable. Hatred of northern values and ideas saturated the southern mind-set. Southern churches did not rush to reunite with their northern brethren. Instead, they nurtured the "old time religion" of the antebellum period as a means to resist northern triumphalism. Southern churches defended, and secured a future for, southern traditions, even as the Union was preserved.

While members of the southern aristocracy belonged to *mainline* churches such as the Presbyterian and Protestant Episcopal, Methodists and Baptists defined the overarching religious ethos of southern Protestantism. Methodist and Baptist worship in the South after the Civil War had several general characteristics. First, most parishes continued to rely on the revival style of worship, although as members became more affluent changes began to take place. Second, African Americans founded separate congregations. No longer would white and black southerners share the intimacy of the plantation system and its interracial worship. As a result, the religious practices of black and white southerners became increasingly distinct.[142] Third, an anti-intellectual atmosphere pervaded southern religion. Most Methodist and Baptist clergy were uneducated and decidedly so.[143] While Vanderbilt, the first southern Methodist institution of higher learning, was established in 1873,[144] and Southern Theological Seminary, its Baptist counterpart, was founded in 1859,[145] southern theological education rejected the so-called northern intellectual trends of scientific and historical-critical methods.

Worship among southern European-American Protestants of the late nineteenth and early twentieth centuries concentrated on the reformation of individual moral behavior, the preservation of as much of the Old South as possible, and the avoidance of the encroachment of the modern era. Ahlstrom writes:

> ... they gave their blessings to the "peculiar institutions" that replaced slavery, inveighed with more consistent vigor against card playing and dancing, than against racism or the unpunished murdering of recalcitrant blacks, and led the general run of people to prize the values and practices of the "old time religion" rather than to ponder the forces that were reshaping modern civilization.[146]

The revival-based worship of southern European-American Protestants was the primary alternative to the liberal traditions of the Northeast. Southern missionaries instituted revival forms throughout the country among their converts.

In the late nineteenth century, vast social changes swept across the US. Chief among them were industrialization, urbanization and the growth of the American empire. Industrialization brought opportunity for economic advancement to many and dire poverty to even more. In general, white southern Methodists and Baptists benefited from these trends. Members entered the ranks of the skilled labor and professional classes. With increasing wealth and education, southern Methodists and Baptists tamed the enthusiasm of their worship. Congregations hired architects to create structures that re-called a past these descendants of frontier settlers had never experienced. They claimed as their own the aesthetic values of southern aristocracy of the late eighteenth and early nineteenth centuries.[147] Methodists who sought to preserve or extend *enthusiast* practices split off into Holiness sects. Holiness adherents emphasized the potential of converts to live a sinless life. While based on Wesley's notion of Christian perfection, these Christians restricted the moral implications to personal and domestic sphere, such as attitudes toward alcohol, gambling, and sexuality. As the perfectionist wing in Methodism reduced its influence through attrition to Holiness churches, those remaining in the denomination began to shape worship along the lines of *mainline* respectability.

Pentecostalism

Just as Holiness communities broke from less demonstrative Methodist churches in the nineteenth century, a fourth pattern of European-American Protestant *enthusiast* worship, Pentecostalism, developed out of the Holiness churches in the early twentieth century.[148] While related to the revival styles that characterized southern *enthusiasm*, Pentecostalism also has unique features. A radical departure from medieval Roman Catholic practices, Pentecostalism aimed for the direct apprehension of the Holy Spirit's power among the worshiping community. Pentecostals have little concern about following traditional orders of Christian public prayer.[149] Pentecostal churches contain frontier missionary impulses, structure their worship at the local level along pragmatic lines, and, most often, practice believer's baptism. Members of the first

Pentecostal communities emerged primarily from southern Methodist or Holiness communities.

European-American Pentecostals trace their roots to Charles Parham, a Holiness pastor and educator, who identified speaking in tongues as *the* sign that one had been baptized by the spirit.[150] Speaking in tongues, or *glossolalia*, is a form of spiritual ecstasy in which the Holy Spirit gives utterance through an individual worshiper in a foreign or unknown tongue. Speaking in tongues indicates that a believer received a second blessing, the baptism of the spirit that was promised to the disciples at Pentecost, a fuller transformation than that effected by water baptism and assurance of one's salvation.[151] Pentecostals exchanged enlightenment moralism and traditional sacramental emphases for ecstatic enthusiasm. White writes:

> Far from being scandalized by the thought of God making direct intervention in worship, that very concept is a basic premise of Pentecostal worship … If the Holy Spirit is present in tongues, then the washing of baptism is hardly a unique experience of grace (although a necessary one in most churches). If the Holy Spirit acts visibly in healing individuals, then the Lord's Supper does not convey a greater presence, although one commanded by Christ and therefore celebrated at least occasionally. In another sense all Pentecostal worship is sacramental in manifesting visibly and audibly within the gathered community the action and presence of the Holy Spirit.[152]

Pentecostal worship is based on four central principles. First, in Pentecostal worship, God is present and active. The Holy Spirit enters persons and gives them gifts for the benefit of the community. Speaking in tongues is the most widely recognized spiritual gift, but there are others such as the ability to interpret tongues, prophecy, and preaching. God bestows these gifts without regard for a person's worldly status, nor upon one's identity or one's role in the institution or ritual setting. God chooses whom God chooses.

Second, given God's freedom to act according to the divine will, worship cannot be tightly confined by rubrics. Pentecostal worship is open to interruptions, to contributions from unexpected sources. Not only is a fixed order rejected in favor of a service based upon a fluid form, but individual pieces of the liturgy are most often spontaneously created rather than scripted. Written prayers are discouraged. To be an effective presider, one must possess an ability to improvise, to facilitate the movement of the service without any predetermined order, and to accept interruptions in the normal plan in order to accommodate revelation from other participants.

Third, in contrast to most Protestants, who consult the gospel texts or Pauline traditions in ordering their worship, Pentecostals justify their liturgical style as a restoration of the forms of prayer and proclamation outlined in the Acts of the Apostles.[153] Pentecostal communities seek to re-create in the present the practices of the early church with their manifest spiritual gifts and millennial expectations. The manifestation of spiritual gifts indicates that modern Pentecostals are true heirs to the promises given to the first apostles. White writes: "… the advent of modern spiritual gifts [is] a sign of the imminent reign of Christ. Worship itself is both a foretaste of the kingdom and a means of advancing its coming".[154]

Finally, Pentecostal communities tend to welcome outcasts.[155] The first members of Pentecostal communities were rural migrant workers seeking employment (often unsuccessfully) in America's rapidly growing cities. Significantly, during a time of intense racial tension, early Pentecostalism was also racially mixed. Blacks and whites worshiped together for at least a decade before separate denominational bodies for African Americans and European Americans emerged.

As Pentecostal churches have grown in size and visibility, European Americans in *mainline* traditions from a variety of backgrounds, rich and poor, in suburb and city, have assumed Pentecostal practices, such as speaking in tongues. These Neo-Pentecostals retain membership in their original churches but add Pentecostal elements to their worship.[156] In this way, Pentecostal traits, such as an emphasis on the present experience of worshipers, embodied responses to the Spirit, renewed attention to rites of healing, and a willingness to allow for spontaneous responses by the congregation, are infiltrating other, more structured styles of worship. Because different types of Christians have received the gifts associated with Pentecostal worship, some see Pentecostalism as the source of a wider restoration of ancient practices, one that will culminate in the return of Christ. Along these lines, Pentecostalism may be characterized as an alternative and *enthusiast* liturgical renewal movement parallel to the liberal ecumenical one of *mainline* traditions.[157]

While Pentecostal practices infiltrate *mainline* churches, American popular culture infiltrates Pentecostalism, especially European-American denominations. Whereas early Pentecostals extolled the pure and remnant qualities of their apostolic restoration, now Pentecostals rejoice in their mass appeal. Pentecostal churches offer members music, entertainment, and literature which employ stylistic patterns that closely parallel, even as they criticize, mainstream cultural norms. They have also been at the forefront of media-based liturgical forms, which imitate US network television talk shows and fund-raising appeals while claiming the status of Christian ritual.[158] Blumhofer writes:

> The Assemblies of God began with professions of allegiance to a higher kingdom, enjoining adherents to live as "pilgrims and strangers" in the world. In time, its adherents improved their economic and social standing and carved out a niche for themselves on the American religious scene. The restorationist urge erupted occasionally as a troubling reminder of their earlier identity, it spawned popular movements that continued to have wide appeal in a constituency that professed to yearn for spiritual authenticity but often yielded to the enticements of the time.[159]

European-American Pentecostal worship has gained legitimacy and respectability in recent decades. European-American Pentecostals now own schools, have built architect-designed houses of worship, and have contributed to the social and political organization of the religious right.[160] While Pentecostals in Brazil have followed the Spirit into positions critical of unjust social power, European-American Pentecostals have generally accommodated to US mainstream culture, shifting rhetoric from counter-cultural prophecy to cultural parroting.[161] European-American Pentecostals have entered into ecumenical conversations. At this point, Pentecostals are influencing the worship of *mainline* churches more than they are being influenced, as they remain loyal to their *enthusiast* worship forms while *mainline* churches attempt to cultivate greater spontaneity.

Enthusiast Convergence

Enthusiast churches with European-American members share frontier patterns in common. The principle of pragmatism and the hymn-sandwich structure of Sunday worship are nearly universal, as they have been since the late eighteenth century. Evangelists employed revival techniques throughout the South until the end of the nineteenth century. Dwight Moody, among others, adapted the revival for urban areas with great success in the early twentieth century.[162] Mission, both within the United States and around the globe, became chief occupations of *mainline* and *enthusiast* traditions as Americans established themselves as world leaders. The revival techniques accompanied missionaries to their fields.

Enthusiast denominations continue to experience convergence. They have reacted against, and organized in response to, theological liberalism. The adoption of "Five Points" as "essential and necessary" doctrines by the Presbyterian General Assembly in 1910, and its proliferation throughout conservative circles, is one example of this trend.[163] Recent *enthusiast* organizations have taken on a more explicit political flavor with Pat Robertson's Christian Coalition, Jerry Falwell's PTL (formerly Jim Bakker's "Praise the Lord" Network), and, most recently, James Dobson's Focus on the Family organization. Worship among evangelicals now serves not only to facilitate praise, but also to organize grassroots believers into a formidable political machine, powerful enough to influence the outcome of national elections.

Finally, descendants of the frontier missionaries have exploited new media technology with unmatched enthusiasm and success.[164] Adaptation of Christian worship for broadcast has only further promoted a convergence of worship styles among evangelicals. The use of choirs, the scripting of worship as a show for those watching, appeals for conversion, action and contributions has made *enthusiast* worship more effective in mission and in political fundraising. *Enthusiast* churches define success as the greatest possible number of converts, subordinating their own traditions to any innovation which provokes response. Of Pentecostals, Blumhofer writes:

> In the Assemblies of God as in Pentecostalism more generally today, popular culture appears increasingly to [set the pace, agenda, and the priorities]. Almost entirely unacknowledged, it influences perceptions of success, goals, professions of belief. Heroes are the media stars and entrepreneurs who lead mega-churches, not those who reflect critically on the relationship between religion and culture. The denomination has grown at least in part because at the grassroots it is so thoroughly attuned to the tastes and jargon of the popular culture and has embraced and exploited modern technology.[165]

Without service books, without institutional control of local orders of service, without adherence to ancient rites outside of references to New Testament proof texts, still *enthusiast* European-American Protestant liturgies have become easily recognizable, even uniform.

In sum, *enthusiast* liturgical traditions stand in tension with their sibling tradition among European Americans, the *mainline*. They are less wedded to published liturgical texts. They encourage more demonstrative responses in the midst of worship. They utilize more experiential modes of articulating religious experience.

Aiming for the conversion of unbelievers rather than the sustaining of established communities, *enthusiast* churches borrow the idioms of popular culture to make their worship accessible to the unchurched, or lapsed, convicting them to join this remnant people. Their "target audience", since *enthusiast* pragmatism borrows freely the vocabulary of the market, has consisted traditionally in those on the margins of white society. Members of lower classes, it seems, respond most readily to ecstatic forms of worship. However, as both Wesleyan and Pentecostal Christians in the US have experienced social mobility, their worship—boisterous when members were mostly poor—has most often become staid. As *enthusiast* communities become secure, their worship style is curtailed by, and serves to inculcate, middle-class sensibilities. *Enthusiast* traditions function best to welcome people into the world of religious symbolism and experience. They offer relief from anxiety by offering converts sure identification among the elect. To speak in tongues assures the Pentecostal convert of her salvation and frees her to participate fully in worship and life as one of God's chosen. Among European-American Protestants, at least, there is no barrier to full assimilation into mainstream culture for those who acquire its values whether through *mainline* or *enthusiast* worship traditions. *Enthusiast* European-American liturgical traditions serve, then, as both an alternative to and a means to enter into *mainline* American Protestant society.

Conclusion

European-American Protestant liturgical traditions adapt easily and radically to the historical context in which they find themselves. They are, therefore, plural in structure and ethos. At the same time, the history reveals a strong tendency towards convergence—albeit not into a single shape but around particular poles: the *mainline* and the *enthusiast* streams. These two streams are distinct primarily because of two factors, the class location of their adherents and their varied responses to the Enlightenment. I comment briefly on these observations here to prepare for the comparative task of Chapter 4.

From Calvin, who cautiously acknowledged that worship should conform to particular historical circumstances, to Finney, who simply threw out the old when it proved unproductive in favor of more effective measures, European-American Protestants have practiced adaptation of worship to particular historical and cultural contexts throughout their 400-year history. The adaptability, and subsequent plurality, of European-American Protestant liturgical traditions is a central theme of this narrative.

However, European-American liturgical traditions also function as part of the forces of assimilation in US society. Those with white skin are encouraged (some would say forced; others would say enabled) to join in the racial/ethnic majority known as "unhyphenated whites". The *enthusiast* stream serves primarily to welcome people into the process of assimilation and to begin the process of joining mainstream society. The *mainline* serves those further along in the process, those who have joined fully in US majority culture.

Where worship once helped European Americans distinguish their ethnic identity from that of others, it now serves primarily to reinforce their participation in the ruling majority. European-American Protestant liturgical traditions shift from pragmatist to restorationist extremes, from demonstrative to restrained behavioral norms, but, in whatever direction a given age is moving, tendencies toward homogeneity are strong. The *mainline* churches currently share common worship patterns based on the new generation of ecumenically created service books. The *enthusiast* stream shares media-centered forms that might be called Broadcast Christianity. Movement toward convergence in European-American Protestant liturgy parallels the forces of assimilation in US culture.

The forces of convergence are powerful and yet have not resulted in a merging of the two streams. This is primarily because of the factor of social class. Connections between socio-economic status and worship style are fundamental but complex. The Pentecostal movement may have begun like the frontier revivals among the disinherited but now attracts members of a variety of classes. *Mainline* and *enthusiast* traditions reflect the different realities of the wealthy and educated versus those of the poor and the marginalized. Yet, as a rule, even poor and marginalized European-American Protestants eventually move up the socio-economic scale, at least in part, because of the cathartic function of ecstatic practice and the discipline of the overall ritual system in which they participate. The difference between *mainline* and *enthusiast* groups is, therefore, not static but again follows a path of convergence as those on the margins move towards the center of socio-economic security. European-American Protestant liturgical traditions celebrate the American dream and confer God's blessings upon those who know its bounty as well as those who aspire to its vision.

Finally, the two streams have been shaped by the Enlightenment, but in different ways. *Mainline* traditions are the worship styles of groups which most easily embraced scientific rationality and enlightenment philosophy. *Mainline* churches have accepted, to various degrees, historical-critical approaches to scripture and doctrine, shaping worship according to the insights of historians, archaeologists and other scientific disciplines. *Enthusiast* Protestants, in contrast, seek a spirituality that returns mystery and mysticism to Christianity in reaction to scientific worldviews. Contesting claims that God is absent from human history, *enthusiasts* testify to God's activity in their lives. While the subordination of doctrinal formulations to insights based upon personal experience makes *enthusiast* movements vulnerable to corruption by charismatic leaders and to captivity in relation to cultural forms that shape such experience unconsciously, *enthusiast* traditions serve those who find *mainline* decorum alienating. *Enthusiast* worship incorporates more senses than eye and ear, expressing with and through the body the joy of God's presence among the gathered community.

European-American Protestant worship is rich in variety, adapting readily to the circumstances of new lands and new peoples. It adapts easily to the vicissitudes of human character as well and so has been often co-opted to serve unjust and violent ends. For example, worship was used as one arena in which European Americans justified the slaughter of Native Americans and the enslavement of Africans in relation to authoritative religious texts and beliefs. While understanding themselves as "good Christians", white Protestants asserted their right to occupy a land belonging to Native peoples and to exploit the labor of the slaves. Members of majority groups who would live in just relations with others must remember worship's capacity to rehearse structures of ideologies of domination. To some description of the interrelationship of the four streams and to investigations of previous examples of interracial services, I now turn in Chapter 4.

Barriers Built, Barriers Broken:
The Intersection of African-American and European-American Liturgical Traditions

African Americans and European Americans have shared nearly 400 years of history on this continent and created both common and distinct cultural traditions. Europeans conquered the Americas, subjugated or eliminated the native population, and imported African captives as slaves. British colonists inverted their claim to found a country on faithful adherence to Christian doctrine through their violence, racism and exploitation. They continued to practice their faith, and their worship flourished in the context of freedom in the new world, yet their creation and support of the peculiar institution undercut their claims of particular righteousness. Africans endured the horrors of capture, transport, sale and perpetual servitude. They survived the onslaught of the doctrine of non-personhood and forged a creative and liberative strain of ritual practice out of the religious worldview of their oppressors. Together Europeans and Africans became Americans. Together, with members of other racial/ethnic groups, they created what is now called American culture.

Religious practice is one of several phenomena that contribute to the process by which groups of individuals become peoples and discrete behaviors and systems of thought become cultures. African Americans and European Americans prayed to the same God and read the same scriptures but often in quite different ways and towards different ends. Sometimes they prayed together and sometimes they prayed separately. Often the styles and content of their prayers necessitated separate spaces. Sometimes dividing walls were dismantled and common prayer again attempted. The separate narratives of African-American and European-American Protestant worship are streams within the larger narrative of liturgical development—a narrative of barriers built and barriers broken.

In Chapters 2 and 3, I utilized the image of a stream to describe the four major divisions in US Protestant liturgical traditions among blacks and whites. In fact, however, the four streams flow side by side within the banks of one great river, the US Protestant context. For this reason, I shift the metaphor now. From this point on, I will speak of the streams that I traced individually above, as currents, to emphasize their interrelationship. In this chapter, I highlight places where the four currents intermingle, inlets and whirlpools where the waters of liturgy have swirled together. In these places of mixture, the currents develop new compositions as they borrow and lend various distinct elements to the others and contribute to the flow of Protestant worship in this country more generally. I speak first about the four currents and the common history in which they developed. Second, I turn to specific occasions when blacks and whites worshiped together. I conclude with some thoughts on the implications of these narratives for multicultural communities today.

Four Currents Flowing Side by Side

By the time a great river reaches the sea, it has encountered, accepted, and assimilated water from many sources. So, too, liturgical traditions are composed out of a variety of religious and cultural materials. Liturgies accept contributions from the culture or cultures in which they are located, incorporating the cultural products of a people into the theological trajectories of the tradition. Protestant worship in the US incorporates a variety of European, African, and Native cultural currencies. Protestant worship continues to change as new cultural challenges arise. In the same way, US culture grew out of the interactions of various peoples and continues to evolve in relation to religious innovations, as well as other types of cultural shifts.

African Americans and European Americans did not exist as peoples until they lived US history. Both groups have created themselves as peoples on this continent in the context of their interrelationship and through many cultural and social performative activities, an important one of which is Christian worship. Culture and religion are dialectically related. They become what they are in relation to each other. Neither is prior. Neither is static. They both emerge as human social constructs and continue to change in relation to one another. African-American and European-American Protestant liturgical traditions contributed to the formation of these groups as peoples, even as these peoples crafted, performed, and continue to adapt these liturgies.

The chart opposite (Fig 1.1) illustrates graphically my overall reading of the history of US Protestant worship in relation to these two racial groups. On the one hand, African-American and European-American Protestant liturgical traditions are distinct. On the other hand, they are mutually interdependent. I image the history of US Protestant worship as a river in which four currents flow. The four currents are divided by islands that distinguish their individual characteristics, placing them in a continuum of time on the horizontal axis and one of cultural composition on the vertical. Between the islands, and in several specific locations, the currents mix together. The second section of this chapter deals with previous occasions of biracial worship. This section concerns the more general schematic that I am proposing: the sources and characteristics of the four currents.

Sources

The river of my graphic has two major sources: Western Christianity and African Traditional Religion. Western Christianity dominates as a source. Only traces of African Traditional Religion remain from the time of the slave trade. But a spectrum remains. Near the upper bank, African influences are strongest; at the lower bank, the European headwaters can still be found in relatively pure form. The chart locates the currents relative to the concentration of each of these sources. I invert the expected order of presentation, listing the currents in order of decreasing concentration of

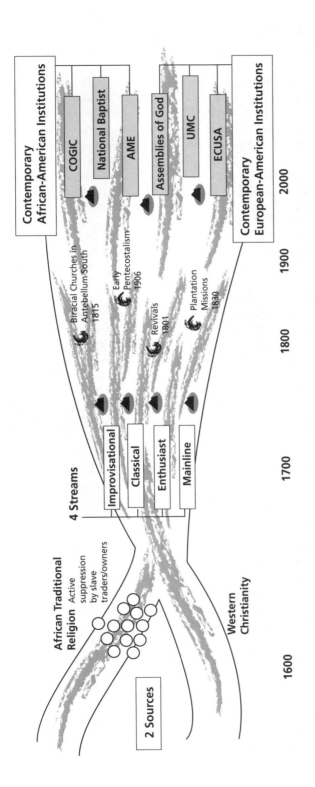

Fig 1.1 Like a River: A Schematic of the History of US Protestant Worship Traditions among African Americans and European Americans

African elements to emphasize the importance of African forms to American cultural forms generally.

Slave traders, owners, and colonial religious authorities dammed the source of African Traditional Religion when they discovered a link between these ritual traditions and slave revolts. But no dam holds all the water back. Traces of African Traditional Religion can still be detected throughout both American culture and the variety of American Protestant worship practices. The traces are, however, most concentrated in the *improvisational* current. The *improvisational* current carries the legacy of the African captives from the "invisible institution" through southern Afro-Baptist churches to modern African-American Pentecostalism, embodied in COGIC, the Church of God in Christ. Like other religious systems that combined African survivals with Christian iconography such as Brazilian Candomble, Haitian Voudoun, and Cuban Santeria, African-American *improvisational* forms use Western Christian language, practices, and imagery to cover a base of African concepts, rhythmic patterns, and ritual principles. In other words, African performative values, ethical positions, and cosmological perspectives lie just beneath the overlay of the rhetoric and practices of the Christian cult.

Classical traditions have a higher ratio of European to African components than the *improvisational* current. Celebrations rely on performative styles similar to those of *improvisational* liturgies but in modulated tones. Worshipers participate actively but in more closely defined roles. The emphasis is on responding to preacher or soloist rather than sharing authority between the pulpit or choir loft and the nave. *Classical* worship bridges the two-ness of being both and neither African and American, which, as DuBois observed, is central to African-American identity. While celebrating their distinct cultural heritage, members of *classical* churches aspire to full participation in American society. Instead of standing as an alternative to the standard fare of US Protestantism, like the *improvisational* current, *classical* churches integrate African communitarian values with European theological and liturgical traditions. Worship reflects both the powerful oratory of African storytelling and the value of educated clerics. Worship relies on polyrhythmic accompaniment but also includes the robed choirs of Finney's revivals. *Classical* churches follow closely the order of service and many of the prayers (especially the sacramental rites, or ordinances) of their European-American counterparts but infuse dialogue, spontaneity and exuberance into these rites. *Classical* worship preserves the structure and content of frontier revivals more closely than the *enthusiast* churches which gave them birth. Leaders of *classical* churches rejected much of the ritual of the slave legacy as they defined themselves as "New Negroes", and, eventually, the "black middle-class". They sought to create a cultural current that nurtured African-American education and economic stability, while, at the same time, gaining respectability in a white supremacist society. So they balance European and African elements delicately. The prominence of the preacher, the dialogical style of performance, the centrality of music, all contribute to a unique set of traditions that allow members both to celebrate their heritage and to integrate themselves further into mainstream society.

Enthusiast churches trace their origins to Europe, specifically England. Europeans also have practiced and continue to practice demonstrative ritual forms. Europeans speak in tongues, fall as if dead, dance and shout. Enthusiasm is not the possession of any one culture, but arises in many contexts. Whitefield and Wesley pursued bold innovations in their contexts, but were not unique in calling Europeans to demonstrate bodily the presence of God in worship. However, it is also true that African practices anticipated many of the forms of enthusiasm that European Americans pursued in frontier revivals. As we shall see below, revivals were interracial gatherings and participants borrowed behaviors and ideas from each other. At camp meetings, African Americans discovered ecstatic and egalitarian versions of Christianity that they could accept and European Americans witnessed, and sometimes came to imitate, African-American ritual practices. European-American enthusiasm, in camp meetings and in the biracial churches of the antebellum South, assimilated aspects of African thought and practice even as they abandoned the egalitarian atmosphere that attracted African Americans to their communities.

Predictably, however, *enthusiast* worship tends to lose its enthusiasm, especially in the face of new social expectations as members gain economic status. *Enthusiast* churches shift their worship towards *mainline* standards of decorum with relative frequency and ease. But in its full flower, *enthusiast* worship mirrors *classical* worship closely and ritual styles reminiscent of the *improvisational* current are not unknown among European Americans. Yet, in most instances, such as the early Pentecostal movement, European-American ecstatic practice functions primarily to assure practitioners that they are truly saved whereas African-American ecstasy seeks primarily to channel transformative divine power into the present social order. *Enthusiast* traditions attracted African Americans and served as their conduit into Christian faith. African Americans and European Americans prayed together at revivals and in southern antebellum parishes, and so learned each others values, faith language, songs, and performative styles. In the end, European-American racism compelled African Americans to form independent communions. Separation ended the period of direct cultural interchange, but African-American influences remain, even as they steadily fade, as *enthusiast* churches converge with *mainline* traditions.

Mainline traditions have the fewest traces of African Traditional Religion. Charles Finney brought his revival system to the east coast establishment and with it some African influences that were prevalent in camp meetings. However, *mainline* traditions developed their primary characteristics in the midst of European reform movements. Reformed liturgies, in theory, reclaimed the liturgy from clerical captivity, restoring a priestly role to the people and the expectation of divine activity in the midst of the gathering. In practice, most of the liturgical acts in Reformed services remain the purview of the ministers since it has proven difficult to shift away from the didactic precedent set when so much had to be taught to the those schooled only in the mysteries of the late medieval Roman Mass. Such discrepancies between Reformed thought and practice continue to this day and have been exacerbated by adoption of the principles of revival, in which the norm of biblicism is replaced with pragmatism, as this tends to increase the focus on the state of individual souls and the neglect of communitarian ethics. The liturgical reform movement highlighted early church practice, enriching contemporary practice with pre-Enlightenment models with their rich symbolic language and action. In *mainline* traditions, African survivals are difficult to detect except as a part of the general African-American contributions to US language and music, or as token inclusion of occasional gospel songs or guest preachers. *Mainline* liturgical traditions overwhelm African cultural practices with European-American individualism and rationality.

Characteristics

The water from the two central sources flows through the landscape of US geography and history. Spatially, the four currents travel from the early, Atlantic coast settlements west with the shifting frontier and then into the great cities. Temporally, they flow from the "pure" covenant communions of seventeenth and eighteenth century New England through the two great waves of Awakenings, the Civil War and the two World Wars to today; and from slavery to emancipation through the great northern migration to ghetto and, more recently, to suburb. To each situation and age, the currents adjust. Individually, the currents remain defiant of cultural pressures in some moments but are readily adaptable in others. Collectively, they influence each other substantially in some locales and separate in order to follow distinct paths in others. In the context of this continent over nearly 400 years, the four currents travel to this present moment even as they continue to evolve. A brief description of their individual characteristics seems appropriate as we envision communities that will grow out of their interaction. I address the currents in the same order as I did in the previous section.

    Improvisational worship reflects the deep yearnings for freedom and salvation that empowered the slaves, with God's help, "to make a way out of no way". As the slaves prayed together for liberation at great risk, so the *improvisational* churches serve the marginalized as safe havens beyond the reach of the stifling powers of white churches. *Improvisational* worship was born in the "invisible institution" of slave religion. As free blacks, along with some slaves, formed their own churches in the late eighteenth and early nineteenth centuries, slave practices were transmitted most purely in the so-called southern Afro-Baptist churches. As Baptists moved towards *classical* models following Emancipation and its attendant economic opportunities, *improvisational* characteristics flowed into Holiness and Pentecostal denominations.

    It has been said that *improvisational* ritual forms are "dance-possible", engaging participants' bodies in rhythmic patterns, not only during designated musical selections but throughout the service.[1] They express the worldview of the participants in dialogical speech and song, empowering the people to affirm, celebrate, and question the insight of leaders. These traditions do not separate spiritual and material concerns, acknowledging the legitimacy of practical as well as metaphysical dilemmas in communal prayers. They stand outside of the dominant cultural ethos and focus on participatory and therapeutic ritual forms in which revelation is not limited to prescribed institutional authorities but percolates up in the midst of the community itself. Oral traditions assume primary authority. Spontaneous rather than scripted ritual texts predominate. *Improvisational* traditions place Christianity at the service of the African-American community in ways which highlight the distinctiveness of black experience within US history and the gifts of African religious traditions when assimilated unapologetically in a fully inculturated form of Christianity.[2]

Free blacks, who could no longer accept the hypocrisy of white Christians who called them brothers and sisters but treated them as second-class citizens, founded the *classical* churches. These communities rejected white caricatures of blacks, reveling in their independence from white ecclesial and social institutions. They celebrate the African-American community as beloved of God, even as they offer hospitality to all who enter their doors. Their worship relies on the contributions of many people—deacons, elders, ushers, nurses, choir members, preachers, assistant pastors, and song leaders. Almost every member has some official role to play and each is recognized for their contribution and empowered by that recognition.[3] *Classical* liturgies provide a sense of welcome and sanctuary that aims to balance the experience of racism and empower participants to remain in the struggle for justice. While *classical* liturgies promote self-esteem among African Americans and contribute to the prophetic critique of white supremacy, they also are subject to internal critique since they tend to promote hierarchical relations within the beloved community based upon characteristics such as gender and class.

Classical liturgies follow the structure of frontier worship. They open with a devotional period that focuses the people on God, gathers their joys and concerns, and involves them in singing God's praise. In the second stage, the preacher addresses the people with scripture, prayer, sermon, and song. In *classical* traditions, proclamation is central, although the act of proclamation is itself dialogical as the people participate through structures of call and response. The service concludes with an invitation to discipleship, an "altar call" in older parlance, now most often termed "opening the doors of the church". Interspersed throughout the service, the choir or choirs perform musical selections (e.g., anthems, gospel choruses, or spirituals) that support the mood of the service and are often chosen in the moment rather than previously scheduled. These services have a predictable structure that adheres closely to the order of service printed in the program. Deftly combining biblical texts, the performative aesthetics of slave religion, and Western Christian traditions, *classical* liturgies produce a new whole—analogous to the development of jazz in relation to European musical forms. *Classical* liturgies address the concrete needs of the community and point to the ultimate fulfillment of God's pledge of salvation and justice. *Classical* worship celebrates African-American wholeness as a present reality and as an eschatological promise.

Enthusiast European-American Protestant liturgical traditions are characterized by a willingness to change in order to attract converts. These traditions reveal the creative potential as well as the pitfalls associated with adaptability. The most sweeping change was the replacement of the rule of biblical warrant, in which every practice required justification through scriptural evidence, with a pragmatic principle, in which whatever worked to convert participants is allowed. The goal of mission efforts became the number converted, not the participation of converts in traditions continuous with historical Christian practice. The change from biblical to pragmatic norms allows for critical reflection on the received tradition and an openness to new insights, but it also carries the risk of turning the Gospel into a commodity to be sold at any price. Despite its adaptability, the form of *enthusiast* worship is fairly stable, mirroring the frontier revival structure—the "hymn sandwich"—of the *classical* churches, but to very different effect. *Enthusiast* worship addresses the anxiety about one's ultimate fate as an individual soul, rather than serving the liberation struggle of a people, as the *classical* tradition does. *Enthusiast* worship centers on the testimony of the converted. Preachers challenge hearers to give themselves to Jesus as they themselves have done. Through one person's preaching another receives a call to testify and so experiential discourse leads to institutional vitality and growth. The intensity of the experience, the depth of transformation it brings about in the convert, and the eloquence of the testimony in conveying these effects to others are the basis for success of *enthusiast* preachers, not educational achievement, family connections, or philosophical acumen.

The populism of *enthusiast* traditions differentiates them from *mainline* denominations and connects them to movements of protest against the social order. But, again, the connections are not simple. Revival preachers have motivated converts to participate in a wide variety of social causes. Their techniques, not their particular message, successfully recruit converts. *Enthusiast* traditions have contributed to both progressive and conservative social movements. For example, revivalists were central in the successful campaign to achieve women's suffrage, but their descendants now collect signatures, money, and foot soldiers for the campaign to deny women the legal right to have an abortion. In still other contexts, *enthusiast* traditions have promoted quietism, revealing their tendency to divide spiritual and material concerns. *Enthusiast* European-American Protestant liturgical traditions have reshaped the American religious scene over and over again. As the worship of *mainline* churches grows formal, renewal movements that emphasize personal investment in religious matters arise. When mass immigration threatens "native" security, when widespread reconfiguration of living arrangements (whether the settling of the frontier or suburban sprawl) displaces masses of people, when the crush of urbanization alienates large groups of people from the religious structures of their past, missionary movements take shape among the unchurched. *Enthusiast* traditions re-integrate displaced people into a well-defined cosmic order and provide relief from anxiety by offering converts sure identification among the elect.

Mainline European-American Protestant worship is a current of liturgical traditions shaped according to the reality of privileged white Americans. *Mainline* European-American churches enjoy the privilege of being the norm against which all other worship in this country is judged. While declining in membership as cultural and religious pluralism increase across the nation, *mainline* Protestant churches continue to carry considerable social influence. Given the security of their position in society, members of *mainline* churches can celebrate in worship the basic goodness of present national patterns and religious metaphors that uphold rather than challenge current social structures. The "stars and stripes" process with the prayer book and once again, for this hour, America is "one nation under God", the Protestant holy land.

At the same time, *mainline* European-American Protestant worship traditions are also dynamic and plural. The principles which govern *mainline* liturgies have been, and continue to be, adapted to the changing context of US society. As an example, while the Puritans rejected the *Book of Common Prayer* (and eventually service books all together) in favor of locally crafted rites, *mainline* denominations now regularly publish and promote the use of worship books. Recent liturgical proposals in *mainline* churches issue most often from denominational worship committees staffed by liturgical experts. Because of extensive ecumenical dialogue and cooperation, *mainline* traditions share many elements in common. However, worship in an Episcopal church and in a Presbyterian one continues to feel quite different.

Mainline European-American Protestant liturgical traditions maintain vitality but frequently lapse into formalism. The revivals of Edwards and of Finney sought to breathe life into dead practices. Nineteenth century restoration efforts and the recent ecumenical movement both attempt to rekindle deep piety by reviving ancient forms of prayer. Yet, for the most part, lay contributions in *mainline* services remain formal, structured, and restrained. *Mainline* worship continues to attend most closely to the congregation's sense of hearing; explaining and persuading, not displaying or performing. Sermons may criticize government or industrial policies but *mainline* worship services, on the whole, do not perform alternative ways of governing or doing business. One might observe, to the contrary, that *mainline* liturgical traditions cultivate members whose bodies function productively in the alienation of late industrial capitalism. In a technology-driven society with its stress, insecurity and rapid change, *mainline* worship provides solace with predictable orders, scripted prayers, and "high art" music. *Mainline* worship supports the status quo by comforting adherents—especially the successful ones—in services that demand little participation and even less community interaction. *Mainline* liturgical traditions have served the powerful center of the population since the founding of the nation. They serve well the secure who support social welfare programs but remain loyal to global capitalism even when it exacerbates economic inequities.

Conclusion

US Protestant liturgical traditions among blacks and whites flow as four currents in one river. They share the sources of European Christianity and African Traditional Religion but in varying concentrations. They flow through the same terrain but on different sides of varying events. The descriptions above reveal differences between the four currents. Many factors contribute to the construction of different groups in a shared historical context. However, the category of social class deserves special attention as it, along with race and culture, sits at the root of many of the differences between the currents.

Social class is the crucial factor in the sub-division of both African-American and European-American Protestant liturgical traditions. *Mainline* liturgies were shaped decisively by the gains and flaws of the Enlightenment, which itself rested on the preceding movements of the Renaissance and the Protestant Reformation. The *mainline* current is set apart from the other three by its allegiance to carefully crafted written prayers, academic sermons, the downplaying of the role of human emotion in the life of faith, and the subjugation of the body to rigid rules of restraint in the ritual context. This "Enlightened" liturgical sensibility is closely connected to issues of class not just because the Enlightenment was primarily a movement among the elite, both intellectual and socio-economic, of the eighteenth century but also because the rituals that it shapes cultivate personal traits and skills that are rewarded in the economic sphere and contribute to the accumulation of wealth. In contrast, the *enthusiast*, *classical*, and *improvisational* currents all are rooted in various folk cultures. These currents acknowledge the importance of gestural and vocal responses to the encounter of persons with deity in the context of liturgy. They value experiential explications of scripture, spontaneous prayers, and first-person testimonials. The *mainline* churches served the landed gentry and the industrial elite of the eighteenth and nineteenth centuries, and now serve upwardly mobile professionals. The other currents took shape among the rugged individualists of the frontier and the undereducated and unskilled laborers of other regions.

Yet, it also true that as economic opportunities emerge, members, especially of the *enthusiast* current, and less so of the *classical*, trade their religious fervor for material success. Members of these currents confine enthusiasm under discipline. They forced themselves into the expectations of industrial capitalism and it paid off. For example, Wesley's appeal to the emotions attracted workers not only because they could comprehend his theological images more easily than the ancient creedal language of the Church of England but also because it addressed their situation of displacement in the new economic structures of their age and helped them to cope in the face of the new demands of industrialism. Similar class divisions exist in the US. Hatch writes:

> ... the Second Great Awakening delineated the fault line of class within American Christianity. Clergy from both ends of the social scale battled for cultural authority. Blessed with a common touch, the insurgents enjoyed the advantage. Embodying the aspirations and values of common people, upstarts hopelessly blurred the distinction between pulpit and pew. Their success may have been the most profoundly democratic upheaval in the early republic. Using every means possible, they gave witness to the message that virtue and insight resided in ordinary people.[4]

Enthusiast and *classical* churches took seriously the needs of the masses and reaped the rewards as both their membership and their social prestige rose dramatically. But such success also resulted in a decline in fervor among the rank and file. Those not yet comfortable with (and/or critical of) decorous liturgies found a new outlet for their more spontaneous expressions. The Holiness movement is one example of the process by which new ecstatic forms emerge as the *enthusiast* and *classical* currents shifted to less spontaneous forms of ritual expression. Many of those disgruntled with the "bourgeoisification" of the *classical* churches turned instead to the *improvisational* current. Shifts in class allegiance contribute to shifts in liturgical idioms and aesthetics. The *enthusiast* and the *classical* currents now approach the *mainline* in cultivating restrained participation rather than ecstatic possession. *Improvisational* communities continue to encounter, demonstrably, a living and active spirit, even as they too slowly "mature" and begin to curb "excesses".

In the end, no direct correlation between the class location(s) of members of a particular community and liturgical style exist. On the one hand, liturgies can inculcate behaviors that fit economic structures. The Methodist discipline tutored day laborers into industrial workers. Slaveholders "improved" their slaves, making them more productive with the help of lessons in obedience and patience from plantation mission preachers. On the other hand, human beings can adapt a variety of modes of ritual performance for a variety of circumstances. The majority of contemporary liturgical scholars, both Roman Catholic and Protestant, consider the High Middle Ages the nadir of Christian liturgical practice.[5] Yet, the popular devotions of many Roman Catholics, especially women, in that period demonstrate that even in the midst of rites that are distant, inaccessible and non-participatory, the people find ways to create meaningful practices. The people of medieval Europe said the rosary, meditated on the visual gospel of the carved walls, and adored the consecrated host, despite the priestly captivity of the rites in a dead language, behind a screen, too distant to participate in and culminating in the transformation of bread into a substance too holy to receive.

The poor can find a place of solace amidst rites of power and privilege. The rich, too, may join in ecstatic rites, although they most often employ the Spirit to quiet their anxiety while leaving intact their privilege. The First Great Awakening swept through the mercantile towns of New England, moving the wealthy as well as the hungry to demonstrative acts of praise. Recent Neo-Pentecostal (or "charismatic," as they are often called when they take place within established churches rather than in separate denominations) revivals have swept up wealthy matrons as well as the marginalized. Consider, too, the Quakers, a small but well-to-do sect, who practice communal mysticism. Whether silence attracts entrepreneurs or provides the discipline for participants to become successful merchants is hard to say. I do not subscribe to theories of economic determinism but am compelled to note the widespread and inverse relation of social power and religious enthusiasm. In this country, where race and class are inextricably linked, the history of the four currents is as much about the consequences of economic disparity as it is about cultural conflicts.

Previous Occasions of Biracial worship

Contrary to what many may think given the legacy of American segregation, the record shows that African-American and European-American Protestants shared the experience of regular Sunday worship together long ago. In this section, I discuss four significant occasions of biracial worship: the frontier camp meetings, the biracial Methodist and Baptist churches of the antebellum South, the plantation missions, and the early Pentecostal revivals. These are certainly not the only instances of joint worship among blacks and whites, but they were central in the establishment of patterns of interaction between African Americans and European Americans. Without undue repetition of the material included above, I will trace the histories of these occasions in order to apply their lessons to worship in contemporary multicultural communities. I am interested in the circumstances that led to such biracial services, the style of worship that occurred, the dynamics between members of the two groups in these services, and the results of these shared experiences.

European-American slaveholders resisted the idea of converting slaves at first. To do so would imply a shared humanity between master and slave. To do so might also allow slaves to claim a right to be freed. The latter problem was solved through laws severing links between baptism and manumission.[6] The former problem remained. At the same time, other European-American Christians felt compelled to evangelize all non-Christians, even those who were slaves. Eventually, the missionaries convinced slave-owners of the benefits of slave conversion.

European-American missionary efforts to the slaves were, on the whole, unsuccessful before the Second Great Awakening. The ritual and theology of *mainline* churches reflected too closely the values of the privileged classes that belonged to them to attract those they owned.[7] Towards the end of the eighteenth century, Methodist and Baptist missionaries attracted large numbers of slaves as well as unchurched whites to Christianity in the context of the Camp Meeting. These missionaries with their fiery rhetoric of human sin leveled the social distinctions on which southern plantation life was built. In the camp meetings and in the numerous Baptist and Methodist congregations that grew out of them, slaves experienced a variety of Christian practice that fueled their own hopes for liberation.

Accepting that African Americans were becoming Christians, slaveholders developed a version of Christianity that better suited their need to control their slaves as an alternative to European-American *enthusiast* worship.[8] The planters as the economic and political elite asserted significant influence over religious institutions and forced reform-minded evangelicals into a new mold in exchange for access to the slaves. Raboteau writes:

> The egalitarian trend in evangelicalism which drove some Methodists, Baptists, and Presbyterians to condemn slavery foundered on the intransigency of that institution in the South. These evangelicals, who had condemned slavery found themselves defending slave conversion for making slaves "better," which was easily transposed into making "better" slaves.[9]

Slaves, for their part, resisted conversion to Christianity at first as well. They rejected the religion of their masters and attempted to preserve their traditional religious practices. But their transportation to a new continent and active suppression by slaveholders broke the integrity of their traditional religions.[10] With no obvious alternatives, and attentive to the liberative strains of revivalist preaching, slaves began to convert to Christianity in substantial numbers during the Second Great Awakening. Slaves, employing creatively the tension between their owners' desire for control and tainted but nonetheless sincere compassion for those with whom they lived and worked, recognized the opportunity that conversion presented. Baptism, while no longer able to confer civil rights did recognize that a soul animated African bodies and that this soul, if not the body, deserved a destiny of freedom.[11] As a consequence, slaves and free blacks approached the altar at camp meetings and waded in the waters of frontier rivers and southern ponds. African Americans also accepted the right hand of fellowship as it was offered by Methodist and Baptist congregations. Worship with whites would never include prayers for emancipation but it did ameliorate the stark and hierarchical relation of the races. While slaves could experience fully satisfying worship only in the "Invisible Institution", they attended worship with whites—sometimes without choice but sometimes willingly—and found that they could influence the religious practice of their so-called betters.[12] Immediately after the Civil War, the ex-slaves separated from whites and formed their own churches, institutionalizing their alternative ritual system.[13] Independent black churches, especially Afro-Baptist communities, continued to practice worship in the style of the "Invisible Institution". Later, these African-American *improvisational* liturgies developed into a tradition which attracted whites to ecstatic forms of worship and led to the final historical example of joint worship—the early Pentecostal phenomenon.

The Camp Meeting: "Separate but Simultaneous" Biracial Worship

The first example of biracial worship is the revival, or Camp Meeting, where large numbers of slaves first heard a version of the Gospel that appealed to them. Itinerant preachers, primarily Methodists and Baptists, spoke of the promise of salvation, of personal transformation, and of the coming Kingdom. Camp Meeting leaders combined highly emotional music, confrontational sermons and exhortations, and vivid and moving prayers, to challenge participants to self-examination, confession and repentance as the first steps towards reconciliation with their Creator. Services continued for three or four days to break the routine of daily life and to weaken the resistance of the unrepentant. Camp meetings were occasions of great festivity, a time for socializing, good food and a bit of leisure. For slaves, the prolonged meetings meant a break from the grueling routine of uncompensated labor, and a taste of freedom as they pursued spirit possession.[14] Camp meetings drew all manner of people—rich and poor, black, white and Native. The Second Great Awakening created new alternatives to the established churches that were controlled by the elite. The largely unchurched population responded with vigor, and American evangelicalism came to dominate the land.

While southern evangelicalism eventually permeated all classes of European-American Protestants, it appealed first and foremost to the inhabitants of the frontier, owners of small farms and the like. These European Americans shared a similar routine of hard labor with the slaves.[15] In addition, most were not wealthy enough to own slaves themselves and so had a different relationship to the "peculiar institution" than wealthy whites. They were primarily illiterate and shared a common love of the spoken word with African Americans. To them, as well as to the slaves, revival preachers appealed with participatory rites of preaching, prayer, and song. New leaders came from the common ranks and were chosen based upon the power of their testimony to their call and their preaching talent, and not because of education or skin color. Blacks were popular preachers among both whites and blacks and were more effective evangelists among slaves than white preachers.[16] Given the characteristics of both members and leaders, it is not surprising that European-American *enthusiast* churches were suspicious of slavery. The Methodists condemned slavery in 1778; the Baptists in 1785.[17]

Evangelical theology emphasized the great divide between God and people. God alone was good; people were sinful and needed God to redeem them. The emphasis on the difference between the divine and the human resulted in a leveling of human distinctions. All were equal relative to God's majesty. All were equal in that all sinned. All were equal in needing to hear God's word and confess their own need for salvation. All who converted were equal in that their righteousness depended not on their own merit but on the unmerited grace of God. These principles encouraged revivalists to address both rich and poor, black and white, slave and free. All were called to conversion and all were welcomed with a sign of fellowship into the fold. Genovese writes: "Blacks responded to the rough-hewn frontier preaching and were, for the most part, welcomed as participants".[18] The existence of a Divine Master deflated the claims of any human master to ultimate authority, just as the reclamation of divine independence from the institutional church and human monarchy during the Reformation diminished allegiance to Pope and King.

Early camp meetings welcomed people of all races to worship together. Later, certainly by the 1830s, at occasions where both African Americans and European Americans attended, whites and blacks separated for some services. European-Americans complained that the exuberance of African Americans disturbed both their own worship services and their sleep—as blacks continued to pray and sing long into the night. Free of competing preachers and close supervision, the slaves "pounded their chests, cried out with great pathos, and danced the 'holy dance' although the last was forbidden by the preachers".[19] In response, Camp Meeting leaders assigned blacks and whites separate spaces on the grounds. Blacks held their worship behind the main pulpit while whites gathered in front. Eventually, a custom of building a wall between the two groups arose. The wall marked the boundary between the races and made it easier to hear each separate service.[20] In other words, the wall created what I call "separate but simultaneous" worship. This pattern would continue throughout the meeting until the last day. To close the meeting, the barrier would be dismantled and all participants would march together around the grounds and celebrate the Lord's Supper.[21]

In the setting of the Camp Meeting, African Americans and European Americans came not only to share the Christian faith but also to re-shape this faith together into a unique American version of Protestantism. The Camp Meeting exposed slaves to European-American *enthusiast* worship and whites to African-American religious sensibilities. Mechal Sobel provides extensive analysis of the mutual influence of whites and blacks in eighteenth century Virginia.[22] For example, she notes that revivals occurred first and lasted longest where whites were in close contact with blacks, that blacks came to accept the idea of a personal God, that whites began to exhibit a greater appreciation of extended family bonds and a stronger attachment to a particular geographic location, and that blacks came to accept a more linear view of time and to expect to go home to God, joining the glad reunion in the Big House after death. In terms of worship, the camp meetings provided an opportunity for whites to hear the African-inspired rhythms of the slave spirituals and blacks to be introduced to European-American camp songs. Whites witnessed the norms of possession that slaves practiced and imitated black exuberance. Blacks copied and extended *enthusiast* preaching styles. Together, whites and blacks crafted a religiosity that supported their common way of life. Sobel writes: "By the end of the eighteenth century, whites and blacks shared family, clan, and even folk histories that could not be separated from each other".[23]

At camp meetings, whites and blacks were more equal than anywhere else in southern society. This is not to deny that European Americans controlled camp meetings. African Americans preached at camp meetings, but they had no freedom to initiate or administer a public event of such magnitude in the antebellum South. Nonetheless, camp meetings were exceptional in accepting the humanity and spiritual practices of African Americans alongside those of European Americans. First, in view of the "separate but simultaneous" services, both white and black styles of worship were seen as legitimate. While whites might decry black enthusiasm and blacks might remain skeptical of white hypocrisy, at a revival they shared together important spiritual experiences. The dismantling of the wall between the races and the joining in the celebration of the Eucharist, while tainted by the never disputed conjunction of skin color and bondage, stands out as an important symbolic gesture of ultimate equality in a society that rigidly guarded distinctions between members of the two races. Second, camp meetings allowed for some expression of African-American authority in relation to European Americans. Black preachers touched the hearts of whites and occasioned them to "get religion" at a time when the legal testimony of African Americans in relation to European Americans was disallowed. Raboteau writes:

> When white sinners were awakened by black exhorters, when masters were converted by the singing, shouting, and praying of their slaves, when white congregations were pastored by black preachers, the logical extreme of revivalistic religion was reached.[24]

Camp Meeting worship recognized both commonalities and distinctions between black and white religiosity. There was a time of separation and a time of unity. There was a time for exhortation of whites to individual moral behavior, which included convictions on the humane treatment of slaves. Most white, and some black, preachers instructed slaves to accept their station and obey their masters, but they also recognized the humanity of slaves, their right to hear the Gospel and be instructed in religious matters, and their ultimate equality with whites in the eyes of God. There was also opportunity for slaves to pray on their own for their own concerns.

Blacks and whites shared the same faith but from radically different social locations that necessitated different ritual expressions. Both groups prayed to Christ, but European Americans sought freedom from the anxiety of personal failings and the hellfire and brimstone to which sin was said to lead, while African Americans, especially those held in bondage, desired freedom from hell in the present. Whites and blacks both expressed their needs in the ecstatic language of the revival—the shout, the jerk, exclamations and acclamations—but, even in the context of shared ecstasy, whites have consistently observed the heightened fervor of black practices. In the antebellum South, separate services provided the only outlet for slaves (and free blacks as well) to fully voice their concerns and express their pain. In describing the opposing interpretations of sermons among blacks and whites, Dvorak writes:

> Whites would derive feelings both of moral earnestness and resolve on their own behalf and of reassurance and righteousness on the question of how society was organized. Even the most disadvantaged whites welcomed this affirmation of the status quo. No matter how disadvantaged, they were white and free. Moreover, whites generally aspired to a bigger slice of the economic and social pie; and in the antebellum South, owning slaves was part of the American dream for most nonslaveholders ... Slaves neither resolved to

obey masters nor celebrated the righteousness of slavery. They heard a different message than divine sanction of their captivity. Blacks—in opposition to whites and for survival—formed a "church within a church".[25]

Camp meetings were temporary and converting occasions. They did not function as churches nor were they meant to. They were instead a form of worship that was to lead sinners into a church or revitalize an existing congregation. On the frontier, churches were few and far between and so camp meetings, along with occasional visits by circuit riding preachers, served as the primary locus of worship for the isolated settlers. Further to the east, however, camp meetings accompanied membership in a specific church that nurtured one's faith on an on-going basis. Camp meetings drew many unchurched people, both black and white, into the faith. The Methodist and Baptist denominations grew at a phenomenal rate and founded numerous churches, many of which were biracial. The reality of whites and blacks worshiping together disturbed guardians of the southern way of life. They responded, first, by denouncing the enthusiasts and, when this proved ineffective, by setting up an alternative. We turn next to some analysis of biracial Methodist and Baptist churches and then to the plantation mission concept that took shape in the 1830s and defined a style of biracial worship in the decades leading up to the Civil War.

Worship in Biracial Baptist and Methodist Churches: "Hospitality that Fades"

Methodist and Baptist missionaries led the Second Great Awakening and reaped its rewards by winning the loyalty of a majority of southern church-goers. They preached successfully to members of both races and so many of their congregations became biracial. Sobel writes:

> Virtually all eighteenth-century Baptists and Methodist churches were mixed churches in which blacks sometimes preached to whites and in which whites and blacks witnessed together, shouted together, and shared ecstatic experiences of "dry" and wet christenings, meetings and burials. A long period of intensive mass interaction ensued.[26]

European-American Baptists and Methodists, but especially Baptists, allowed slaves and free blacks some measure of freedom to determine how they would worship. On occasion, European-American Baptists even confronted legislatures who restricted the churches' right to license African-American preachers.[27] In addition, white Baptists sometimes encouraged black autonomy in instances where legislators restricted independent worship. As a group, these European-American Christians were exceptional in resisting compromises between Christianity and slavery. They were committed to the principles that God and not human government determined who would carry the gospel message and that every local community had the right to worship God in their own way. Even these commitments would be attenuated as northern abolitionist fervor grew and southern defensiveness increased in turn. But, while these principles held, slaves and free blacks found a relatively hospitable place to practice their new-found religion in Baptist and Methodist biracial churches.

Worship in the biracial churches followed the frontier format. Services were held throughout the day on Sunday. The sermon was paramount while songs and prayers both led up to and followed after that central event. The presence of two racial groups is most notable in issues of architectural setting, the delivery of and responses to the sermon, and in the development of the rites of initiation.

The seating was most often segregated. Whites required both slaves and free blacks to sit in galleries or back rows.[28] Dvorak observes that, although white evangelicals were more egalitarian than mainline churches, they maintained hierarchical seating patterns. Separating not only black from white, the pews were also employed to denote the relative status of whites. In contrast, she finds no evidence of any such patterns among African Americans whether in their own sections or in independent churches.[29] Among European Americans seating was an important symbolic reinforcement of the established social hierarchy.[30] African Americans, in contrast, apparently marked no distinctions among themselves in seating patterns or other symbolic means. On the one hand, the seats for blacks were, in terms of sight and sound, good seats and showed that whites accommodated blacks and desired their presence. H.N. McTyeire challenged churches where space had not been designated:

> Sometimes a portion of the church has been assigned to them, roomy and comfortably seated … and sometimes this has been overlooked, and they are left to stroll around, or listen to the sermon at the window, or under the poor shelter of an arbor. They have been invited to the gospel feast, but no places have been provided for them. With hungering, unfed souls they look on—the spectators of others' piety and not partakers of the common grace.[31]

On the other hand, segregated seating represented an insurmountable barrier between the races that not even Christian fellowship could overcome. Dvorak writes: "There was no route—ritual or generational—by which the worshiper in the gallery or balcony or back of the church could ever approach services as fully assimilated, equal members of the congregation".[32] Blacks, easily identified by the color of their skin, were set apart in a manner that demonstrated their inferior social status in a setting that purported to, and, in fact, did, welcome them more fully as equals than elsewhere in antebellum society.

Both blacks and whites preached in biracial services. In the aftermath of slave insurrections, whites sometimes restricted the ability of blacks to preach, but these restrictions were unevenly enforced and, for the most part, quickly lifted. The preaching abilities of uneducated African Americans continued to impress many white evangelicals. As noted above in relation to camp meetings, black preachers were successful in converting both whites and blacks and were significantly more effective than whites in evangelizing slaves. The importance of blacks being accepted as spiritual authorities in a society that systematically denied them authority in material matters cannot be underestimated. Blacks preached in a style that was effective for both blacks and whites. They ignored the supposed distinctions between preaching for white and black parishioners. White preachers continued to preach one sermon for whites and then another, often at the end of the service, to "accommodate the incapacity of the slaves".[33] African Americans responded with more vigor to preaching in general and especially to the artistry of black preachers. While *enthusiast* worship was built upon the expectation of provoking vocal and gestural responses in the congregation and had European as well as African precedents, blacks pushed whites to fuller praise while whites remained more likely to limit the range of acceptable behavior.[34] Sobel writes:

> White Methodists were certainly emotional and vocal, but the shout, involving ecstatic movement as well as vocalization, had come into the tradition from the black experience via the revivals. It was the way to get "happy," "ecstatic," or "high." It involved singing, rhythm in body motion, clapping, and vision travels.[35]

When a sermon helped someone to "get religion", they were offered the right hand of fellowship as a sign of their acceptance as a member of the church. Because so many members would initially convert and be baptized at the Camp Meeting, a separate rite developed for entry into a specific local community. Parallel to the separation of baptism and confirmation in the Roman and other subsequent Western traditions, conversion and rites of reception to membership became distinct experiences on the frontier. Throughout the late eighteenth century, most Baptist and Methodist churches performed the same rites of welcome for both white and black members. This equality of ceremony faded after 1830 as abolitionist critique of slavery became more pronounced. In addition, where early membership lists included blacks equally (although separately) with whites, later lists do not include blacks by name or, in some instances, at all.[36]

In seating arrangements, the giving of and responding to sermons, and rites of initiation, European-American Baptists and Methodists demonstrated both their desire to welcome African Americans as full and equal members of their churches and their ultimate inability to escape the cultural norms of their time. *Enthusiast* worship assumes that participants are equal before God and, thereby, encourages members of the community to treat each other equitably. Both the rhetoric and performative style of frontier worship proclaim that all are equal in needing to hear and respond to the Word. Yet some are white and some are black. As the number of blacks grew relative to the number of whites, as whites discovered the ability of blacks to act on their desire to be free and revolt, and as whites continued up the economic ladder and became further wed to the slave economy, European-American leaders of antebellum Baptist and Methodist churches marked the distinction between the races more and more forcefully. Raboteau writes: "Fellowship required that church members be treated alike; slavery demanded that black members, even the free, be treated differently".[37]

For their part, African Americans discerned the gap between white rhetoric and white ethics, and therefore remained aloof from Christian fellowship. How, an ex-slave asks, could he love his pastor who preaches "Do unto others" when he sees that preacher whip and beat his slaves.[38] African Americans participated in biracial worship but found different meanings in the texts and rites than whites intended for them to find. When addressing slaves, white preachers emphasized Jesus's meekness and humble obedience to God. In contrast, slaves found in Jesus a fellow-sufferer and the King of Glory who was coming to overturn the order of the day and set them free. Whenever an opportunity appeared, blacks separated themselves into independent churches in order to escape their second class status in biracial churches. Indeed, as many white critics predicted, the experience of leadership roles and institutional independence, especially in Baptist circles, encouraged and prepared African Americans to run their own institutions.[39] The movement to autonomy, sanctioned by Baptist principles, became a full-scale exodus in both the Methodist and Baptist denominations after the Emancipation Proclamation.[40]

Worship in the biracial churches demonstrates the ability of worship to function in a culture as means of reforming and buttressing the social order simultaneously. Sparks writes: "When a congregation gathered at the riverside and sang and prayed as blacks and whites were ritually immersed, race could be temporarily transcended".[41] While, in some times and places, blacks and whites were baptized in the same manner, other liturgical acts only reinforced the distinctiveness of the races and the so-called superiority of whites. Blacks and whites might be washed in the same living water, but they could not even sit in the same pew much less eat together at the Lord's Table. Dvorak makes much of the fact that whites and blacks worshiped together at all.[42] But she also notes, as we saw above, that full inclusion was excluded as a possibility. Southern plantation life brought masters and slaves into intimate relationship in many aspects of life including public prayer. Yet, this style of worship also contributed to the rationalization of southern paternalism and the maintenance of slavery as a social institution.

The populist and democratic values of American evangelical Protestantism acquiesced to the economic self-interest of European Americans. Because of pressure from the planter class and because of the rise in socioeconomic status of their own members, *enthusiast* churches made peace with slavery. Sobel writes:

> The Baptist church of the 1750's, and 1760's, and 1770's, had been a church of the dispossessed. Black slaves and poor whites had suffered for their faith; blacks had been whipped and whites jailed and hounded out of Virginia. They had prided themselves on being a church of the lowly and persecuted. However, by the late 1780's, many white Baptists had moved up in social class, and many of the "middling sort" now joined them, along with a few from the elite. This new Baptist church began to be self-conscious about its relationship with blacks and its attitude toward slavery.[43]

The rise in status of members of European-American *enthusiast* churches resulted in a decline in the hospitality offered to African Americans by these churches. Whites grew more fearful of black rebellion as the number of slaves relative to the white population grew and as insurrections such as the one led by Denmark Vesey erupted. In addition, abolitionist sentiments in the North were becoming strident. Southerners felt obligated to defend their way of life. In response, slave-owners developed a version of the Christian faith that addressed both slave control and northern criticism—the plantation mission.

The Plantation Mission: "You have heard … but I say … "

Plantation missions developed as a specific strategy to govern black religiosity. They represent less an instance of biracial worship, although they did include both white and black participants, as an attempt by one group to impose an interpretation of Christianity, which, not incidentally, upheld a social order from which they stood to benefit, upon another group, who served as the labor base for that order. As *enthusiast* missionaries attracted slaves and the slaves showed signs of hearing a promise of liberation in Christianity, the planters recognized the need to create and enforce, as best they could, an alternative interpretation. Genovese writes:

> After the Denmark Vesey plot, however, despite the momentary hysteria over the alleged role of the churches in encouraging slave insurrection, South Carolina's great planter aristocracy began going to church, or rather making sure that the slaves were going. As was to happen in Virginia a decade later, once faced with an insurrection of slaves who displayed religious inclinations, the slaveholders sobered up. If the slaves were going to get religion, then religion had to be made safe for slaveholders.[44]

The Vesey uprising occurred in 1821 and the Turner insurrection in 1831. It is not coincidental that plantation missions became prominent fixtures on the southern landscape following these violent episodes.

The slave insurrections were, however, not the only factor precipitating the organization of these new institutions in which a missionary came to live among the slaves. Plantation missions were also founded to support the sincere efforts of missionaries who desired slaves to hear the gospel. Charles Colcock Jones, a Presbyterian minister and the most visible advocate of plantation missions, was adamant in his pleas for the evangelization of the slaves.[45] He regarded his mission to slaves as a part of the sweeping social reform movements of the period, most of which derived their impetus and power from the Second Great Awakening. Jones believed that, as *enthusiast* churches campaigned for temperance and women's suffrage, they should also contribute to the conversion of the "heathens" within their own borders in order that America remain an exemplary Christian nation.[46]

Jones was pragmatic in his campaign. He recognized that joining the abolitionist ranks would mean losing access to the slaves. Planters would not permit a missionary to criticize slavery itself. He, therefore, set about to perfect the master-slave relationship, placing all parties in a covenant bond subject to Christian law. He preached obedience to the slaves and responsibility to the planters. Jones established The Lincoln County Association as a model plantation in which slaves were treated humanely and therefore worked efficiently without resistance.[47] He recruited missionaries and raised funds to support them. Many responded and each had their own reasons for living and working among the slaves. Raboteau writes:

> The desire to evangelize the poor, the desire to make slaves docile, the desire to create a model plantation, and the desire to defend slavery against abolitionist attacks were all reasons for supporting plantation missions.[48]

Plantation missions were, finally, an answer to abolitionist criticism from the North. In a strange twist of logic, southern apologists justified slavery as a divinely sanctioned mission to Africans. Never before had missionaries captured their potential converts, dragged them forcibly from the mission field to the home country, and exploited their labor. Yet, the argument continued, if Africans lost their freedom, self-determination, and ties to kin and country but gained the Gospel, were they not better off? Abolitionists accused southerners of neglecting the spiritual needs of slaves. Southern missionaries, in response, re-doubled their efforts to convert slaves in order to justify the existence of slavery.

The worship of plantation missions emphasized instruction. Simultaneous with Baptist and Methodist biracial worship described above, and in conjunction with efforts to stamp out independent African-American worship in both its visible and invisible forms, the missions multiplied during the 1830s. Jones proposed that every plantation include a chapel structure on-site and employ a missionary. He insisted that slaves hear preaching every Sunday and catechetical lectures on a weekday evening. Preachers should speak in a manner accessible to uneducated slaves. The lectures should explain doctrines necessary to salvation but not threaten the social order. He encouraged the planters and their families to participate in the religious instruction of the slaves in bible studies in order to form familial bonds among plantation residents.[49] Jones provided a catechism which proved popular.[50] He accepted the restriction that instruction proceed orally so that slaves did not need to learn how to read in order to participate in the worship or classes. He trained missionaries to read aloud the questions and answers that he provided while the slaves repeated them until they could do so from memory. Jones also insisted that instruction continue beyond the experience of conversion so that the slaves would not be left to their own interpretations but remain under white supervision. Finally, Jones agreed that all activities would be subject to the prior of approval of the owners.[51]

The dynamic between whites and blacks in the plantation missions was exceptionally rigid. Worship in the plantation missions was altered to serve the needs of planters. It consisted almost exclusively in preaching obedience to the slaves. There might be some singing and a prayer for conversion, but the biblical passages to be read were limited to those portions of scripture that justified slavery as divinely sanctioned. While purportedly for the spiritual benefit of slaves, mission worship served as an instrument of social control for the planters. Missionaries insisted upon the right to comment upon any unjust treatment of slaves by planters and overseers, but they could not challenge the right of one human being to own another. Slaves understood the hypocrisy on which the missions were built and took what they could from the services. Jones himself reports that on one occasion, as he preached about slave obedience, half of the gathered audience walked out and the rest seemed not to listen.[52] The slaves perfected a "hermeneutic of suspicion" in which they differentiated between the gospel of their masters and the gospel of God.

Plantation missions resulted in several major shifts in European-American Protestant practice. First, the missions allowed religious practice to be shaped by the social elite to their own despotic ends. Where the sixteenth century reformers had sought to free local communities to follow the Bible rather than ecclesial or secular powers in determining the shape of worship, slave-owners dictated the worship practices of the missions. Slaves received a misshapen gospel subject to the whims of the ruling class, rather than one defined by the freedom of the divine spirit. Second, in opposition to the Protestant tenet that all Christians should have access to and knowledge of the entire biblical witness, slaves heard only those parts of scripture that lent support to slavery. Whitemarsh B. Seabrook insisted that slaves become "intimately acquainted" only with "the prominent portions of scripture which shew the duties of servants and the rights of masters".[53] Third, the missionaries accepted an uncharacteristic separation of religious education and the imparting of literacy. The Protestant reformers translated scripture and liturgy into the local vernacular so that worshipers could understand the content of the prayers. The slaves were not taught to read and so were denied access to the full biblical texts. Planters were afraid, and rightfully so, that giving slaves access to the full biblical witness might lead to insubordination. Slaves pursued literacy specifically to gain access to the bible throughout this period, and leaders of rebellions, such as Denmark Vesey, quoted biblical apocalyptic extensively in their recruitment and motivation of followers. Thus, Reformed Christians, defenders for over 300 years of the importance of direct access to scripture, now restricted the communication of the message of Christianity to oral means, and the inheritors of a predominantly oral culture strove for literacy in order to access scripture without the interference of the owners. Finally, missionaries accepted a split between spiritual and material realities, the repudiation of which had been central to their ancestors. The forebears of the Baptists, the Puritans and Separatists, had sought to integrate faith and life. Now Baptists and Methodists declared their religion was concerned only with the spiritual, and not the civil, status of slaves.

The worship of the plantation missions helped to define and enforce these compromises. Texts were carefully chosen to support enslavement and to encourage obedience of slaves to their masters. White missionaries, dependent on planters for their careers and in many instances their paychecks, led the services. Occasionally, black preachers were invited to the pulpit, but only if they were willing to avoid criticizing the institution of slavery and to promote obedience. Northern whites were welcome to witness the success of the plantation missions among the slaves but not to address the slaves, because owners feared abolitionist rhetoric.[54] The entire system of the missions came to support the preservation of the southern antebellum social order. Its modifications of the extremes of behavior such as slave revolts and the violence of owners only reinforced the staying power of the slave economy.

Worship in the plantation missions could not challenge slavery directly. However, Christian missionaries and the slave converts made use of Christian teachings, even the corrupt ones available to them, to influence the relations of masters and slaves in the midst of the "peculiar institution". Such indirect challenges did not go completely unnoticed. Seabrook warned of the dangers implicit in the instruction of slaves, no matter how controlled the content of the teaching. He criticized Jones for allowing blacks to preach, for insisting on the participation of masters in slave instruction as if white aristocrats were on the same plane as slaves, and for accommodating the slaves with special sermons. Raboteau writes:

> Inherent in the recognition of the slave's claim to humanity and even more in the assertion of his right to Christian instruction was, as Seabrook astutely recognized, an implicit threat, even though muted, to the practice of slave management and control.[55]

The plantation missions introduced many slaves to Christianity. The gospel evaded the confines created by the planter class and served not only as an ideology to promote slave obedience but also as a resource for revolt against the injustices of slavery. Yet the missions recall for multicultural communities today the capacity of

Christianity to be used for the support of unjust social systems. Religious thought and practice can, in fact, be molded by a particular group to reinforce their view of reality and subjugate others. The slaveholders succeeded in their design to promulgate a version of Christianity that supported their privilege. However, their success was not total. Religion can also escape the grasp of those who abuse its authority. The slaves understood that Christianity promised good to them even while the form in which it was made available to them only defended their perpetual servitude. They listened to preachers who told them to obey, to accept their fate, to wait for freedom in heaven. Then, they went out to the brush arbors and felt the Spirit move and knew that Jesus meant for them not bondage but freedom. The slaves re-tooled the Christianity of the missions in the "Invisible Institution" and, as soon as they were able, in their own churches after the Civil War. They practiced their own version of this new religion, an ecstatic version which would blossom again in the early twentieth century in the Pentecostal movement, where African Americans would once again worship with European-American Christians.

The Early Pentecostal Revivals: "Short-lived Ecstatic Biracial Community"

The vast majority of African-American and European-American Protestants worshiped in distinct racial enclaves from 1865 to 1906. Forty years of separate practice reinforced and accentuated the differences between black and white worship styles. The significant interaction between 1790 and 1865 gave way to a new era of independent development. European-American *enthusiast* churches sub-divided into new denominations. Some communities, including many Methodist churches, followed *mainline* trends towards text-based liturgical forms and dogmatic theological language. Others, such as Holiness communities, strove to preserve folk-based sanctification themes. Similarly, African-American churches split along class lines, but their independence in the context of the racist backlash after Reconstruction insured their continued focus on their own survival in a culture hostile to their well-being and allowed for the preservation of the slave legacy among, especially, southern Afro-Baptists.

Despite all this, a new form of biracial worship arose in the early twentieth century, countering the well-established traditions of racial segregation in US Protestantism. In 1906, in the city of Los Angeles in an abandoned church, African Americans and European Americans again found themselves side by side on their knees praising God. This surprising phenomenon developed out of several factors: first, continuing development of the Methodist traditions; second, a reassertion of African-American folk ritual forms as members of Afro-Baptist and Holiness denominations reunited in new institutions; and, third, the personal contributions of several charismatic leaders, the most important of which were William Seymour and Charles Parham.

In Chapter 3 I traced the origins of Methodism to Wesleyan interpretations of Anglican spirituality. Wesley emphasized human participation in the conversion process and the transformative consequences of sanctification on both the personal and social levels. The discipline of Methodism, for the most part, however, led not to social flux but to the formation of successful industrial laborers and entrepreneurs in the booming economy of early American industrialism. The success of many Methodists led to a decline in religious enthusiasm. MacRobert writes:

> The now predominantly middle-class churches began to adopt the values of secular culture. Conversion, personal piety, and social service were replaced by education, prestige, and materialism.[56]

Those who enjoyed less prosperity became dissatisfied with the complacency of Methodism in its accommodationist forms and sought a new and revitalized style of practice. Holiness revivals took place in the North just before the Civil War and, later, in the South as well. The Holiness communities placed more emphasis on Wesley's perfectionist themes, challenging each other to live out a strict moral code and to worship with exuberance.[57] Holiness practices attracted African Americans. The opportunity to worship with enthusiasm and the doctrine of perfectionism resonated once again with African survivals in the *improvisational* current of African-American liturgical traditions. Many African-American Holiness adherents emerged from Methodist traditions such as the AME and AMEZ denominations. Others, however, unlike most of their European-American counterparts, left various Baptist conventions to join Holiness Churches.[58] In any case, distinctions between white and black Holiness traditions emerged quickly. MacRobert writes:

> Wesley had taught that sanctification had both individual and social dimensions but most white Holiness people stressed the former at the expense of the latter. For black Christians, on the other hand, the experience of the Spirit was more than personal Holiness, it was also power from God to triumph over injustice and oppression in the social sphere.[59]

The early twentieth century was also a period of great racial animosity in the US. The failure of Reconstruction allowed southerners to wreak their vengeance upon former slaves. The rising popularity of Social Darwinism provided "scientific" evidence of white superiority. The implementation of Jim Crow laws justified legally the prejudice that lurked in white hearts. Lynchings and other forms of white violence raged throughout the South. Yet, even in this context, a new occasion of biracial worship evolved.

Many European-American Pentecostals acknowledge Charles Fox Parham as the founder of modern Pentecostalism. He precipitated the first large scale instance of speaking in tongues in the modern era, when he encouraged his students to reflect on the second chapter of Acts. He also formally proposed that speaking in tongues be accepted as *the* form of evidence that one had been baptized by the Spirit. His notion that sanctification would be accompanied by a sign and that this sign would be the ability to speak in foreign or unknown languages served as the doctrinal foundation upon which Pentecostalism was built. He himself could not sustain a revival, however. Agnes Ozman, a student in Parham's Bethel Bible School in Topeka, Kansas, spoke in tongues in January 1901. By 1903, however, Parham had to close this school and his followers disbanded. He opened another school in Kansas City later that year and, when that effort also failed, he moved to Houston and tried again.

William Seymour was born in Louisiana in 1870. He was a self-educated son of slaves. He was an African-American who found himself engaged in racial reconciliation throughout his life. At the age of 25, he moved to Indiana and joined a Methodist church, a black congregation in a majority white denomination. Five years later, he found himself in Cincinnati and joined a Holiness Church that was consciously interracial. After a bout with smallpox in which he lost the use of one eye and suffered severe scarring, he set out to find members of his family who had been scattered by slavery and Emancipation. He ended up in Houston and at Parham's school.

The contrast between Parham's and Seymour's theological understanding of race relations could not be more stark. Parham was a committed white supremacist. His Holiness beliefs were linked to "the British-Israel" theory, a claim that the English colonists in America were the ten lost tribes of Israel and were destined to form the new people of God through which all the world would be blessed.[60] Parham believed that white people were the one race that had descended directly from Abraham and so were the sole heirs to the covenant. In Parham's school, Seymour had to listen to the lectures outside in the hall, through a half-opened door. In addition, he had to sit in the back of the chapel during worship and could not come forward to receive communion.[61] Yet Seymour, despite all the prejudice to which he was subjected, left Houston in order to accept a call to serve an integrated church in Los Angeles. He had a vision of the Pentecostal phenomenon that would bridge rather than emphasize the racial divide in America. MacRobert writes:

> For Seymour, the baptism of the Holy Spirit was much more than a glossolalia experience, it was the fulfillment of Joel's prophesy that once again the barriers between the races would be broken down by the coming of the Spirit as on Pentecost.[62]

Seymour quickly offended his new church community by insisting, as Parham had taught him, that sanctification would be accompanied by the baptism of the Spirit and manifested in the speaking of tongues. After he gave a sermon on the second chapter of Acts, the pastor locked the doors to him. But several members of that church encouraged his work and on Friday 6 April 1906, while Seymour led a small service at the home of Richard and Ruth Asbery, another outburst of *glossolalia* erupted. This one did not stop for three years!

Crowds flocked to Seymour and his fledging community. While only African Americans were present on 6 April, whites, blacks, Asians, Hispanics, rich and poor alike soon came to hear Seymour preach. He moved his congregation into an abandoned chapel at 312 Azusa Street. Neglected and used for storage, the building was full of crates and boxes. Seymour and his followers cleaned up, but had no time to renovate. They spread sawdust on the floor and made benches using planks and boxes. The pulpit was simply a stack of crates. They placed the benches in a full circle around the pulpit so that worshipers could see each other, rather than the backs of each other's heads. This make-shift theater-in-the-round functioned to demonstrate the equality of all who came to experience the power of the Spirit. No one in Seymour's care was relegated to the hall, unless the crowd filled the room to overflowing. All were welcome and all were expected to participate not just by watching or listening, but by demonstrating their encounter with the Spirit in word, gesture, or dance.

The Pentecostal eruption in Los Angeles had roots in both African-American *improvisational* and European-American *enthusiast* currents. Out of white Methodism came the idea of Christian perfectionism and the need for a manifestation of the encounter between a believer and the Spirit that answered definitively the anxiety of whether one was saved. From African-American traditions came the gestural vocabulary, the liberative ritual forms, and tendencies towards social activism. At Azusa Street, a praxis-based version of Christianity that incorporated African ritual forms in the cause of Christian restorationism engaged both black and white Americans.

The worship at Azusa Street was every bit as demonstrative as that of the frontier revivals. Seymour expected the congregation to re-enact the story of the first Pentecost as recorded in *The Book of Acts* with a tangibly present Spirit and *glossolalia* in their worship every night. They called upon the Holy Spirit to come and enliven the gathered community, creating both chaos and possibility. Shouts rang out; worshipers jerked and danced; converts fell as if dead; black, brown, white, yellow and red bodies piled up entangled in the sawdust upon the floor. In a time of widespread segregation, worship at the Azusa mission demonstrated that all God's children needed divine care and all could manifest God's presence in worship.

The "interracial infancy" of the Pentecostal movement quickly attracted notice and criticism.[63] Visitors from across the country and across the globe descended upon Los Angeles to experience the power of a living and active God. Converts carried the promise that anyone could receive the gift of tongues and all, thereby, were equal to more than fifty countries in less than two years. However, critics also arose. They cited not only the excesses of enthusiasm so frequently rejected among more rationalistic Christians, but the fact of interracial mixing in itself. Parham was appalled by Seymour's interracial fellowship.[64] While visiting Azusa Street in 1907, Parham condemned Seymour's biracial vision. MacRobert writes:

> Black and white were worshiping God together and whites were engaging in the same motor behavior as blacks: shouting, jerking, dancing, falling down, and speaking in tongues "under the power" of the Holy Spirit. Parham went to the pulpit and began to rebuke the worshipers for what he described as "animalism".[65]

Parham, an advocate of the freedom of the Spirit to act demonstrably in the present, clearly had limits in mind about the manifestations that action could take in the midst of the worshiping community. Apparently, African-American modes of ecstatic behavior were beyond his pale.

Parham attempted to take over Azusa Street, but the people rejected him. In response, he set up an alternative revival elsewhere in Los Angeles, but it failed after only two months. Seymour remained in control of Azusa Street and the mission remained interracial. However, other crises slowed the momentum of the revival. The energy of Azusa Street declined because of scandal surrounding Seymour's personal life, the loss of the mailing list that supported the circulation of Seymour's newspaper, *The Apostolic Faith*, and the loss of members to rival evangelists and their doctrinal innovations. For example, William Durham claimed that sinners were fully cleansed at the time of conversion and Christ required no second step such as Spirit baptism after his initial "finished work". Durham successfully recruited members from Azusa Street when he moved to Los Angeles from his mission in Chicago in 1911.[66] Another rival, Elmer Fisher, founded the Upper Room Mission, which eventually attracted most of the white participants from Azusa Street.[67] By 1914, the Azusa Mission had only 20 regular worshipers, most of whom dated to the time of Seymour's pre-Azusa Street home-based meetings, "plus [as the records indicate] a few white women".[68] Seymour re-wrote the constitution at this time in order to insure that African Americans would remain in control of the institution. He died in 1922 at the age of 52, brokenhearted over the decline of the mission.[69] The original mission, 312 Azusa Street, was demolished in 1938.

Seymour's Pentecostal revival represented a counter-cultural movement of interracial fellowship in a time of intense animosity between European Americans and African Americans. White and blacks participated together in the ecstatic worship forms of the African-American *improvisational* current. Seymour presided over an encounter between a mixed congregation and the Holy Spirit which resulted in the formation of an interracial community of believers. The congregation experienced their equality and went home to testify that the power of God breaks down barriers between races.

Soon, however, this concord evaporated as whites withdrew into their own denominational structures. MacRobert writes:

> White Pentecostals were unwilling to challenge the racist laws and mores of the United States or to stand up to the criticism of the mainline denominations who sought to discredit them by pointing to their interracial character and black roots. Instead, they yielded to the pressures of segregated American society and the apartheid of American Christianity, and pointed heavenward when challenged on the question of origins. The divisions in the Pentecostal movement were caused by (or justified in terms of) many interrelated factors—disagreements over doctrine, struggles for power and dominance, desire to achieve "respectability", social diversity and geographical location—but the end result demonstrated that white Pentecostals did not wish to maintain an interracial movement, submit to black leadership or recognize the black origins of their movement.[70]

While schisms within the Pentecostal movement are regularly described as resulting from doctrinal controversies,[71] these mask the underlying discomfort of whites with institutions, and the forms of worship in use within them, created by and for black people. Whites simply could not accept that the message of the Spirit present in these revivals might indeed be, at least in part, that the divisions between white and black Americans must, and could, be healed. Instead, they resumed their interest in correct formulation of doctrine, the definition and enforcement of individual morality, and the building of respectable social institutions. MacRobert writes: "White Pentecostals valued and retained glossolalia but neglected or rejected the equality and unity which the Spirit brought to Azusa Street".[72] African Americans accommodated whites into their ecstatic worship and sparked the revival that brought Pentecostalism to churches throughout the world. However, European Americans could not accept African-American leadership in either the ritual setting or institutional governance. Instead whites, in the phrase of Leonard Lovett, attempted to "Europeanize" Pentecostalism and, when they could not, they left.

The loss of interracial fellowship was crucial and shifted the very identity of Pentecostalism. From a movement concerned primarily with the present experience of worshipers, the movement divided over cultural differences that became manifest as members of different groups performed their encounter with the Spirit. Especially among European Americans, Pentecostalism became yet another instance of Christians seeking assurance of their individual salvation through exclusive formulations. African Americans, less concerned with preserving doctrinal purity than with praising God and opening themselves to the fresh word of the Spirit, continued to seek shared fellowship but were repeatedly rejected. European Americans again created a situation in which African-American religious practice, instead of serving the whole community, was defined (by outsiders) as an "ethnic" community. MacRobert writes:

> With the redrawing of the color line by the white Pentecostals, the black worshiping community became an ethnic community, as it had been in Africa and during slavery. There the black person in a racist society, could have his humanity and dignity affirmed. There he could find an outlet for the self expression, creativity and diverse abilities which were stifled by white society. Self determination and leadership could develop in an environment which was not disadvantageous to those who had limited education and a black culture as well as a black skin. Oral liturgy and narrative theology—the heritage of West Africa and slavery—were not overwhelmed by the literary or systematic methods of Western Christianity.[73]

In subsequent years, African-American Pentecostals have preserved their ecstatic worship traditions to a greater extent than European-American Pentecostals. While both groups have experienced a rise in socioeconomic status and have moved from the inner city to the suburbs and from storefronts and rural chapels to established sanctuaries, the upward mobility of whites has been more rapid and widespread. African-American churches continue to emphasize participation and the empowerment of lay people. European-American congregations have adopted a more passive stance in their worship. MacRobert writes:

> Early Pentecostal (and a great deal of contemporary black Pentecostal) worship was holistic and all-embracing—heart and mind and body and emotions were given over to the celebration of life and hope. Worship was social and communal, not individualistic and private. It built up the Christian community and incorporated the individual into the family of God. All were able to participate in the worshiping community through music and singing, rhythmic motion and antiphonal responses, testifying and simultaneous praying, governing and leading, even cooking and cleaning. No one was excluded on the grounds of illiteracy or lack of ability, for what was done was not primarily for man to glory in or for people to be entertained by. It was done for God and it sprang not from the intellect but from the heart. To sing or testify or pray was a liberating experience. Neither the words nor the music were to be judged but rather the sincerity of the speaker or singer. For many white Pentecostals these activities soon became threatening rather than liberating. The illiterate, inarticulate or unmelodious fell silent for fear that their performance was deficient. The community was once again reduced to an audience.[74]

In addition, attention and energy shifted from the mission of renewing the church through active encounter with the Spirit into institutional maintenance, the defense of doctrinal purity, education, and clericalism.[75] European-American Pentecostalism, which served first as a correction to the excesses of Enlightenment rationalism, now includes an ironic amount of abstract theological speculation. Each successive controversy serves to limit the freedom of the Spirit. MacRobert writes:

> In this attempt to fit the presence and power of the Holy Spirit into existing theological categories, most of the white Pentecostals and also—though to a lesser extent—many of the black ones, demanded that the Church "control" the Spirit and make his manifestations subject to ecclesiastical interdict. Being possessed by the Spirit gave way to possessing the Spirit.[76]

The early Pentecostal revivals, and especially the Azusa Street Mission experience, demonstrate that African-American ecstatic ritual forms can serve as the basis for the worship life of a multicultural community. Perhaps this short period of intense religiosity was an anomaly in US Protestant liturgical history. Indeed, African Americans and European Americans returned to racially segregated worship quickly, despite the success of Seymour's work. Perhaps the mission context of Azusa Street allowed whites to feel comfortable with *improvisational* forms since most would not become full members but were passing through, getting a charge to renew their batteries of faith, and then returning to their more established and less enthusiastic congregations. Indeed, eight years after the revival began, less than ten whites still worshiped with the Azusa Street congregation. However, Pentecostal restorationism in the context of the racially divided US society, not surprisingly, tackled this very division and performed racial equality in its liturgy, an equality directly counter to the cultural context, just as the first disciples broke through the linguistic divisions of first century Judaism to preach the gospel of reconciliation.

Lessons from these Four Previous Examples of Biracial Worship

The historic occasions, which we have been discussing, when African Americans and European Americans worshiped together, hold many lessons for those contemplating US Protestant worship today. I consider four of these here before concluding this chapter.

A Variety of Dynamics   These instances of biracial worship reveal the variety of dynamics that have occurred between European Americans and African Americans in Protestant worship in this country. First, the Camp Meeting provides an example in which the two groups worshiped simultaneously but separately. There was some recognition that the worship of African Americans and European Americans was different and yet that both were legitimate expressions of praise. Camp meetings included time for separate worship and for a rite of unity, the breaking down of the barrier that divided the two services.

Second, in biracial Methodist and Baptist churches in the antebellum South, whites included blacks at first but then found it necessary to accommodate to the wishes of the elite and to emphasize distinctions between the groups. Even before the hospitality of whites foundered and despite severe sanctions, African Americans held their own services in addition to the biracial liturgies and, at the close of the Civil War, quickly took advantage of the opportunity to form their own congregations. European-American *enthusiast* communities in the antebellum South, despite their rhetoric of hospitality, reflected the social hierarchy in seating patterns, in preaching, and in rites of initiation. While purporting to accept all converts as children of God, European-American "enthusiasts" came to accept assumptions of white supremacy and to rehearse these in their liturgies.

Third, in the plantation missions, slave-owners, and the missionaries that accepted their terms for access to the slaves, created forms of worship to explicitly serve the interests of the elite. The gospel was twisted. Biblical texts were carefully selected to disguise the message of liberation. The most extreme edges of violent treatment of slaves were buffed away, strengthening the institution of slavery itself. Spiritual and material concerns were torn asunder and the latter excluded from prayers. Worship declared the righteousness of injustice and the perversity of the hope for liberation. The cult was inverted. And, yet, the gospel message of freedom could not be confined. It broke from the grasp of the powerful and spoke a healing word to the suffering—as slaves met Jesus out in the brush.

Finally, in the early Pentecostal period, African Americans reestablished the ecstatic forms of Christian worship that had been long forgotten. Montanus and his spirit-filled followers were rejected as heretics in the third century.[77] While the risks of abuse of possession-based cults are significant, Christianity lost a good deal of vitality and flexibility when ecstasy was relegated beyond the bounds of "orthodoxy", or "right praise".[78] European-American *enthusiast* worship provided a much-needed corrective to the heady rationalism of the *mainline* churches, but African Americans have clearly established the norms that define the performative modes and interpretations of Christian spiritual possession in the US. The Azusa Street revival and its ecstatic forms attracted whites, both European Americans and Europeans, with its renewal of apostolic Christianity and its radical equality in a time of severe racial animosity. But just as quickly as they had come, whites split off again, unwilling to submit to African-American spiritual authority.

Not only do the four examples of biracial worship reveal that worship can display a variety of dynamics between racial groups, but also that a variety of ritualized race relations can be performed in a society simultaneously. Differences in theological perspective, cultural norms, and class location make for a variety of liturgical forms in any given moment. The camp meetings, the biracial Methodist and Baptists services, and the plantation missions happened during overlapping periods in the eighteenth and early nineteenth centuries but encouraged contrasting perspectives on black–white relations.

Ritual is Polyvalent   Further, even in the same ritual, participants can experience quite different notions of what it means to be a community. While the white members of antebellum Methodist and Baptist biracial churches considered their worship inclusive of, and appropriate for, the slaves and free blacks who joined their churches, the exodus reveals that African Americans did not experience these forms of worship as conducive to their own well-being. This confirms one of the ways in which ritual is polyvalent, in which it can mean many things at the same time. On the one hand, this makes ritual difficult to plan and interpret—as, for example, some will be offended while others applaud a given service. On the other hand, ritual's ambiguities allow participants enough space to take what they need from it. Even with contrasting understandings of a rite, participants from different perspectives may still find a place to be engaged in praise in a single service. This allows us some confidence that worship in a multicultural context can satisfy the spiritual hungers of a variety of people—those who seek assurance and those who seek liberative, transforming power. The interplay of the central metaphors of the constituent groups will determine and produce shared metaphors that guide the developing traditions of the integrated community.

Cycles of Segregation and Integration   Throughout the history of US Protestant worship, African Americans and European Americans have come together to worship and each time they have eventually split apart again. Whites have most often determined the style of worship of mixed groups, but blacks have influenced even the most tightly controlled forms, or, at least, provided a critique of white control by setting up an alternative liturgy of their own. In the early Pentecostal movement, African Americans were the primary institutional leaders. Whites left the interracial Pentecostal churches, but blacks have left mixed churches too. Whites left primarily because they could not gain institutional control. Blacks leave most often when white actions toward blacks belie their rhetoric of equality. African Americans and European Americans live in proximity and members of both groups aspire to reconciliation. However, with rare exceptions, US Protestants have not yet found liturgical forms that legitimate both African-American and European-American traditions; hold the groups together in a semblance of community; and forge one people out of two, one liturgy out of several currents, one Body out of diverse members.

A Complex Relationship Between Worship and Culture   Ritual is part and parcel of culture, while also, as a mode of performance, providing a means through which to judge and transform culture. Christian rites juxtapose the ancient stories of Jesus, and other representatives of God's people, with the present reality of the gathered community in activities that use ordinary things such as bread and water to re-imagine the world and its future. Particular local communities perform these rites in their own language and with their own local representations of ancient stories and ordinary objects. Holy symbols take local form. Divinity takes on the body of particular, culturally bound objects and actions. This is the scandal of the incarnation that animates Christian belief. Christian rites, therefore, never stand outside, above, or in opposition to culture, but rest instead within a culture, even while breaking open the particular to speak a word of healing and transformation.

In the past, European Americans have subordinated the ethics of the gospel to their own interests and yet God's promise of liberation has still landed on the ear of those who were meant to hear only a command to obey. While slave-owners forced missionaries to teach obedience rather than freedom, Methodists and Baptists did their best to welcome slaves and free blacks as equals in their churches, while the slaves themselves met secretly to practice their own version of the faith. When Methodists and Baptists began to succumb to the temptation to perform white supremacy rather than equality, African Americans left these churches to worship in ways that allowed them to feel affirmed as children of God.

Liturgies alone, even ones that claim to recognize all people as mirrors of God's image, cannot solve the problem of racism. Ritual does not function on a purely pragmatic level. Ritual is also intimately tied to cultural context and so will not easily overturn ideologies in the context of which it takes its particular, local form. Yet ritual can serve to negotiate symbols that support and sustain a culture, provide a vision of an alternative future, and rehearse that vision as African Americans, European Americans and members of other groups form communities of love.

Conclusion

In my renderings of the histories of Protestant worship in this country in Chapter 2 and Chapter 3, and in my comparative work in this chapter, I have sped across time and space. I highlight various turning points and central figures in both European-American and African-American liturgical traditions to offer worship leaders and members of contemporary multicultural communities a set of narratives in common for their complex work of worshiping towards reconciliation in their own place, in their own time. The narratives make clear the intransigence of obstacles to inclusive, multicultural worship. African-American and European-American liturgical traditions flow together as currents in a single river and yet remain in tension. The previous occasions of biracial worship are, primarily, examples of failed attempts to cultivate mixed communities that would come to live together as members of the One Body.

Perhaps multicultural worship is simply too difficult to sustain. African Americans and European Americans live in proximity but in different cultural worlds. They share a national history and geographical boundaries. But each group, in itself plural and with some resonance across racial lines, has distinct cultural idioms, worldviews, and theological perspectives. Reflecting on a different but parallel context, Hollenweger writes:

> As to the de facto segregation into white and black Christianity in Britain, the reason now seems clear. They are two cultures, an oral, narrative, inclusive black culture and a literary, conceptual, exclusive white culture. The two integrate very badly and only if some of the black and white Christians become "bi-lingual".[79]

While Hollenweger's characterization of both black and white cultures is simplistic, it is true that divisions between African-American and European-American cultures are substantial. Perhaps praying separately is right, or even necessary.

Perhaps advocacy for multicultural worship is also misguided. Mark Francis emphasizes that every person is entitled to worship in her/his own cultural idiom even if that requires that on a regular basis each racial/ethnic group worship separately.

His perspective is shaped by the difficulties experienced in multicultural US Roman Catholic communities. He writes:

> It can be asserted that, as far as possible, different cultural groups of the parish have a right to worship regularly in their own language and in their own cultural idiom ... The African-American Catholic bishops, in speaking about the liturgy, eloquently stated that more is at stake than simply "accommodating" different cultural groups. There is an important pastoral/theological issue involved: "All people should be able to recognize themselves when Christ is presented, and should be able to experience their own fulfillment when these mysteries are celebrated." This recognition becomes much more difficult if multicultural worship is proposed as the norm.[80]

On the whole, US Protestant communities are more segregated than Roman Catholic parishes. At the same time, Protestant churches that are multicultural do not usually have the luxury of allowing each constituent group to take charge of their own service each week. There is usually only one, or perhaps two, services each Sunday. The African-American bishops' challenge to create services where all who attend can recognize themselves in the mysteries must be kept in mind, but cannot be resolved simply by dividing congregations into sub-groups for their own distinct liturgies. Perhaps worship across lines of difference increases rather than mollifies tensions.

Without ignoring the difficulties of creating felicitous multicultural liturgies, the reasons for pursuing them outweigh the objections. First, multicultural Protestant communities exist, and they must have worship in which to engage. Second, multicultural worship can balance the gifts, and faults, of various groups and create vital and beautiful worship. Finally, Christian communities are called to break down, rather than accept as inevitable, dividing walls.

First, while most African-American and European-American Protestants have worshiped separate from each other since the end of the Civil War, there have always been, and will continue to be, significant exceptions to the rule. At present, many *mainline* communities in urban areas are experiencing a significant decline in membership and in response to the changing demographics of their neighborhoods are reaching out to new constituencies. These "white" churches are fighting for survival by opening themselves, not without hesitancy and marked ambiguity, to the richness of alternative liturgical traditions as so-called minority groups join them in prayer. As we recall from the opening chapter, The Riverside Church in New York City has been interracial, in intention since its founding and in reality for more than a generation, but still shifts cultural modes with awkwardness. Congregations that face issues of diversity with less experience can learn from places like Riverside, but all multicultural communities need to develop models that will move them beyond guest and host dynamics to new levels of unity in diversity. Multicultural worship is happening and so experiments and continuing research should proceed.

Second, most worship traditions among US Protestants have for a long time served the needs of one specific racial/ethnic group. The worship of homogenous groups can neglect or even resist the adaptations necessary to insure continuing vitality. Among African Americans, worship has served as a means to challenge white supremacy, while providing a context for African-American faith and hope to thrive.

Among European Americans, worship has, too often, simply provided assurance of the righteousness of individuals and the justice of current social structures. The juxtaposition of African-American and European-American liturgical traditions breaks both open and reveals richer, more faithful, and more self-critical worship. Over a hundred years ago, H.N. McTyeire recognized that better worship occurs in mixed groups:

> It is desirable that white and colored worship together: one reason among many is this, that no distinction of religion arise between them. Religion appears in its loveliest form where rich and poor, bond and free, meet together, and pray to a common Father through a common Savior, drinking into one Spirit, offer up songs and prayers, and hear what all have equal interest in. The attempt to make the services intelligible and interesting to an audience thus composed, must ever impart to them excellent qualities of strength and perspicuity, simplicity and earnestness.[81]

The historical record shows that distinctions of religion do, in fact, arise between groups of Christians who live in different social locations. African-American and European-American Protestants are Christian, but differently so. As groups, they emphasize different theological and ethical perspectives based on their distinct historical experiences and, especially, their historical relationship to each other. Nonetheless, worship in communities that have members from both of these groups, and perhaps others, can be more vital than that of homogenous groups. Balancing individual and communal orientations, carefully crafted scripts with spontaneous responses of praise, the repertoires of two great musical canons, and the wisdom of people who live in various locations within society, multicultural worship becomes a thing of great power and beauty.

Finally, Christians are called to live as a unified Body of Christ in the world. While praying in a foreign tongue or through alien symbols represents a substantial barrier to full, conscious, and active participation in worship, the possibility of efficacious multicultural worship is not thereby excluded, but is, instead, recognized as difficult to fully and justly achieve—difficult, but not impossible. To ask African Americans to pray in a European style is unjust and destroys both the prayers and those who pray. African Americans must find in any worship in which they participate affirmation that they, as individuals and as a group, are bearers of God's image. The same is true of European Americans and any other worshipers. But to bear God's image is not only to sanctify one's own particular cultural roots but also involves opening oneself to the possibility of being changed. Members of multicultural communities must stand firm in their individual identities, but as members of a community, one people gathered in God's name. The dividing wall between constituent groups will come down as people, in part through the liturgy, move into deeper levels of relationship that respect diversity while celebrating a common bond of love.

CHAPTER 5

"Discerning the Body":
US Racism, Protestant Worship and Sacramental Theology

"Whoever, therefore, eats the bread or drinks the cup of the Lord in an unworthy manner will be answerable for the body and blood of the Lord. Examine yourselves, and only then eat of the bread and drink of the cup. For all who eat and drink without discerning the body, eat and drink judgement against themselves. For this reason many of you are weak and ill, and some have died. But if we judged ourselves, we would not be judged. But when we are judged by the Lord, we are disciplined, so that we may not be condemned along with the world" (I Corinthians 11:27–32, NRSV).

In this concluding chapter, I will concentrate on three lessons drawn from my historical narratives of Protestant worship among African Americans and European Americans. First, white supremacist ideology has distorted Protestant worship traditions in the US and is an example of why a theo-ethical critique of European-American ways of praying is necessary. Second, African-American Protestant liturgical traditions represent a challenge to the norms of the ecumenical liturgical reform movement. Third, the narratives remind us all that the Body of Christ *is* multicultural. Each of these lessons prompts Christians to discern the Body as they worship, to recognize the Body's diverse members and to pray in ways that celebrate the pluralism of the Body and the equality of all who belong to it.

Racism and the Integrity of Protestant Worship

In the relations between African Americans and European Americans, Christian worship has served more often as a dividing wall than as a bridge. Instead of discerning themselves as members of the same body, these groups found and, for the most part, still find, it necessary to pray separately. White racism is the central cause of the segregation of US Protestant churches. European-American Protestants demonstrate in their liturgies that they believe that whites are superior to blacks. In response, the vast majority of African Americans removed themselves from white-dominated churches. The exodus of blacks from biracial churches indicts the European-American traditions of unethical liturgical practice. The effects of racism on Protestant worship in this country occupies my attention in this section.

European-American Protestant liturgical traditions came to full flower in the freedom of the so-called New World. On the margins of European society, these "pure" and "dissenting" Christians became the ruling elite of a new land. Their worship came to support them in their new status as central powers and to celebrate their privilege. In the matter of race relations, this was particularly true. In the context of slavery, European-American Protestant worship marked Africans and African Americans as inferior. Through their language, architecture, and art, whites pushed blacks to the margins of Christian community. White preachers addressed the slaves with sermons "accommodated to their incapacity". White congregations designated specific pews in which the slaves might sit. White artists portrayed God and Jesus in their own image, denying that Africans might also reflect the divine reality. The liturgies performed an understanding of the Body of Christ not as a society of equals but as a hierarchy of caste.

At the same time, European Americans distanced themselves from African-American styles of praise. European-American Protestant traditions, in general, speak of God in the language of dogmatic theology, encourage an aesthetic of decency and order, and countenance gestural and emotional restraint. African-American commitments to storytelling, improvisation, and embodied responses to word and song are unwelcome. In the camp meetings, where even whites were less restrained, whites built walls between themselves and black worshipers to buffer the sounds of boisterous praise and excruciating *pathos*. European-American worship, in its *mainline* current, and today in a growing number of *enthusiast* churches, is oriented to a script, whether published or merely customary, that controls closely the content, form, and length of a service. In contrast, the characteristic freedom of most African-American traditions is palpable.

Because of their desire to worship freely, without the oppressiveness and hypocrisy of white services that welcomed with one hand and confined with the other and without the constraints of European-American liturgical norms, most African-American Protestants left white churches. African Americans demonstrated a remarkable willingness to pray with whites even in situations of disparity, but, eventually despairing of the ability of whites to repent of their racism, the vast majority left biracial churches. Many Blacks preferred to establish new worship traditions rather than reform white ones. They met, at great risk, in the alternative ritual space of the "Invisible Institution". Later, they formed independent churches and denominations to shelter their own distinct style of worship.

The process through which African Americans established traditions independent of white control is important. First, blacks worshiped with whites. Second, they left to escape white hypocrisy. Third, in the context of freedom, they developed their own culturally distinct ritual styles. Fourth, they established, in independent ecclesial institutions, their own alternative current of Protestant worship in the US. This independent current, which is itself divided into two sub-traditions, combined African survivals with the worship practices of European-American enthusiasm. It is three generations of reforms removed from medieval Roman liturgical traditions and, with rare exceptions, has not joined in the contemporary ecumenical liturgical reform movement.[1] While the relation of African-American Protestant worship to the advances in *mainline* liturgical reforms is the subject of the next section, it is important to say here that the separation of black and white institutions and their worship has separated African-American Protestant traditions from many of the riches of historic Christian liturgy. There was cost as well as gain to the separation for African Americans. That being said, there was little choice. To pray with one's oppressors in a manner that supports the structures that oppress you is death-dealing. To have no option to pray for one's own freedom is unacceptable confinement.

Racism made, and makes, a mockery of the Body of Christ. It is not the only example of the ethical failing of Christians, but it is a critical one in the history of this country. Other failings include anti-Semitism, sexism, classism, and heterosexism. Others have noticed this tendency of Christians to deny in their lives, and in their worship, the ethical ideals they profess. Few have been so radical in their critique as Tom Driver.[2] He contends that the ethical failings of Christians stem not only from human imperfection, as is often claimed, but from central theological commitments of the churches, including what is taught about Christ. Further, changes in our ethics—whether the swing from support to repudiation of slavery, or the more recent shift among many Protestants to accept women as presiders at the table—should be reflected in changes in basic theological tenets as well.[3] Following Rosemary Radford Ruether, Driver contends that as the church grew from marginal, ecstatic community into imperial institution a christological paradigm-shift occurred.[4] Three aspects of that shift are important to our discussion here. First, Christianity shifted focus from the present–future to the past. Christ was declared a static, once-and-for-all embodiment of perfection rather than a spiritual companion to be encountered in the present and traveled with into the future. Second, Christ became the center of history rather than one who is leading us toward a new age, an age of justice and peace. Third, as the church looked back to Christ as the once-and-for-all embodiment of God and itself as the extension of that perfect life, the mission of the church became the expansion of its social power rather than the performance of freedom in service of the world's liberation. Christ, the dynamic force of the relation between God and humanity, became trapped in a static identity.

Driver proposes to shift the paradigm in order to save Christ for our time.[5] He removes Christ from the center, freeing Christ to change as history progresses and freeing us to act responsibly for the realization of God's reign on earth. Driver would encourage us to wed ourselves not to the Jesus of ancient texts but to the one who comes among us now, especially in the context of Christian sacramental practice. If we expect to recognize Christ in the breaking of the bread as the early Christians did, we may find ourselves caught up by the Spirit of the living God with whom we might find and follow pathways to justice and peace.[6] Unfortunately, the *mainline* traditions, which are Driver's primary audience, have almost entirely abandoned postures of expectation and instead gather to remember a past-perfect Christ who holds no promise of liberation and dissipates our ability to act ethically. Driver's critique certainly fits my own reading of the history of European-American liturgical traditions. Even the *enthusiast* current has become wedded to forms of liturgy that support, mostly by ignoring, oppressive social structures. European-American rites have lost their critical, "anti-structure" function.[7] In other words, most European-American Protestant liturgies no longer function to provide a "liminal" context, a space outside of the constraints of the social order in which alternative human relations might be experienced and perhaps adopted as a part of the historical development of human societies.[8] They did this, certainly, at the time of the Protestant Reformation, and, somewhat more ambiguously, on the American frontier, but not often since. The value of eschatological expectation and the ethical dimensions of liturgy are returning to the fore in contemporary liturgical theology; however, most proponents remain tied to christocentric models which, if Driver is correct, undermine the very goals they advocate.[9]

African-American traditions, in general, appear to me more closely aligned with Driver's ideal. In general, African-American worship looks toward the present-future more than to the past, remembering in ways that sustain action for liberation.[10] The prayers, songs, and sermons are not confined to texts or strict formats but open to the leading of the spirit. African Americans "have" church rather than go to church. Worship is an event to be experienced rather than a script to be followed. There is an active role for all participants. Everyone can contribute to the event through testimony, shout, and dialogical response to preaching and praying. In addition, African-American worship stands outside the social order in that it is a home for a people on the margins. This is a historical, not an essential, aspect of African-American worship. Certainly, there are congregations of elite African Americans that do not fit this description. Certainly, there are African-American styles that are closely allied with the social relations of the wider society, and which replicate hierarchical systems that value men over women, the rich over the poor, the middle-aged over both the young and old, the educated over those wed to folk ways, the ordained over the lay. But in the main, African-American church communities condone less stratification, do not manifest hierarchy to the same degree ritually, and respect a wider variety of persons than white churches. Most importantly, African Americans expect to meet God on Sunday and to join with God in the struggle for liberation.

Ritual systems stand in a variety of relations to the social systems in which they function. Driver contends that ritual has three social gifts, in ascending order of value: order, community, and transformation.[11] Applying these categories to the currents in US Protestant worship outlined in my narratives is instructive. The *mainline* current places emphasis on order, celebrating the way things are, assuring people of their place in this order, and anticipating their welcome into God's reign with approximately the same level of respect to which they are accustomed in this world. *Enthusiast* and *classical* traditions are not so tied to ritual's ordering function, although adherents claim knowledge of God's eternal structures upon which rest their hopes. These traditions are more concerned with the formation and maintenance of community, as, respectively, "a faithful remnant" and "the beloved community". *Enthusiast* communities identify themselves as a remnant over against the corruption and relativism of liberal theological traditions and the evils of secular society. *Classical* churches simply know that God is present among them, working out their collective salvation and liberation. It is this confident hope, or expectation, that bridges ritual's gifts of community and transformation. And, it is in the *improvisational* current that such ritualized expectation, and its transformative potential, is most fully present.

The emphasis of each of these currents in US Protestant liturgical traditions on order, community, or transformation, corresponds with the relative social power of the group. Groups tend to adopt more hierarchical and less ecstatic forms of ritual as they rise in social status. Both the European-American and African-American Methodist churches are more exclusive, class-bound, and liturgically stable than they were when they were founded. The dynamics of this "solidification" are difficult to define. In its initial stages, the Methodist sacramental system provided release and discipline that shaped bodies to fit the socio-economic structures of the time.[12] Further, the values emphasized by Methodist preachers encouraged educational achievement and economic advancement among participants, and the participants, as they rose in social status, came to appreciate more predictable and literary rites. In addition, even as one group rises in status and its worship becomes less hospitable to those who have not yet "made it", the newly marginalized create a system of new, more enthusiastic rites. In ritual, those on the periphery define, or rediscover, a liminal space to rehearse less oppressive relations and recover from the onslaught of violent oppression. Meanwhile, the powerful seek comfort and assurance of righteousness in forms of worship that do not threaten change. Cultures shift; cults shift. Both adjust to human need and human vision. Rites offer solace, rehearse domination, and contribute to the evolution, for good and ill, of human societies. Rites distorted by racism proceed. Other rites make space for healing. Perhaps, one day, liturgies, too, may perform reconciliation between African Americans and European Americans.

The "Shape" of the Ecumenical Liturgical Reform Movement and African-American Liturgical Innovations

Striking differences remain between African-American and European-American Protestant liturgical traditions. Of course, a spectrum of styles exists within each of these culturally distinct families of rites as well. But it is the reconciliation of these peoples for, and through, worship that I am interested in promoting. The arrogance of European-American liturgists remains a critical stumbling block. Having experienced a monumental convergence of liturgies across the ecumenical spectrum based upon the common heritage of the ancient church orders, many European Americans approach liturgical scholarship with the assumption that a single "shape" of Christian public prayer exists, is known in its basic contours, and needs now to be implemented. This attitude is reflected in the most recent generation of worship books produced by and for the *mainline* churches. These new collections of prayers, both for public and private use, share not only common assumptions about what prayers are but share many of the same texts as well. This attitude remains a barrier to inter-racial dialogue. Continuing controversies over the topic of liturgical inculturation reflect the depth of the impasse. I reflect on the challenge that African-American traditions represent for the ecumenical liturgical movement in this section.

The contemporary ecumenical liturgical reform movement began in the mid-nineteenth century, but has many precedents.[13] Christians have experienced, since the founding of the church, change in the manner of their praying. Some changes have been heralded as significant clarifications of the gospel. Others have resulted in regret, causing reformers to hearken back to a "golden age" in order to restore former integrity. The Protestant Reformation of the sixteenth century sought to restore the orders of the ancient church.[14] Nineteenth-century opponents of the frontier revival style looked back to Wittenberg and Geneva.[15] While US Protestants divided into "New" and "Old" schools, European Roman Catholics were rediscovering the riches of medieval liturgy. These two branches of a liturgical restoration movement eventually joined forces in the decades just prior to and following the Second Vatican Council. Widely ecumenical, as representatives of the central *mainline* denominations (Anglican, Lutheran, Presbyterian, Methodist, and, even, the United Church of Christ) joined Roman Catholic leaders and scholars in detailed study of ancient documents in hopes of revitalizing contemporary liturgical practice, the conversation was (and in many quarters, remains) almost exclusively "white".

Dom Gregory Dix's *The Shape of Liturgy* was central to the restoration efforts.[16] Published in 1945, Dix's work proposes that, although Christian liturgies (and he is particularly interested in eucharistic prayers) follow a diversity of orders and utilize various theological and metaphorical languages, there remains an underlying unity, which he names the "shape". Dix's "shape" refers specifically to the four-fold action of taking, blessing, breaking, and sharing the bread and cup. While many of Dix's specific conclusions have been questioned, his approach remains influential. Many liturgical experts remain committed to the ideal of discovering and defining the one "shape" of Christian worship that reflects and fosters a shared identity among all Christians.

A more recent and well-received treatment of the "shape" is contained in Gordon Lathrop's *Holy Things*. Lathrop uses the term *ordo* to denote the *sine qua non* of Christian worship. For Lathrop, the *ordo* refers to the largest patterns of actions in which Christians engage rather than the elements of any particular set of prayers. He writes:

> These are abiding and basic characteristics of Christian worship: Christians meet on Sunday while maintaining a lively sense of the week. The Sunday meeting is marked by both word and meal. Christian prayer is thanksgiving and beseeching. People are brought into the community by instruction leading to bath and the meal. In the spring, "Christ our passover" is proclaimed.

> Thus, a significant pattern is discoverable in the texts and practices of Christian worship. There is a design, an *ordo*, and it is one that is especially marked by juxtaposition as a tool of meaning ...

> ... these juxtapositions of the *ordo* have thrived because of the particular Christian interest in speaking of God by speaking of Christ. One text next to another text; the texts next to the meal; the meeting next to the week; lament next to thanksgiving; the bath next to the name; the fire, bath, and meal next to both springtime and the old stories; all these patterns are turned to this christological end. In the synaxis, the expected religious meanings of the texts are turned upside down when they are applied to this Christ and to those who are with him. In the eucharist, the old hope for God that the texts engender is newly enlivened, and now from the depths of human need, by this bread that speaks of the death of Christ. In the prayers, that very God who is praised as creator of all is also known as present in the cross to all the misery that everywhere cries out for mercy. In the bath, the hope for God's day and God's reality is given in the name of Jesus Christ. At *pascha*, human longings for liberation and cosmic fecundity are used to tell the meaning of baptism into Christ. The various paradoxical pairs that have been so necessary to Christians in order to speak faithfully of God—human and divine, letter and spirit, now and not yet, hidden and revealed, immanent and transcendent—correspond, in conceptual language, to the ways the liturgy presents the faith.[17]

I quote Lathrop at length because I enjoy his language and agree with him that juxtaposition is key to faithful Christian worship. Juxtaposition continually breaks open the familiar, prevents the rhythms of the liturgy from becoming routine, and helps Christians avoid the trap of inertia.[18] Lathrop is a constructive theologian, as is Driver. Lathrop is less radical but presents to us a scheme of worship that is dialectical, affirming of pluralism, centered in action and encounter, committed to the fate of those outside the circle. It is precisely because I appreciate his approach that I bring Lathrop into juxtaposition with the narrative of African-American Protestant traditions; for here, I detect a different "shape".

The *ordo* of "Black Worship" has been parsed by James Cone as "preaching, singing, shouting, conversion, prayer, and testimony".[19] We can fit African-American worship into much of Lathrop's scheme. Yes, there is a Sunday meeting. Yes, there are texts. Yes, the meal and bath are practiced, and with great passion. Certainly, there is juxtaposition. But Cone's list, a list internal to this community and one that would receive wide assent, is centered not on "holy things" but what might be called "holy practices", and, primarily, actions, not of the ordained leadership, but of the congregation. The pastor preaches but the people's responses help the sermon move along, and all sing, all shout, all experience conversion, all pray, and all give testimony. The central juxtaposition here is not word and table but word and people, perhaps Word and voices.[20] The table is not mentioned.

The disparity between the *ordo* of the almost entirely white ecumenical liturgical reform movement and the *ordo* of African-American Protestant worship leads me to two further topics. First, weekly gatherings at table will not soon be an element of African-American worship. Second, contemporary liturgical theologians must embrace diversity on a deeper level.

The Place of the Table in the African-American Ordo

A central aim of the ecumenical liturgical reform movement is increasing the frequency of eucharistic celebration in all churches. While weekly communion among Roman Catholics is now commonplace it is only relatively recently so and, outside of the Episcopal Church USA and some Lutheran bodies, remains rare across US denominations. The reform movement considers this a failing to be corrected. African-American Protestant churches, on the whole, however, continue, without apology, non-eucharistic worship as the norm at their Sunday assemblies. I am interested in the discrepancy and have several nascent theories about why this may be so. First, African Americans were introduced to Christianity through European-American *enthusiast* traditions in which the sacraments were not as prominent as preaching, song, or the experience of conversion. Although many camp meetings culminated with a gathering at table on the final day, revivals were infrequent (most often annual or semi-annual) and, on frontier and plantation, there were few ordained ministers to administer the sacraments in the interim. Second, as we saw above, in most situations where the Lord's Supper was held in biracial contexts, it performed separation and white superiority rather than unity and equality. Third, as African Americans reclaimed the meal rite, most traditions concentrated on its significance as a re-enactment of the Last Supper. For most African-American Protestants, the meal rehearses Jesus's preparation for his suffering and death and there is little emphasis on themes of resurrection and eschatological expectation. Occasions for lament and the rehearsal of the conviction that, as the hymn says, "earth has no sorrow that heaven cannot cure" is critical to African-American piety but, perhaps, not an action appropriate for weekly celebration. Finally, in African-American traditions, the experience of encounter between God and God's people is present as tangibly on Sundays without "the ordinance" of the Supper as it is when bread is broken and wine poured. In other words, we need to consider whether the sensible elements serve as necessary correctives in traditions in which proclamation of the Word involves only passive listening on the part of the people. When Word does not provide tangible evidence of God's grace, then, one might say, we must go to the Table. However, in African-American understandings of preaching, which are dialogic and involve the people with the Spirit in a manner more akin to Spirit possession than a lecture hall, the necessity of balancing Table and Word diminishes. In an atmosphere of call and response, the community itself becomes a living symbol of God's presence, relieving bread and wine of a good portion of their symbolic burden.

These all may be but temporary obstacles to the institution of weekly celebrations of the Lord's Supper as an integral part of an African-American *ordo*. There are many African Americans in Lutheran, Roman Catholic and Anglican traditions who do, in fact, participate in the sacrament of the table on a weekly basis. However, my argument is that the liturgical reform movement should reconsider its claim that non-eucharistic liturgical celebrations are necessarily incomplete. African-American Protestant worship traditions facilitate an embodied encounter of God with God's people; for me, this is the *sine qua non* of Christian sacraments. African Americans already participate fully, actively, and consciously in worship, another, and perhaps more critical, stated goal of the liturgical reform movement. Among African Americans, worship is already the cornerstone of the week, the shelter from the stormy blast, an earthbound semblance of the eternal home. African-American worship is not defective because it is not eucharistic, rather it shows the larger church that the Spirit will not be confined, loves no particular historic form of the liturgy but all gatherings in faithful hope, and is present not *ex opere operato* but because of a promise.

The Challenge of Pluralism for Contemporary Liturgical Theology

The complex history of US Protestant worship in which schism is frequent, adaptation to cultural shifts is dramatic, and captivity to oppressive ideologies is not unknown requires new approaches to questions about the relationship of worship and culture than the academy has pursued thus far. Two observations that begin this work must suffice here.

Liturgies are Local "Inculturation" is the term presently in vogue to describe the process by which Christian worship comes to life in a new cultural environment. Anscar Chupungco, a Roman Catholic scholar from the Philippines, has been its primary interpreter.[21] Chupungco carefully reflects on the process by which the "typical editions" of the Roman Catholic rites can be expanded, translated, and supplemented in a given context.[22] He proceeds with caution since Rome is in the midst of reasserting its authority over the worship of all Catholics.[23] While I appreciate Chupungco's constraints, I advocate stronger notions of adaptation than the term inculturation can convey. "Incarnation" was once used in this same arena and strikes me as more appropriate, not despite the doctrinal conflation of christology and ecclesiology it may imply (a principal reason it fell out of favor) but because of it.[24]

The church is the Body of Christ. There is no other Body. The church represents God in specific local communities just as Jesus was God in the flesh of a first century Palestinian Jewish man. So, too, the church is the Body of Christ concretely and not abstractly. Just as Jesus, as God-in-flesh, healed many with infirmities by touching them and shared actual food and wine with friends and strangers, the church and its members are to embody such tactile love in the world. While failing in many concrete, historical moments to live up to its ideals, still the visible church—as a multitude of particular communities made up of broken, conflictual, faithful people who occupy the pews of brick and mortar buildings—is the only Body God has on earth. The hands of these people are the only hands that God has to feed hungry people, to heal the sick, and to comfort the broken-hearted.

An emphasis on local incarnations of Christian liturgy implies radical pluralism. Liturgies are local acts. Consider the following scenario. People gather. They bring not a book but stories within their hearts, told in rhythms of their grandmother's wit. They bring drums rather than assembling in proximity to an organ. They gather around a pot rather than a table. They sing and dance. They know Christ is with them, not as memory, but in the flesh, and they dance some more. Could this not be authentic and Christian?

Paul Bradshaw is a critic of the convergence of Christian worship in the ecumenical reform movement. While he appreciates the importance of the tremendous strides towards re-unification among the churches and is grateful for the insight of ecumenical scholarship on the liturgy, he is troubled by the prospect of homogeneity that he notes is pervading the new liturgical publications. He posits a division among liturgical scholars: the lumpers and the splitters. He identifies as a "splitter", while Lathrop, for instance, is a "lumper".[25] Bradshaw cautions us to avoid the trap of seeking one apostolic shape to which we might return. He believes that Christian worship began as diverse local gatherings with many shapes and should remain so. He also cautions us now from following the present path of convergence too far. He writes: "In general, I would hope to see a valuing of deep diversity and pluriformity in liturgical theology and practice as a good thing".[26] Christian communities need to search, in conversation with their traditions, authentic and local ways of praying.

Liturgies and Social Location   Many have spoken about the relation of liturgy and culture. Most often they address the need for Christians to be both authentic to who they are, as persons shaped inescapably by their cultural environment, and transformed by the norms of a gospel that stands above, beyond, or outside of that ethos.[27] My historical narratives show, however, that the challenge is not simply a matter of discerning the proper relation between a culture and a religion. The location of a group or individual within a culture will affect her/his approach to religion and spiritual practice. In the US, we often speak in terms of a "white" as opposed to a "black" culture. The narratives show that within the one large, cultural mixing bowl, there are many sub-cultures, divided not so much by the identity of their constituents as by the relations of one group to another. Cultural difference is a part of a larger question about the relationship of individuals and groups within a society.

In regard to African-American and European-American Protestant worship traditions, it is the relationships between groups that most accurately account for differences in worship style. Between whites and blacks, the differences derive in large part from racist attitudes, and the ritual structures that proceed from and support them. African-American worship serves those who live on the underside of white supremacy. While African-American religious life is much larger than a series of communal responses to racism, these traditions are unique sanctuaries for a people who suffer daily indignities and provide an alternative arena where one is honored and accorded dignity. African-American worship heals the wounded, comforts the disconsolate, and empowers the weary. In contrast, most examples of European-American worship rest on white privilege, support the status quo, and provide solace to those who benefit from oppressive structures. Further, within each of the racial groups, distinctions in performative style arise primarily from differences in the relative status of sub-groups based on social class. The differences between the worship of the poor and of the rich, again, illustrate the way in which alienation, in this instance from economic structures, encourages liminal ritual modes that serve to shelter the oppressed from suffering and rehearse alternative futures.[28]

I would venture that, in fact, African-American traditions perform a different theology to European-American traditions because of the difference in social location of the two groups. In general, European-American traditions, especially those in the mainline current, concentrate on a rather abstract and distant God who is unlikely to take much of an active role in our daily lives, much less this service. This divine parent has mostly left it up to the people to figure things out, and this is accompanied by anxiety that they are not up to the task. The work of worship is then to provide a message of comfort that, despite appearances, all is well with the world, that "I'm okay and you're okay". Focusing on solace, a progressive, prophetic consciousness atrophies. In contrast, and again in a general sense, among African Americans, the primary mover is Spirit. The ecstatic streams of Christian worship live still among these, and other, marginalized Christians. They meet Jesus as an Ancestor, as a living Spirit. They walk with him and talk with him in the here and now. They know all is not well with the world. In fact, much needs overturning. With Jesus, they seek freedom, dignity and full citizenship in a land that denies their full humanity.

The difference in social standing, and the subsequent difference in theological perspective, accounts, in part, for the difference in the "shape" or *ordo* of European-American and African-American Protestant worship. Ecumenical liturgical theology needs to account for the relationship between the *ordo* it has discovered and promoted, and the ties of those who follow it with social power. I do not mean to imply that praying the juxtaposed poles of Lathrop's *ordo* results in unethical worship. To the contrary, juxtapositions break open the routinization to which all rites seem subject, allowing for eschatological expectation to arise. However, it seems more than coincidental that those who hold positions of privilege and live in relative comfort pursue with vigor rites shaped primarily by a process of historical restoration and presented in published, and therefore static, form. Lathrop's *ordo* is not, and should not be, shared by all Christian communities. There are other juxtapositions and other ritual means to facilitate the encounter of God and God's people. African-American traditions provide testimony that other authentic "shapes" exist. As James White has written, "The continuing existence of a variety of peoples is the best argument for a pluralistic approach to Christian worship".[29]

The Multicultural Body of Christ

The Body of Christ is, always has been, and always will be multicultural. At its origins, the church encountered and dealt creatively with cultural difference. In addition, the church is compelled to reach continually beyond its present configuration in order to provide hospitality to the stranger. The narratives of worship among African-American and European-American Protestants is primarily a story of the failure of these churches to break down the dividing wall of race, but there were also moments when just relations were forged. Both the failures and the real, if fleeting, successes provide lessons for members of multicultural communities who would like to better understand the role of cultural conflict in liturgical settings.

The church's birth story is one of cross-cultural encounter. In the second chapter of the book of *Acts*, the Spirit falls upon the apostles in the marketplace of Jerusalem so that the speech of these Galileans becomes intelligible to Jews gathered from the corners of the empire. The crowd drawn to the wind, the tongues of the fire, and the first occasion of Christian *glossolalia* had made pilgrimage for a festival called PentecFost, the culmination of the fifty days of the Passover celebration. They were all Jews, but they came from many lands and shared different languages and customs. To this culturally mixed crowd came testimony of "God's deeds of power" (2:11). The crowd does not share a single language that transcends their varied backgrounds. Instead, the text says, "we hear, each of us, in our own native language" (2:8). The hearers were "cut to the heart" (2:37). The small group of Galileans then baptized 3,000 converts and this multicultural community "devoted themselves to the apostles' teaching and fellowship, to the breaking of bread and prayers" (2:42).

Further, there is a dynamic within the church to constantly expand its own boundaries. Jesus scandalized both the religious authorities of his day and his own friends by eating with sinners, by befriending women and children, by touching the unclean. It is true as well that, by not accepting his dismissal of her request to heal her daughter, the Syro-Phoenician woman challenged Jesus's own presuppositions about who might receive divine power (Mark 7:24–29). At the end of his earthly ministry, Jesus commissioned his friends to make "disciples of all nations" (Matthew 28:19). Soon after that first Pentecost, Peter came to realize through a dream that "God shows no partiality" (Acts 10:34) and the church accepted Gentile members. The church as the Body of Christ is continually called to open itself to the excluded and pursue reconciliation among its members.

But living in diversity is not easy. Paul endeavored to help the church in Corinth maintain a status-free ritual environment. He writes:

> Now in the following instructions I do not commend you, because when you come together it is not for the better but for the worse. For, to begin with, when you come together as a church, I hear that there are divisions among you; and to some extent I believe it…when you come together, it is not really to eat the Lord's Supper. For when the time comes to eat, each of you goes ahead with your own supper, and one goes hungry and another becomes drunk. (I Corinthians 11:17–21)

After exploring a proper understanding of the supper and giving warning about the consequences of improper celebrations (the passage which serves as the epigraph to open this chapter), Paul continues: "So, then, my brothers and sisters, when you come together to eat, wait for one another. If you are hungry, eat at home, so that when you come together, it will not be for your condemnation" (11:33–34). Condemnation comes not from getting the prayers wrong, from using the wrong *ordo*. Condemnation comes from not discerning the Body, from not waiting for one another, from not sharing food with those in need.

Sharing at table graciously, living as a Body, has been no easier in more recent days. The rich lord over the poor, men over women, the owners over the laborers and the enslaved, the ordained over the lay. We must learn from our failures to pray in ways the promote equality, that set aside the distinctions of value under which we live in our daily lives. First, we must be suspicious of rites that resist critique and change. The slaves understood that worship in the plantation missions sustained their status as chattel and so they prayed their prayers for deliverance elsewhere. Adrienne Rich warns us to be aware of the power of human artistic forms to "reorganize violence", "translating violence into patterns so powerful and pure / we continually fail to ask are they true for us".[30] Voices which protest the exquisite violence of our rites are critical to the continuing evolution of Christian ways of praying. All members of the Body need a place at the table. No authority is entitled to say, "I have no need of you" (I Corinthians 12:21). Outsiders, affected by the ethical consequences of our rites, should be heard as well. The churches are human institutions that can never embody ethical, or any other kind of perfection. This means both that we cannot be scandalized by ethical failure and that we cannot cease the ethical critique of ourselves, our practices.

Second, we are free to experiment with new forms of prayer. Jesus said, "The sabbath was made for humanity and not humanity for the sabbath" (Mark 2:27). Juan Segundo, in his text on sacraments, echoes Jesus: "The sacraments were made for the Church and not the Church for the Sacraments".[31] The sacraments, and all other forms of Christian worship, are to serve human need. So, we are free to change worship to meet our needs, to do justice. We are constrained only by our conscience, and conscience understood in a collective, not individualistic, sense. "All things are lawful but not all things are beneficial. All things are lawful but not all things build up. Do not seek your own advantage, but that of the other" (I Corinthians 10:23–24). In cross-cultural dialogue, the assumptions of those on either side, and especially those with racial privilege, can serve as stumbling blocks for all. As a multicultural Body, a community must make plain these assumptions, engage in dialogue, and then pray with a sense of freedom and responsibility. Most importantly, experiments in multicultural worship need thorough and on-going evaluation. To reveal the form of authentic local rites will take time. Patience, courage, and compassion are required.

The Body of Christ has been and always will be multicultural. Among African-American and European-American Protestants, however, shared membership in the Body has not been discerned well or often. Communities with black and white members must be prepared to negotiate across the chasm that white racism has torn between these peoples. To dismantle the dividing wall, members of these groups must accept a final, difficult implication. Praying together will not only entail painful acts of confession, compromise, and conversion, it will also lead ultimately to the emergence of a shared identity, a shared culture. Christ promises to make a new thing and not simply to bring two antagonistic parties into proximity. African Americans and European Americans share a language, a geography, and some cultural currency already, but, by engaging ritually in a shared, communal life, members of multicultural communities risk losing cherished parts of themselves in exchange for the promise of greater wholeness. "For he is our peace, in his flesh he has made both groups into one and has broken down the dividing wall, that is, the hostility between us" (Ephesians 2:14). African Americans and European Americans who pray in ways that honor difference, perform equality, and expect reconciliation will be rewarded by failed experiments, continued misunderstandings, and, perhaps, glimpses of a better way.

Notes to text

Notes to Chapter 1

1.   These words remain prominently displayed on the worship bulletin to this day.
2.   See Tom F. Driver, *Christ in a Changing World: Toward an Ethical Christology* (New York: Crossroad, 1981), 1–4.
3.   This is an insight shared by strange bedfellows. For example, both Gustavo Gutierrez, the Peruvian liberation theologian, and Aidan Kavanagh, a conservative, liturgical historian speak of theology as occurring after and deriving from Christian practice. Gutierrez articulates his theological method, a hermeneutical circle of praxis, study and reflection in *A Theology of Liberation: History, Politics, and Salvation*, revised edn, trans. Sister Caridad Inda and John Eagleson (Maryknoll: Orbis Books, 1988). Kavanagh writes of the on-going life of the prayer as primary theology, in *On Liturgical Theology* (Collegeville: The Liturgical Press, 1992), 73–95.
4.   Kavanagh, *On Liturgical Theology*, 77.
5.   Robert Taft, "How Liturgies Grow", in *Beyond East and West: Problems in Liturgical Understanding* (Washington: The Pastoral Press, 1984).
6.   Taft, "How Liturgies Grow", 170–1.
7.   Taft, "How Liturgies Grow", 167–8.
8.   Tom F. Driver, *Liberating Rites: Understanding the Transformative Power of Ritual* (Boulder: Westview Press, 1998), 212.
9.   Mina Pendo, *A Brief History of the Riverside Church* (New York: The Riverside Church, 1957), 41.
10. James White, *Protestant Worship: Traditions in Transition* (Louisville: Westminster/John Knox Press, 1989).
11. White, *Protestant Worship,* 119.
12. The final sentences are Fosdick's, from *Church monthly*, Summer 1946, while the full passage can be found in Pendo, *Riverside Church*, 52.
13. Quoted in Robert Oates Miller, *Harry Emerson Fosdick: Preacher, Pastor, Prophet* (New York: Oxford University Press, 1985), 229–30.
14. Ryan, Halford. *Harry Emerson Fosdick: Persuasive Preacher* (New York: Greenwood Press, 1989), 3.
15. Ryan, *Fosdick: Persuasive Preacher*, 10.
16. Ryan, *Fosdick: Persuasive Preacher*, 10.
17. Pendo, *Riverside Church*, 53.
18. George Younger, conversation with author, The Riverside Church, New York City, 4 March 1995.
19. Sally Norris, conversation with the author, The Riverside Church, New York City, 23 February 1995.

20. James Cone, *Martin, Malcolm, and America: A Dream or a Nightmare* (Maryknoll: Orbis Books, 1991), 237.
21. Barbara Butler, conversation with the author, The Riverside Church, New York City, 22 February 1995.
22. Susan Chin, conversation with the author, The Riverside Church, New York City, 25 February 1995.
23. *Acting On Faith*, video, The Riverside Church, New York City (n.d.).
24. *Acting On Faith*, video, The Riverside Church, New York City (n.d.).
25. Leo S. Thorne, ed., *Prayers from Riverside* (New York: The Pilgrim Press, 1983), vii.
26. James Forbes, conversation with author, The Riverside Church, New York City, 29 March 1995.
27. Manuel Ortiz clarifies the distinctions between a "multicongregational" church and a multicultural or, in his terms, "multiethnic" (MEC), one in *One New People: Models for developing a Multiethnic Church* (Downers Grove, Illinois: InterVarsity Press, 1996). Of multicongregational situations, he writes:

> 1. The multicongregational church uses one facility for several language groups (congregations). 2. Language, more than anything else, seems to be what keeps congregations separated ... 3. There are different levels of interinvolvement in each congregation. Some churches come together more often than others. 4. Usually the English-speaking church owns the church building and determines the use of facilities and the events for any kind of combined effort. The other language groups tend to go along with the requests from the English-speaking church. 5. There is very little sharing of ministry projects. This is not always true, but it seems to be more common than not. (65)

Of multiethnic situations:

> There must be sufficient representation of any particular ethnic group in order to claim that a church is multiethnic. It is not enough to have a smattering of one culture or another ... [And, second] the church has biblically contextualized its ministry to the multiethnic context in which it finds itself demographically. This includes reforming the structure and administration of the body to represent the church biblically in the same way it did when it was a homogenous church ... Thus the effective MEC is more than just a variety of cultures meeting under one roof ... The qualitative aspect also has to do with matters of reconciliation and justice. (88–89)

28. James Forbes, conversation with author, The Riverside Church, New York City, 29 March 1995.
29. Members included: Sarah Cunningham, Gwen Shepard, George Younger, Elsa Callender, Carol Fouke, and Rose Marie Wildman from the Commission; Forbes and Sally Norris, representing the clergy; Organist Tim Smith; and at-large members Chenault Spence from the Social Justice Commission, Susan Chin, a former chair of the Trustees, Arelis Figueroa, a new member, Leo Thorne, and Barbara Butler.
30. James Forbes, conversation with author, The Riverside Church, New York City, 29 March 1995.
31. The term "spine" was proposed by Chenault Spence. For him, the word evokes

more than "order of service". He explains:

> The word 'spine' has a sense of suppleness and flexibility and yet strength and familiarity
> as well. I believe that continuity between services is important because you can then ask
> people to try something new and they will be comfortable enough to go along. If people
> are uncomfortable they will resist change.

The "spine" formulated in the December meeting consists of several components: actors (God and the congregation (who have various roles)), elements (preaching, prayers, and music are the most essential), and movements (gathering, sharing the Word, and responding/going out into the world).

32. James Forbes, conversation with author, The Riverside Church, New York City, 29 March 1995.
33. George Younger, conversation with author, The Riverside Church, New York City, 4 March 1995.
34. Roundtable Meeting, author's unpublished field notes, The Riverside Church, New York City, 12 December 1994.

Notes to Chapter 2

1. James Washington writes: "African Americans in the Western Hemisphere represented the first sustained blending of African ethnic groups to occur in the history of African people" (*Frustrated Fellowship: The Black Baptist Quest for Social Power* (Macon: Mercer University Press, 1986), 198).
2. Joseph Murphy begins to compare the wider field of "ceremonies of the African Diaspora" and indicates continuities among a variety of Latin, Caribbean, and North American groups. See his *Working the Spirit: Ceremonies of the African Diaspora* (Boston: Beacon Press, 1994).
3. C. Eric Lincoln and Lawrence H. Mamiya, *The Black Church in the African American Experience* (Durham, North Carolina: Duke University Press, 1990), 1.
4. My terms may suggest that I value the stream I call *classical* over the *improvisational.* My intention is quite the opposite. The term *classical* does imply longevity, respectability, and perhaps some type of normative standard. For me, however, just as the term *classical* in discourse about music tends to promote confined and false notions of what constitutes "good" music, representatives of the institutions I categorize as *classical* claim priority within African-American traditions. This hubris compels me to choose this term. Members of the African Methodist Episcopal Church and related denominations, at least until recent decades, have too often spoken pejoratively about other, folk-based streams. My narrative should make clear that *classical* traditions, while laudable in many respects, tend to mirror hierarchical social structures, and that *improvisational* traditions are much closer to my ideal of worship as a complex of transformative and counter-cultural performances. *Improvisational* liturgies adapt readily to changing circumstances, combine various cultural traditions into new coherent forms, and remain open to a living Spirit in the context of communal prayer.

5. In contrast to my current reading, Mechal Sobel and Alfloyd Butler are examples of scholars who find the evidence compelling enough to date African-American traditions back into the late seventeenth and early eighteenth century. See Sobel, *The World They Made Together: Black and White Values in Eighteenth Century Virginia* (Princeton: Princeton University Press, 1987); and Butler, *The Africanization of Christianity* (New York: Carlton, 1980).

6. Washington, *Frustrated Fellowship,* ix–xi.

7. E. Franklin Frazier, *The Negro Church in America* (New York: Schoken Books, 1964), 9–14; and Lincoln and Mamiya, *The Black Church*, 347.

8. Mary Berry and John Blassingame discuss both the liabilities and rights of slaves in West Africa, demonstrating that, while burdensome, slavery in West Africa had a more limited and short-lived impact on its victims than did the system employed in America (*Long Memory: The Black Experience in America* (New York: Oxford University Press, 1982), 3–7).

9. Albert J. Raboteau informs us that because of the relatively small number of slaves imported to the American colonies, the astounding rate of reproduction among slaves in the colonies and the relatively low concentration of slaves on American plantations, "[in] the United States the gods of Africa died" (*Slave Religion: The "Invisible Institution" in the Antebellum South* (Oxford and New York: Oxford University Press, 1978), 86).

10. Genovese warns us to avoid two pitfalls:

    the facile tendency to assume that southern slaves passively absorbed a religion handed down from above and completely relinquished their African heritage without replacing it with anything new; and the mechanistic error of assuming that religion either sparked the slaves to rebellion or rendered them docile. The religion fashioned by the slaves of the Old South did not replicate that fashioned by the slaves of Brazil or Saint-Dominique or Jamaica, but it did display the same creative impulse to blend ideas from diverse sources into the formulation of a worldview sufficiently complex to link acceptance of what had to be endured with a determined resistance to the pressures for despair and dehumanization. (*Roll, Jordan, Roll: The World the Slaves Made* (New York: Pantheon Books, 1974), 183).

11. Cone, "Sanctification, Liberation and Black Worship", in *Theology Today*, 35 (July 1978), 150.

12. Cone, "Sanctification", 141.

13. Raboteau writes: "From the abundant testimony of fugitive and freed slaves it is clear that the slave community had an extensive religious life of its own hidden from the eyes of the master. In the secrecy of the quarters or the seclusion of the brush arbors ("hush harbors") the slaves made Christianity truly their own" (*Slave Religion*, 212).

14. Joseph Murphy, *Working the Spirit*, 147.

15. Berry and Blassingame, *Long Memory*, 7.

16. See Cone, "Black Worship", in *The Study of Spirituality*, eds. Cheslyn Jones, Geoffrey Wainwright and Edward Yarnold (New York: Oxford University Press, 1986), 483; Frazier, *The Negro Church*, 17; and Lincoln and Mamiya, *The Black Church*, 347.

17. Henry H. Mitchell, *Black Preaching: The Recovery of a Powerful Art* (Nashville: Abingdon, 1990), 86–7.
18. The debate about what cultural forms survived the Middle Passage, which dates back to E. Franklin Frazier's challenge, in *The Negro Church*, of Melville Herskovitz's findings that African cultural forms were preserved in African-American life in *Myth of the Negro Past* (Boston: Beacon Press, 1941 and 1958) continues. Berry and Blassingame find it necessary to reassert the existence of "African survivals" (*Long Memory*, 15ff), while Henry Mitchell, an Afro-centric homiletician, still uses phrasing such as "… language changes had robbed them of their proverbs and other holy wisdom" (*Black Preaching*, 56–57).
19. Peter Paris, *The Spirituality of African Peoples: The Search for a Common Moral Discourse* (Minneapolis: Fortress Press, 1995), 21–22.
20. While Raboteau has already told us that the Gods of Africa die in this country, he does not dismiss the evidence for African survivals. He writes: "… slaves brought their cultural past to the task of translating and interpreting the doctrinal words and ritual gestures of Christianity" (*Slave Religion*, 126).
21. Raboteau, *Slave Religion*, 127.
22. Cone, "Black Worship," 484. Wyatt Tee Walker pushes further. He writes: "… it is more accurate to conclude that the Africans were not Christianized; the ancestors of Afro-Americans Africanized Christianity" (*The Soul of Black Worship* (New York, Martin Luther King Fellows Press, 1984), 50–1).
23. Mitchell, *Black Preaching*, 23.
24. Williston Walker, et al., *A History of the Christian Church*, 4th edn (New York, Charles Scribner's Sons, 1985), 574; see also Lincoln and Mamiya, *The Black Church*, 348.
25. Raboteau, *Slave Religion*, 125–6; and Nathan Hatch, *The Democratization of American Christianity* (New Haven, Yale University Press, 1989), 102–5.
26. See John Boles, "Introduction", in *Masters and Slaves in the House of the Lord: Race and Religion in the American South, 1740–1870*, ed. John Boles (Lexington, University Press of Kentucky, 1988), 5; and Raboteau, *Slave Religion*, 98–9 and 122ff.
27. Mitchell points out that because few independent black congregations existed and separate services were also rare, black preachers, from the earliest times, preached to white congregations, and were quite popular (*Black Preaching*, 24–27).
28. Melva W. Costen, *African American Christian Worship* (Nashville: Abingdon Press, 1993), 30.
29. Mechal Sobel, *The World They Made Together*, 180ff.
30. Williston Walker, *History of the Christian Church*, 599.
31. From Whitefield, *Three Letters* (1740), quoted in Sobel, *The World They Made Together*, 182.
32. On Whitefield's movement from criticism to acceptance of slavery, see Allen Gallay, "Planters and Slaves in the Great Awakening", in *Masters and Slaves in the House of the Lord: Race and Religion in the American South, 1740–1870*, ed. John Boles (Lexington, University Press of Kentucky, 1988), 19–36.

33. Sobel, *The World They Made Together*, 236.
34. Lincoln and Mamiya, *The Black Church*, 50.
35. Lincoln and Mamiya, *The Black Church*, 50. Hatch contends that American Methodists—due to the pragmatism of Francis Asbury—encouraged democratic reform and the participation of all worshipers as equals to a greater degree than Whitefield or Methodists in England (*Democratization*, 50).
36. See Lincoln and Mamiya, *The Black Church*, 66; and Raboteau, *Slave Religion*, 134.
37. Washington, *Frustrated Fellowship*, 205.
38. White, *Protestant Worship: Traditions in Transition* (Louisville: Westminster / John Knox Press, 1989) 180.
39. Sobel, *The World They Made Together*, 180.
40. Costen, *African American Christian Worship*, 33.
41. Raboteau, *Slave Religion*, 162.
42. Wilmore, *Black Religion*, 70–71.
43. Boles, "Introduction", 11.
44. Boles, "Introduction", 10.
45. Costen, *African American Christian Worship*, 65.
46. Boles, "Introduction", 9.
47. Lucretia Alexander in *The American Slave: A Composite Autobiography*, ed. Rawick, 8:1, 35; quoted in Raboteau, *Slave Religion*, 214.
48. Costen, *African American Christian Worship*, 48–9.
49. Costen, *African American Christian Worship*, 39–49. It is important to note that she also states that no simple listing of the forms employed in the secret meetings can be reconstructed as: various groups would have their own personalities, secrecy would necessitate flexibility, and "music, movement, and song were apparently constant dynamics, providing the foundation upon which all elements were carried out" (*African American Christian Worship*, 40).
50. Cone discusses Miles Mark Fisher's study of slave spirituals. Fisher notes how spirituals indicate earthly aspirations for freedom in veiled language. One example is the song "Steal Away", which Fisher says "served as a means to convene secret meetings during the early part of the nineteenth century" (*The Spirituals and the Blues* (New York: The Seabury Press, 1972), 16). See also Raboteau, *Slave Religion*, 231ff.
51. Because they met in secret and at great risk, slave worship leaders could not hold services in an established location. Each time they had to choose a spot, direct others to this place, and craft some semblance of sanctuary out of the natural surroundings. Leaders broke the branches of trees or otherwise marked a trail into the brush so that participants could find their way. To deaden the sound of their songs and prayers, the slaves put up wet blankets or directed their voices into an overturned pot or into a pot filled with water. As pots are employed in some West African rites, some also see these practices as cultural survivals. See Costen, *African American Christian Worship*, 38–41; and Raboteau, *Slave Religion*, 215–19.
52. Raboteau, *Slave Religion*, 219.

53. Evans Crawford, *The Hum: Call and Response in African-American Preaching* (Nashville: Abingdon, 1995), 30 and 38.

54. Lincoln and Mamiya discuss the musical qualities of all aspects of African-American worship, in preaching and prayer as well as actual songs (*The Black Church*, 348–9).

55. Costen, *African American Christian Worship*, 50–54. While historians trace the shout to the Sea Islands, similar activities are recorded in descriptions of worship elsewhere—both in the praise houses where slaves could worship openly and in the secrecy of the invisible institution.

56. This description was penned by Harriet Ware, an abolitionist teacher from Boston who observed black worship in the Sea Islands of South Carolina in 1862. It is included in *Letters from Port Royal Written at the Time of the Civil War*, ed. Elizabeth Ware Pearson (Boston, 1906), and quoted in Joseph Murphy, *Working the Spirit*, 148. Murphy goes on to cite scholars such as Sterling Stuckey and Margaret Washington Creel, who have found similar ceremonies in various African rituals (147 and 149). Costen also quotes this passage, *African American Christian Worship*, 53.

57. Murphy, *Working the Spirit*, 198.

58. Walter Pitts, *Old Ship of Zion: The Afro-Baptist Ritual in the African Diaspora* (New York: Oxford University Press, 1993).

59. Murphy, *Working the Spirit*, 174.

60. Payne's description can be found in Charles S. Smith, *The History of the AME Church*, Vol. 2 (New York: Johnson Reprint Corp, 1968), 284–5. It is also appears in Mitchell, *Black Preaching*, 43.

61. Lincoln and Mamiya, *The Black Church*, 354.

62. Cone, "Black Worship," 484.

63. In his taxonomy of "infelicitous" rituals, Ron Grimes notes: "Ritual 'defeat' is more common than might be supposed, because ritual competition and conquest are widespread" (*Ritual Criticism* (Columbia, South Carolina: University of South Carolina, 1990), 203). The theological and kinesthetic vocabulary of African-American Christians performs a different cosmology from the European-American forms on which they build.

64. DuBois, *The Souls of Black Folk*, in *Three Negro Classics*, ed. John Hope Franklin (New York: Avon Books, 1965), 215.

65. Lincoln and Mamiya, *The Black Church*, 51.

66. James Cone, *Martin and Malcolm and America* (Maryknoll: Orbis Press, 1991), 6–7.

67. Carol George, *Segregated Sabbaths: Richard Allen and the emergence of independent Black churches 1760–1840* (New York: Oxford, 1973), 55.

68. Ann Lammers, "The Rev. Absalom Jones and the Episcopal Church: Christian Theology and Black Consciousness in a New Alliance", *Historical Magazine of the Protestant Episcopal Church*, 51:2 (June 1982), 172.

69. The time of quiet contemplation before attending to business and the wedding rite provided for members seem a rare instance when African Americans adopted rituals in the manner of the Society of Friends. Allen characterized Quaker worship styles as inappropriate for most African Americans because of

the emphasis on discernment rather than demonstration. See George, *Segregated Sabbaths*, 57; and Lammers, "Absalom Jones," 168.

70. Carolyn Stickney Beck, *Our Own Vine and Fig Tree: The Persistence of the Mother Bethel Family* (New York: AMS Press, 1989), 95–109.

71. The components of the Supper are an Invitation, a confessional rite, the First Collect, a musical interlude, the Second Collect, music, prayers of Adoration and Humiliation, more music, the Consecration, and the Distribution. The dependence of the AME on Wesleyan traditions is evident but not total.

72. Beck, *Our Own Vine and Fig Tree*, 110.

73. Berry and Blassingame, *Long Memory*, 57.

74. See Boles, "Introduction", 17. Boles attempts, unsuccessfully in my opinion, to uncover a history of Southern antebellum religion in which blacks and whites worshiped if not in equality at least in ways not contrary to the gospel.

75. Lincoln and Mamiya, *The Black Church*, 54. The AME is only one of the many independent black churches. Others include the African Methodist Episcopal Zion Church whose first congregation was formed in New York City in 1796, the Union American Methodist Episcopal Church (established 1805), The Church of Christ (Disciples of Christ) (1871), and the Church of the Living God the Pillar and Ground of Truth, Inc. (the first ecclesial body to be established by a black woman, Mary Lewis Tate (1903)). Costen provides a chronology of the founding of numerous denominations in *African American Christian Worship*, 83–6.

76. White, *Protestant Worship*, 171. I discuss frontier worship and its relation to European-American Protestant liturgical traditions in Chapter 3.

77. This shorthand designation of the two structures risks deceiving the reader about both. I refer by the word "ancient" to the complex history of Christian worship, which is itself based upon the complex history of Jewish public prayer. See, among others, Paul Bradshaw, *The Search for the Origins of Christian Liturgy: Sources and Methods for the Study of Early Liturgy,* 2nd edn (Oxford: Oxford University Press, 2002). The earliest prayers that remain juxtapose two actions. The first involves gathering around the Word and the second around the Table. See, for instance, the 2nd century document by Justin Martyr, in Jasper and Cuming, *Prayers of the Eucharist: Early and Reformed* (Collegeville: The Liturgical Press, 1990), 25–30; and commentary upon it in Gordon Lathrop, *Holy Things: A Liturgical Theology* (Minneapolis: Augsburg Fortress, 1993), 43–53. It is the move from Table as a response to the Word to conversion as a response to the Word that I highlight here. At the same time, Lester Ruth reminds us to keep such claims nuanced and supple—since Eucharistic practice was also central in the lives of many early US Methodist communities. See his *A Little Heaven Below: Worship at Early Methodist Quarterly Meetings* (Nashville: Kingswood Books, 2000).

78. White, *Protestant Worship*, 174.

79. White, *Protestant Worship*, 180.

80. Rhys Isaac, *The Transformation of Virginia 1740–1790* (Chapel Hill: University of North Carolina Press, 1982), 306–7.

81. On African-American participation in camp meetings, see Charles Johnson, *The Frontier Camp Meeting* (Dallas: SMU Press, 1955), 180ff.
82. See the centennial edition of Cartwright's autobiography, published as Peter Cartwright, *Autobiography* (Nashville: Abingdon Press, 1956).
83. I do not mean to neglect the importance of missionary preachers in the intervening centuries of Christian history. Certainly, the mendicant orders of medieval Europe preached in order to convert lapsed Christians to deeper levels of piety and non-Christians to the faith. However, the Franciscans and others structured their appeals as homiletic invitations into the Church and its liturgy. On the frontier, the appeal became the liturgy itself.
84. White, *Protestant Worship*, 183–184.
85. White, *Protestant Worship*, 190. Obviously, a vast body of literature on black preaching has also developed. One scholar who emphasizes this dialogic character of this rich tradition is Evans Crawford. See his *The Hum: Call and Response in African American Preaching* (Nashville: Abingdon Press, 1995).
86. While the Jubilee Singers and many other groups which followed their lead brought a neglected portion of the slave heritage to mass audiences throughout the country, they were not without critics. For instance, while Zora Neale Hurston appreciates the choral arrangements as an example of African-American artistry, she denies that the new adaptations are, in fact, spirituals: "The jagged harmony is what makes it, and it ceases to be what it was when this is absent. Neither can any group be trained to reproduce it. Its truth dies under training like flowers under hot water" (*The Sanctified Church: The Folklore Writings of Zora Neale Hurston* (Berkeley: Turtle Island, 1981 (originally published in *The Negro*, 1934)), 80).
87. H. Richard Niebuhr identifies the process through which new church movements that address the needs of the disinherited become established. Niebuhr uses the example of New England Puritans, exiles from their own land who desired a fully faithful lifestyle. With their emphasis on asceticism and discipline, the Puritans soon found themselves a rich and comfortable ruling class (*The Social Sources of Denominationalism* (New York: Holt and Co., 1929), 19–24). The moral teachings of the Free African Society assumed a similar form and, in the long term (although the continuing presence of racism slows the journey to prosperity for African Americans), had the same result.
88. White, *Protestant Worship*, 188.
89. Gayraud S. Wilmore, *Black Religion and Black Radicalism: An Interpretation of the Religious History of Afro-American People*, 2nd edn (Maryknoll: Orbis Books, 1984), 165.
90. Wilmore, *Black Religion*, 160.
91. Cone, *Martin and Malcolm and America: A Dream or a Nightmare* (Maryknoll: Orbis Books, 1991), 8.
92. Wilmore, *Black Religion*, 177. I place King in my narrative at this point with some trepidation. It is clear that his "Afro-Baptist" roots are crucial to his own views and to the energy out of which the civil rights movement grew. As historians neglect the Baptist rather than Methodist roots of black holiness churches, I risk obfuscation when placing King in the *classical* rather than

improvisational movement of African-American liturgical history. However, his education, his northern connections, and the growing middle class values of urban southern black Baptists (albeit, slower and with more ambiguity than northern Methodists), justify this categorization. I consider King a "prophetic" *classical* liturgist. I am grateful to James Washington for the historical insights on which this claim is built.

93. Wilmore, *Black Religion*, 177.
94. Lincoln and Mamiya, *The Black Church*, 384.
95. Raboteau, *Slave Religion*, 139–140.
96. Costen, *African American Christian Worship*, 50.
97. Raboteau, *Slave Religion*, 187–188.
98. Raboteau, *Slave Religion*, 207.
99. Raboteau, *Slave Religion*, 208.
100. Costen, *African American Christian Worship*, 50.
101. Costen, *African American Christian Worship*, 51.
102. From Sir Charles Lyell, *A Second Visit to the United States of North America*, Vol. 2 (New York, 1850), 14–16; quoted in Raboteau, *Slave Religion*, 199.
103. In this section, I concentrate on locating Pentecostalism in the spectrum of African-American Protestant religiosity. In Chapter 3, a parallel section touches on the European-American lineage of Pentecostal worship. And, finally, in Chapter 4, I examine the interracial character of the early Pentecostal revivals. My intention is for each section to have enough historical facts to stand on its own as a narrative of Pentecostal origins while avoiding undue repetition among the three.
104. Lincoln and Mamiya write:

[Charles Harrison] Mason's work is especially notable because it took place amid the rising tide of racism that swept through the country from the end of the Civil War through Reconstruction, past the turn of the century, and on into World War I with its crest in the orgy of racial hatred and violence that gripped the nation in the 'Red Summer of 1919.' The decorated black American soldiers returned from their overseas' service with the French forces only to discover that, far from proving their worth in the eyes of white Americans, they had instead proven the depth of white racism. The stories of urban warfare, suppression, lynchings, and burnings alive—even of veterans still in uniform—portray the urgent background against which the labors of Mason were consummated in the early years. (*The Black Church*, 83)

105. "Weird Babel of Tongues", in *Los Angeles Times*, April 19, 1906; quoted in Frank Bartleman, *Azusa Street: The Roots of modern day Pentecost* (Plainfield, New Jersey: Logos International, 1980 (first printing 1925)), 174–175.
106. Walter Hollenweger, *The Pentecostals* (Minneapolis: Augsburg Publishing House, 1972), 23–4. Current scholarship on the origins of Pentecostalism agree that the practices emerge from the African survivals of slave religion which heighten the ecstatic forms of European-American revivalism while the teachings of perfectionism and the necessity of a glossolalia experience were first promulgated by Parham and other whites out of the Methodist/Holiness traditions. Debates rage over the relative importance of these two

sources. Hollenweger is supported by Carter Woodson (*The History of the Negro Church* (Washington, DC: Associated Publishers, 1972)); James Tinney ("William J. Seymour: father of modern day Pentecostalism", *Journal of the Interdenominational Theological Center*, 4:1 (Fall, 1976), 34–44; Cheryl Townsend Gilkes ("Together in Harness: women's traditions in the Sanctified Church", in *Signs: Journal of Women in Culture and Society*, 10:4, (Summer 1985), 678–699), and Iain MacRobert (*The Black Roots and White Racism of Early Pentecostalism in the United States of America* (New York: St. Martin's Press, 1988). Vinson Synan (ed., *Aspects of Pentecostal-Charismatic Origins* (Plainfield, NJ: Logos International, 1975)) is the primary voice within Pentecostalism that emphasizes the European-American contributions.

107. Daniels, David D., *The Cultural Renewal of Slave Religion: Charles Price Jones and the Emergence of the Holiness Movement in Mississippi, 1865–1901* (New York: unpublished dissertation, Union Theological Seminary, 1994).
108. Lincoln and Mamiya, *The Black Church*, 80.
109. Hurston, *Sanctified Church*, 103.
110. Lincoln and Mamiya, *The Black Church*, 81.
111. Daniels, *The Cultural Renewal of Slave Religion*, 188–192.
112. Wilmore, *Black Religion*, 153.
113. White notes: "… all Pentecostal worship is sacramental in manifesting visibly and audibly within the gathered community the action and presence of the Holy Spirit" (*Protestant Worship*, 200).
114. White, *Protestant Worship*, 192.
115. White, *Protestant Worship*, 201.
116. See Lincoln and Mamiya, *The Black Church*, 348–9.
117. White, *Protestant Worship*, 198.
118. Lincoln and Mamiya, *The Black Church*, 82–3. A history of the FBI available on the Internet informs me that the FBI was not so named until 1935. In 1908, a body of Special Agents was formed in the Justice Department. They were called the Bureau of Investigation, beginning in 1909, and merged with the Division of Investigation, an agency established to deal with crimes related to Prohibition, to create the present bureau. (I thank Tom Driver for observing the anachronism of the acronym.)
119. Lincoln and Mamiya, *The Black Church*, 81.
120. For discussion of "nihilism" as a description of African-American reality in post-modern US culture, see Cornel West, *Race Matters* (Boston: Beacon, 1993), 12ff.
121. Lincoln and Mamiya, *The Black Church*, 82.
122. White, *Protestant Worship*, 200–201.
123. Lincoln and Mamiya, *The Black Church*, 79.
124. Crawford uses the blues term "riff" to describe African-American spiritual practices that go beyond a given text in response to the needs and mood of the context (*The Hum*, 72–75).
125. Driver, *Liberating Rites: Understanding the Transformative Power of Ritual* (Boulder: Westview Press, 1998), 52–75.

126. My term *voudoun* refers to the syncretistic Haitian religion that combines elements of Roman Catholicism with elements of African Traditional Religion and which is sometimes pejoratively designated "voodoo".
127. Irene Monroe, Annie Ruth Powell and Delores Williams are among the first to publish critical evaluations of Black Church worship from a womanist perspective, which is a movement related to but distinct from feminism inspired first by the thought of novelist Alice Walker. Their essays—entitled, respectively: "The Ache Sisters: Discovering the Power of the Erotic in Ritual" (127–136); "Hold on to Your Dream: African-American Protestant Worship" (43–54); and "Rituals of Resistance in Womanist Worship" (215–224)—appear in Marjorie Procter-Smith and Janet R. Walton (eds), *Women at Worship: Interpretations of North American Diversity* (Louisville, Westminster / John Knox Press, 1993).
128. Cone, "Sanctification", 141.
129. Lincoln and Mamiya, *The Black Church*, 348.
130. Portia K. Maultsby, "Music in the African American Church", in *The Encyclopedia of African-American Religions*, eds. Larry G. Murphy, J. Gordon Melton, and Gary L. Ward (New York: Garland Publishing, Inc., 1993), 520.
131. Quoted in Maultsby, "Music", 523.
132. Costen, *African American Christian Worship*, 110.
133. Maultsby, "Music", 524.
134. Lincoln and Mamiya, *The Black Church*, 373.
135. Pastor Lucas attended Union Theological Seminary in the City of New York during the same years as the author and shared his sung speech in James Chapel on a number of occasions.
136. Jon Michael Spencer, *Sing a New Song: Liberating Black Hymnody* (Minneapolis: Fortress Press, 1995), 4. See also Obery M. Hendricks, Jr, "'I am the Holy Dope Dealer': The Problem with Gospel Music Today", in *African American Worship: Faith Looking Forward: The Journal of the Interdenominational Theological Center*, 27: 1/2 (Fall 1999/Spring 2000), 7–59.
137. Lincoln and Mamiya, *The Black Church*, 376.
138. West, *Race Matters*, 104–5.
139. Crawford, *The Hum*, 30.
140. Raboteau describes West African religious traditions as "danced" (*Slave Religion*, 15). See also Hurston, *Sanctified Church*, 103; and Pedrito U. Maynard-Reid, *Diverse Worship: African-American, Caribbean & Hispanic Perspectives* (Downers Grove, Illinois: InterVarsity Press, 2000).
141. Crawford, *The Hum*, 41.

Notes to Chapter 3

1. However, unlike most Africans, most Europeans chose to cross the Atlantic Ocean. Many were fleeing persecution because of their religious convictions. Some came as economic refugees or as indentured servants, in contractual bondage as an uncompensated laborer for a specified period, but not in perpetuity.

Poor and working class Europeans shared living conditions similar to those of African slaves, but their full humanity was not questioned. Further, while their right to function as citizens was partial (only property-owning white males could vote), it was real. The difference between poverty and slavery would become increasingly important as race categories solidified in the eighteenth century. By way of contrast, the formation of a "white" identity masked the reality of class divisions among whites.

2.   I do not mean to imply by this statement that the rituals, texts and prophets of other religious traditions do, or do not, function similarly. I do repudiate Christian triumphalism but do not desire to erase Christian particularity in simple universalism either. Adequate comparative work is beyond the scope of this chapter.

3.   The Spanish and French, and long before either of these the Vikings, arrived on North American shores earlier but lost or sold their holdings within current US borders to the British or, after independence, to the US itself in due course. The history of Spanish and French influences on European-American Protestant worship is beyond the scope of this chapter because the primary expression of citizens of these two countries is Roman Catholicism. For the most part, French culture became concentrated in the Canadian province of Quebec, or was subject to the inescapable process of assimilation of European Americans into "unhyphenated whites". Hispanic Americans, while initially Roman Catholic, are a growing segment of both the US population in general and of Protestant churches in the Western Hemisphere. Characteristics of Hispanic liturgies must be delineated and incorporated into discussions of multicultural liturgy, but would lead us beyond the parameters of this study.

4.   Hilrie Shelton Smith, Robert T. Handy and Leffert A. Loetscher, eds, *American Christianity: An Historical Interpretation with Representative Documents*, Vol. I (New York: Charles Scribner's Sons, 1960), 7.

5.   Sydney E. Ahlstrom, *A Religious History of the American People* (New Haven: Yale University Press, 1972), 97–8.

6.   See John Dillenberger, "An Introduction to John Calvin", in *John Calvin: Selections from his writings*, ed. John Dillenberger (Missoula, Montana: Scholar's Press, 1975).

7.   Dillenberger, "Introduction", 3.

8.   I follow James White's categorization of Protestant liturgical traditions according to their degree of continuity with medieval Roman Catholic practices. In this scheme, "right" identifies those most similar while "left" indicates relatively more radical departures. See James F. White, *Protestant Worship: Traditions in Transition* (Louisville: Westminster/John Knox Press, 1989), 21–24. On Calvin versus Luther, see White, *Protestant Worship*, 68. For Calvin versus Zwingli, see Nicholas Wolterstorff, "The Reformed Liturgy", in *Major Themes in the Reformed Tradition*, ed. Donald K. McKim (Grand Rapids: Eerdmanns, 1992), 291–3.

9.   Dillenberger, "Introduction", 4; and White, *Protestant Worship*, 63–4.

10.   Charles Washington Baird, *Eutaxia, or the Presbyterian Liturgies: Historical Sketches* (New York: M.W. Dodd, 1855), 13–18.

11. John Calvin, "Short Treatise on the Holy Supper of Our Lord Jesus Christ", in *John Calvin: Selections from His Writings*, ed. Dillenberger (Missoula, Montana: Scholar's Press, 1975), 510.

12. Calvin, "Short Treatise", 510.

13. Nicholas Wolterstorff, "The Reformed Liturgy", 292.

14. John Calvin, *Institutes of the Christian Religion*, ed. John T. McNeill (Philadelphia: Westminster Press, 1960), III.x.30.

15. White, *Protestant Worship*, 67.

16. Calvin, *Institutes*, III.xx.49.

17. Calvin, "Short Treatise," 536. See also R.C.D. Jasper and G.J. Cuming, eds, *Prayers of the Eucharist: Early and Reformed* (Collegeville, Minnesota: The Liturgical Press, 1990), 213–214; and White, *Protestant Worship*, 68.

18. Baird notes that the psalms constitute the people's office in the Genevan liturgy. He writes:

> The Reformers of Scotland did not, as we often hear, deprive their ritual of a responsive and popular character. They did no more than separate the functions of minister and people into the distinct areas of reading and singing. The Psalms are the responsive part of Calvin's liturgy. These choral services embodied the acts of adoration, praise and thanksgiving, which are scarcely noticed in the forms of prayer, while in the latter the offices of intercession, supplication, and teaching were assigned to the minister alone" (*Eutaxia*, 26–7). This answers, but, only in part, Wolterstorff's criticism that Presbyterians spend more time being exhorted to praise than in praising. ("The Reformed Liturgy", 296)

19. White, *Protestant Worship*, 66.

20. White, *Protestant Worship*, 65.

21. Quoted in Baird, *Eutaxia*, 40 (emphasis added).

22. White characterizes Calvin's eucharistic piety as penitential, one of several remnants of the late-medieval period, wherein one must be forgiven before participating in the sacrament rather than receiving assurance of forgiveness through the rite itself (*Protestant Worship*, 66).

23. White, *Protestant Worship*, 65.

24. Alistar E. McGrath, *Reformation Thought: An Introduction* (Oxford: Basil Blackwell, 1988), 92.

25. The 1549 *Book of Common Prayer* was the first "common" and "prayer" book to be published in England. It was to be sold for only two shillings and it was designed to facilitate lay participation in morning, evening and Sunday devotions. See White, *Protestant Worship*, 96–7.

26. Ahlstrom writes: "… the expansion of Reformed and Puritan convictions had revolutionary implications; it was a threat to arbitrary and despotic governance" (*A Religious History*, 116).

27. White, *Protestant Worship*, 125.

28. Ahlstrom, *A Religious History*, 139.

29. Horton Davies, *The Worship of the American Puritans, 1629–1730* (New York: Peter Lang, 1990), 4.

30. White, *Protestant Worship*, 125.

31. Davies, *American Puritans*, 15–17.

32. White, *Protestant Worship*, 119.
33. Davies, *American Puritans*, 273.
34. Davies, *American Puritans*, 41.
35. Davies, *American Puritans*, 79.
36. Davies, *American Puritans*, 82.
37. Davies, *American Puritans*, 77.
38. Davies, *American Puritans*, 187.
39. White, *Protestant Worship*, 119–120.
40. White, *Protestant Worship*, 125.
41. Davies, *American Puritans*, 276.
42. White, *Protestant Worship*, 128.
43. Davies, *American Puritans*, 275.
44. Davies, *American Puritans*, 151.
45. Davies, *American Puritans*, 69–70.
46. Ahlstrom, *A Religious History*, 159–160.
47. McGrath, *Reformation Thought*, 27–49.
48. Williston Walker, Richard A. Norris, David W. Lotz, and Robert T. Handy, *A History of the Christian Church*, 4th edn (New York: Charles Scribner's Sons, 1985), 571–572.
49. White, *Protestant Worship*, 52–3.
50. White, *Protestant Worship*, 53.
51. White, *Protestant Worship*, 107.
52. White, *Protestant Worship*, 130.
53. Ahlstrom, *A Religious History*, 300.
54. See Edwards, *A Narrative of the Surprising Work of God* (New York: American Tract Society, 1735).
55. Edwards mentions his disagreement with his grandfather's lenient policies on church membership in a letter to Thomas Foxcroft of May 24, 1749. The letter can be found in John E. Smith, Harry S. Stout, and Kenneth P. Minkema, eds, *A Jonathan Edwards Reader* (New Haven: Yale, 1995), 308–9.
56. Edwards, *Surprising Work*, 17.
57. See Edwards, "A Treatise Concerning the Religious Affections", in *A Jonathan Edwards Reader*, eds. John E. Smith, Harry S. Stout, and Kenneth P. Minkema (New Haven: Yale, 1995), 149.
58. Ahlstrom, *A Religious History*, 286–287.
59. Edwards, "Religious Affections", 151.
60. John Smith, Harry S. Stout, and Kenneth P. Minkema, "Editors' Introduction", in *A Jonathan Edwards Reader*, xxxvi.
61. Smith, et al., "Editors' Introduction", xxxiv.
62. Walker, et al., *History of the Church*, 578.
63. Cedric Cowling traces the geographical origins of New Lights and Old Lights back to England and reflects upon the environmental factors that shaped the two schools (*The Saving Remnant: Religion and the Settling of New England* (Urbana: University of Illinois Press, 1995)).
64. Charles Grandison Finney, *Revivals in Religion* (Chicago: Moody Press, 1968 (originally published in 1868)), 195.

65. Finney, *Revivals*, 12.
66. Finney, *Revivals*, 10.
67. Ahlstrom, *A Religious History*, 460.
68. Jacobus Arminius (1559/1560–1609), a Dutch Protestant, asserted that God did not decree the eternal fate of all human beings before creation, but, instead, offers grace through Christ to all, who may, in turn, accept or reject it. Theodore Beza, Calvin's successor in Geneva, and many other "orthodox" Reformed theologians resisted Arminianism with vigor. See Walker, et al., *History of the Church*, 538–542.
69. Finney writes: "Many good men have supposed, and still suppose, that the best way to promote religion, is to go along uniformly, and gather in the ungodly gradually, and without excitement. But however such reasoning may appear in the abstract, facts demonstrate its futility" (*Revivals*, 11).
70. Ahlstrom writes: "In Finney's theology sin was a voluntary act and theoretically avoidable, hence holiness was a human possibility" (*A Religious History*, 460).
71. Ahlstrom, *A Religious History*, 461.
72. Ahlstrom, *A Religious History*, 444. Other causes include the Presbyterian insistence on formal creeds and catechesis, educated clergy, and regular worship and teaching opportunities—practices difficult to maintain on the frontier.
73. Ahlstrom, *A Religious History*, 423.
74. Ahlstrom, *A Religious History*, 468.
75. Ahlstrom, *A Religious History*, 651.
76. Ahlstrom, *A Religious History*, 657.
77. Ahlstrom, *A Religious History*, 655.
78. Ahlstrom, *A Religious History*, 659.
79. Ahlstrom writes: "Between 1846 and 1860, churchmen gradually converted the antislavery movement into a massive juggernaut, and dedicated the South to preserving a biblically supported social order. To these opposing causes, moreover, they transmitted the overcharged intensity of revivalism, carrying it even to the troops when war finally came" (*A Religious History*, 673).
80. Quoted in Ahlstrom, *A Religious History*, 687.
81. Ahlstrom, *A Religious History*, 678.
82. Ahlstrom, *A Religious History*, 921.
83. PC(USA), *Book of Common Worship* (Louisville: Westminster/John Knox Press, 1993), 6.
84. White, *Protestant Worship*, 178.
85. Julius Melton, *Presbyterian Worship in America: Changing Patterns since 1787* (Richmond, Virginia: John Knox Press, 1967), 60.
86. Baird, *Eutaxia*, 5.
87. White, *Protestant Worship*, 165.
88. White, *Protestant Worship*, 132. Julius Melton discusses the link between aesthetics and the rise in class location of Presbyterians in the late nineteenth century: "Americans were discovering beauty … America's higher standard of living had brought Presbyterians and their churches in touch with expensive furniture and with the world of color" (Melton, *Presbyterian Worship*, 114).

89. Von Ogden Vogt, *Art and Religion* (New Haven: Yale University Press, 1921), 23.
90. See Walter Rauschenbusch, *For God and the People: Prayers of the Social Awakening* (Nashville: Abingdon, 1909), 12.
91. Vogt, *Art and Religion*, 151.
92. Reinhold Niebuhr, *Moral Man and Immoral Society: A Study in Ethics and Politics* (New York: Charles Scribner's Sons, 1932), xii.
93. White, *Protestant Worship*, 73.
94. The fourth-century church order, *The Apostolic Constitutions*, was rediscovered and published in 1563, but most other ancient liturgical documents known today were not discovered until after 1850. For a helpful schematic, see "Figure 4.1: The Publication of the Pieces of the Puzzle", in Paul Bradshaw, *The Search for the Origins of Christian Liturgy: Sources and Methods for the Study of Early Liturgy,* 2nd edn (Oxford: Oxford University Press, 2002), 74.
95. PC(USA), *Book of Common Worship*, 3–6.
96. White, *Protestant Worship*, 167–169.
97. White, *Protestant Worship*, 114.
98. White, *Protestant Worship*, 55–56.
99. White, *Protestant Worship*, 133–134.
100. Paul F. Bradshaw, "The Homogenization of Christian Liturgy—Ancient and Modern: Presidential Address", in *Studia Liturgica*, 26:1 (1996), 1–15.
101. White, *Protestant Worship*, 215–6.
102. Virgil Funk, "The Liturgical Movement (1830–1969)", in *The New Dictionary of Sacramental Worship*, ed. Peter Fink (Collegeville, The Liturgical Press, 1990), 695–715.
103. *Baptism, Eucharist and Ministry*, Faith and Order Paper No. 111, World Council of Churches, Geneva, 1982. For reflection on the document and specifically on the inevitability of its failure to unify liturgical practice because of its structure as a "consensus statement", see Peter Fink, "Diversity in Communion, or whatever happened to *BEM?*", *Proceedings of the North American Academy of Liturgy* (1994), 4–5.
104. For reflection on the interrelationship of the liturgical movement and feminist scholarship, see Marjorie Procter-Smith, *In Her Own Rite: Constructing Feminist Liturgical Tradition* (Nashville: Abingdon, 1990).
105. Janet Walton, "The Missing Element of Women's Experience", in *The Changing Face of Jewish and Christian Worship*, eds. Paul F. Bradshaw and Larry A. Hoffman (Notre Dame: Notre Dame University Press, 1991), 199–217. See, as well, her *Feminist Liturgy: A Matter of Justice* (Collegeville: The Liturgical Press, 2000).
106. Marjorie Procter-Smith, *Praying with Our Eyes Open: Engendering Feminist Liturgical Prayer* (Nashville: Abingdon, 1995).
107. See Mary Collins, "Principles of Feminist Liturgy," in *Women at Worship: Interpretations of North American Diversity*, eds Marjorie Procter-Smith and Janet R. Walton (Louisville: Westminster/John Knox, 1993), 9–24.
108. On the conversion focus of frontier worship, see White, *Protestant Worship*, 178. On the necessity of reviving current Christians in order to evangelize the unchurched, see Finney, *Revivals*, 15. On the emphasis on speaking in tongues

as necessary evidence of one's true and final conversion in Pentecostal churches, see White, *Protestant Worship*, 194–5.

109. In his classic text, H. Richard Niebuhr identifies the regular occurrence of ecstatic worship patterns among various "disinherited" groups of American Protestants (*The Social Sources of Denominationalism* (New York: Henry Holt and Company, 1929). On the coincidence of ecstatic forms of worship in peripheral groups, although far from the US context, see also I.M. Lewis, *Ecstatic Religion: A Study of Shamanism and Spirit Possession*, 2nd edn (London: Routledge, 1989). And, to illustrate the reverse argument that gains in economic security and denominational affiliation are interwoven, Max Weber, *The Protestant Ethic and The Spirit of Capitalism* (New York: Charles Scribner's Sons, 1958 (first published in article form 1904–5, ET 1920–1)).

110. A significant exception to this rule is Methodism begun and shaped by John Wesley, a well-educated and privileged preacher, who, nonetheless, reached out primarily to the poor. See White, *Protestant Worship*, 152.

111. White, *Protestant Worship*, 179.

112. Whitefield first toured Georgia in 1738. He traveled in the Middle colonies in 1739. He went to Boston and points north, before returning again to the South, in 1740. See Ahlstrom, *A Religious History*, 283–4.

113. Frank Lambert discusses Whitefield's use of popular media to spread word of his activities and to create a mass-market image of himself. It seems the tendency for *enthusiast* preachers to seek to be counter-cultural while employing the media and vocabulary of popular culture has long roots. Frank Lambert, *"Pedlar in Divinity": George Whitefield and the Transatlantic Revivals, 1737–1770* (Princeton: Princeton University Press, 1994), 8.

114. Harry S. Stout emphasizes Whitefield's skills as a stage actor in his biography. While Stout spends considerable time describing Whitefield's preaching, he mentions few details of the ritual activities surrounding the sermons. Harry S. Stout, *The Divine Dramatist: George Whitefield and the Rise of Modern Evangelicalism* (Grand Rapids: Eerdmanns, 1991), 93–4.

115. Whitefield's journey from prophecy to compromise is told by Allen Gallay in "Planters and Slaves in the Great Awakening", in *Masters and Slaves in the House of The Lord: Race and Religion in the American South, 1740–1870*, ed. John B. Boles (Lexington, Kentucky: University Press of Kentucky, 1988), 19–36.

116. In matters of affiliation, Whitefield serves again as an early precedent to contemporary *enthusiast* patterns. See Stout, *The Divine Dramatist*, 91.

117. White, *Protestant Worship*, 151.

118. White, *Protestant Worship*, 153.

119. Weber writes:

In the place of the humble sinners to whom Luther promises grace if they trust themselves to God in penitent faith are bred those self-confident saints whom we can rediscover in the hard Puritan merchants of the heroic age of capitalism and in isolated instances down to the present. On the other hand, in order to attain that self-confidence intense worldly activity is recommended as the most suitable means. It and it alone disperses religious doubts and gives the certainty of grace. (*Protestant Ethic*, 11–12)

120. E.P. Thompson, *The Making of the English Working Class* (New York, Pantheon Books, 1964), 362.
121. Thompson, *English Working Class*, 368–9.
122. White, *Protestant Worship*, 158.
123. Asbury crafted a Camp Meeting system. He held meetings between wheat/hay harvests and corn cutting instead of irregularly, advertised for them instead of relying on word of mouth, and defended them from critics instead of acquiescing to denominational pressure. See Charles Albert Johnson, *The Frontier Camp Meeting* (Dallas: Southern Methodist University Press, 1955), 86.
124. Nathan O. Hatch, *The Democratization of American Christianity* (New Haven: Yale University Press, 1989), 55.
125. Johnson, *The Frontier Camp Meeting*, 14.
126. White, *Protestant Worship*, 172.
127. Johnson, *The Frontier Camp Meeting*, 17.
128. Johnson, *The Frontier Camp Meeting*, 5.
129. Johnson, *The Frontier Camp Meeting*, 208–209.
130. See Kenneth Brown's assessment of Johnson's definition and attendant theory in *Holy Ground: A Study of the American Camp Meeting* (New York: Garland Publishing Ltd., 1992), 3–22.
131. Brown, *Holy Ground*, 5.
132. Johnson, *The Frontier Camp Meeting*, 168.
133. Johnson, *The Frontier Camp Meeting*, 123.
134. Johnson, *The Frontier Camp Meeting*, 124–131.
135. Johnson, *The Frontier Camp Meeting*, 214.
136. Johnson, *The Frontier Camp Meeting*, 93.
137. Johnson, *The Frontier Camp Meeting*, 240–241.
138. Hatch notes: "Modern church historians ... have had difficulty identifying with dimensions of their own ecclesiastical heritage that are diametrically opposed to the modern embrace of intellectual, liturgical, and ecumenical respectability" (*The Democratization of American Christianity* (New Haven: Yale University Press, 1989), 224).
139. Hatch, *Democratization*, 225–6.
140. Ahlstrom, *A Religious History*, 717 (note 5).
141. Ahlstrom, *A Religious History*, 670–673.
142. Ahlstrom, *A Religious History*, 716.
143. Even in 1927, only four percent of Methodist clergy had seminary degrees. See Ahlstrom, *A Religious History*, 728.
144. Ahlstrom, *A Religious History*, 718.
145. Ahlstrom, *A Religious History*, 721.
146. Ahlstrom, *A Religious History*, 716.
147. White, *Protestant Worship*, 188.

148. The reader is advised that parallel but distinct discussions of the origins of Pentecostalism in the US also occur in appropriate sections of both Chapter 2 and Chapter 4.

149. White, *Protestant Worship*, 192–193.

150. Walter J. Hollenweger, *The Pentecostals* (Minneapolis: Augsburg Publishing House, 1972), 24.

151. White, *Protestant Worship*, 195.

152. White, *Protestant Worship*, 200.

153. Edith Blumhofer, *Restoring the Faith: The Assemblies of God, Pentecostalism, and American Culture* (Urbana, Illinois: University of Illinois Press, 1993), 3.

154. White, *Protestant Worship*, 199.

155. Blumhofer, *Restoring the Faith*, 4.

156. White, *Protestant Worship*, 199.

157. See Blumhofer, *Restoring the Faith*, 6; and Hollenweger, *Pentecostals*, xviii.

158. Blumhofer, *Restoring the Faith*, 7.

159. Blumhofer, *Restoring the Faith*, 8–9.

160. White, *Protestant Worship*, 206.

161. White, *Protestant Worship*, 205.

162. Ahlstrom, *A Religious History*, 743–8.

163. The Five Points required affirmation of biblical inerrancy, "the Virgin Birth, the 'Satisfaction Theory' of the Atonement, the Resurrection 'with the same body', and the miracles of Jesus" (Ahlstrom, *A Religious History*, 814).

164. White, *Protestant Worship*, 191.

165. Blumhofer, *Restoring the Faith*, 7.

Notes to Chapter 4

1.   Zora Neale Hurston, *The Sanctified Church* (Berkeley: Turtle Island Foundation, 1981 (first published 1926)), 103.

2.   I will speak further about theories of inculturation in Chapter 5. The term refers to processes whereby Christianity is transformed within a given culture so that it speaks in accessible ways to members of that culture. See Anscar Chupungco, *Liturgical Inculturation: Sacramentals, Religiosity, and Catechesis* (Collegeville: A Pueblo Book, 1992).

3.   Where Pentecostal churches emphasize the equality of all in their need for God and in their ability to channel the spirit for the community, *classical* churches create layers of offices so every one can experience responsibility. James Cone writes:

Black people who have been humiliated and oppressed by the structures of white society six days of the week, gather together each Sunday morning in order to experience another definition of their humanity. The transition from Saturday to Sunday is not just a chronological change from the seventh to the first day of the week. It is rather a rupture in time, a Kairos-event which produces a radical transformation in the people's identity. The janitor becomes the chairperson of the Deacon Board; the maid becomes the president of Stewardess Board Number I. Everybody becomes Mr. or Mrs., or Brother and Sister. ("Sanctification, Liberation, and Black Worship," *Theology Today*, 35 (July 1978): 140).

4. Nathan Hatch, *The Democratization of American Christianity* (New Haven: Yale University Press, 1989), 226.

5. Theodor Klauser describes the development of the now pervasive scholarly consensus regarding the period 1073 to 1545:

> "Investigations of more recent years ... have not demanded that we should add any entirely new details to this (from the liturgical point of view) somewhat sorry picture, which in no way measures up to the romantic idealization of the Middle Ages which prevailed a few decades ago. It has been possible, however, to delineate more clearly the most important outlines and in the process, it has become ever clearer that the most important feature of this period is not that the old and new episcopal sees of the West began to follow the Roman liturgy, nor the fact that in this process there came an increasing measure of liturgical uniformity. Of at least equal importance though of much greater consequence is the fact now long observed, namely of a change in the relationship of the people to the liturgy. For the liturgy, which was once and always should be the common act of priest and people, became now exclusively a priestly duty. The people were still present, but they devoted themselves during the sacred action to non-liturgical, subjective, pious exercises. (*A Short History of the Western Liturgy: An account and some reflections*, 2nd edn, trans. John Halliburton (Oxford: Oxford University Press, 1979 (German original 1965)), 97).

6. Albert J. Raboteau, *Slave Religion: The "Invisible Institution" in the Antebellum South* (New York: Oxford University Press, 1978), 99.

7. Mechal Sobel, *The World They Made Together* (Princeton: Princeton University Press, 1987), 178.

8. Eugene Genovese, *Roll, Jordan, Roll: The World the Slaves Made* (New York: Pantheon Books, 1974), 186.

9. Raboteau, *Slave Religion*, 145.

10. Genovese, *Roll, Jordan, Roll*, 184.

11. Genovese, *Roll, Jordan, Roll*, 183.

12. Sobel, *The World They Made Together*, 233.

13. The separation of blacks from the white churches of the South happened so universally and rapidly it has been characterized as an "exodus". See Kathleen L. Dvorak, *An African-American Exodus: The Segregation of the Southern Churches* (Brooklyn: Carlson Publications Inc., 1991).

14. Charles A. Johnson quotes a passage from John Long's *Pictures of Slavery*: "By no class is a camp meeting more hailed with more unmixed delight than by the poor slaves. It comes at a season of the year when they most need rest. It gives them all the advantages of the ordinary holiday, without its accompaniments of drunkenness and profanity. . . they can jump to their hearts' content" (*The Frontier Camp Meeting* (Dallas: SMU Press, 1955), 114).

15. Sobel, *The World They Made Together*, 64.

16. Raboteau, *Slave Religion*, 135.

17. Sobel, *The World They Made Together*, 209. Of course, the denominations also quickly changed their official position. The Methodists acquiesced to slavery in 1779 and the Baptists in 1793.

18. Genovese, *Roll, Jordan, Roll*, 185.
19. Johnson, *The Frontier Camp Meeting*, 114.
20. Johnson, *The Frontier Camp Meeting*, 46.
21. On the dismantling of the wall, see Dvorak, *African-American Exodus*, 20, and Johnson, *The Frontier Camp Meeting*, 46. On the marching ceremony, see Dvorak, *African-American Exodus*, 11.
22. See Sobel, *The World They Made Together*, 79–229.
23. Sobel, *The World They Made Together*, 233.
24. Raboteau, *Slave Religion*, 148.
25. Dvorak, *African-American Exodus*, 22–23.
26. Sobel, *The World They Made Together*, 180.
27. Raboteau describes a petition to this effect written by a group of white Baptists in Georgia in 1863 (*Slave Religion*, 195–6).
28. David Reimers points out that segregated seating patterns developed in the North even earlier than in the South. He writes:

    The increasing numbers of free Negro Christians in the northern states due to the emancipations of the Revolutionary era raised the problem of race relations within the churches. Patterns of segregation appeared, and with the passage of time, racial segregation became the main characteristic of Negro-white relations within Protestantism. Segregation in the churches assumed a variety of forms, often interrelated, all-Negro denominations, all-Negro conferences, all-Negro congregations, and "Negro Pews" in mixed churches. (*White Protestantism and the Negro* (New York: Oxford University Press, 1965),11).

29. Dvorak, *African-American Exodus*, 18–20.
30. Horton Davies notes that hierarchical seating patterns can be traced to the Puritan churches of the seventeenth centuries (*The Worship of the American Puritans 1629–1730* (New York: Peter Lang, 1990), 233–234).
31. H.N. McTyeire, *Duties of Masters to Servants* (Charleston: Southern Baptist Publication Society, 1851); quoted in Dvorak, *African-American Exodus*, 60.
32. Dvorak, *African-American Exodus*, 170.
33. Larry Jones, "Biracial Fellowship in Antebellum Baptist Churches", in *Masters and Slaves in the House of the Lord: Race and Religion in the American South, 1740–1870*, ed. John Boles (Lexington, Kentucky: University Press of Kentucky, 1988), 56.
34. Randy Sparks, "Religion in Amite County, Mississippi, 1800–1861", in *Masters and Slaves in the House of the Lord: Race and Religion in the American South, 1740–1870*, ed. John Boles (Lexington, Kentucky: University Press of Kentucky, 1988), 67.
35. Sobel, *The World They Made Together*, 224.
36. Sparks, "Religion in Amite County", 70–71.
37. Raboteau, *Slave Religion*, 181.
38. Raboteau, *Slave Religion*, 293–294.
39. Raboteau, *Slave Religion*, 178–180.
40. Dvorak, *African-American Exodus*, 1.
41. Sparks, "Religion in Amite County", 79.

42. Dvorak describes biracial worship as establishing "ritual commensality" between blacks and whites. Her term "commensality" entails sharing a table, forming a group by establishing who is included and who is excluded by the invitation to table fellowship. European Americans did share their tables with African Americans but at a separate seating and with no intention of acting on the experience of unity that the Eucharist should foster (*African-American Exodus*, 15).

43. Sobel, *The World They Made Together*, 207.

44. Genovese, *Roll, Jordan, Roll*, 186.

45. Raboteau, *Slave Religion*, 152ff.

46. Raboteau, *Slave Religion*, 157.

47. Raboteau, *Slave Religion*, 153.

48. Raboteau, *Slave Religion*, 174.

49. Raboteau, *Slave Religion*, 161–162.

50. Charles Colcock Jones, *A Catechism for Colored Persons* (n. p., 1834).

51. Raboteau, *Slave Religion*, 162.

52. Raboteau, *Slave Religion*, 294.

53. Seabrook, in *The Management of Slaves* (1834); quoted in Raboteau, *Slave Religion*, 169.

54. Raboteau, *Slave Religion*, 159.

55. Raboteau, *Slave Religion*, 171.

56. Iain MacRobert, *The Black Roots and White Racism of Early Pentecostalism in the United States of America* (New York: St. Martin's Press, 1988), 38.

57. MacRobert, *Black Roots and White Racism*, 37.

58. In Chapter 2, I discussed links between African-American Pentecostalism and Afro-Baptist churches following the Civil War. I hypothesize that Methodism has more affinity to African-American sensibilities because of the strong unity between head and heart, theological speculation and song, in Wesleyan piety, in contrast to the more dualistic strains of Puritan and Reformed thought that stands behind Baptist theology. I think of Richard Allen's loyalty to Methodist theology despite being betrayed by that church. Many ex-slaves joined Baptist institutions because of the promise of greater local autonomy. However, when Holiness congregations split from stifling Methodist hierarchies, large numbers of African Americans returned (or turned for the first time) to communities with Wesleyan roots.

59. MacRobert, *Black Roots and White Racism*, 50.

60. MacRobert, *Black Roots and White Racism*, 61.

61. MacRobert, *Black Roots and White Racism*, 51.

62. MacRobert, *Black Roots and White Racism*, 55.

63. MacRobert, *Black Roots and White Racism*, 82.

64. Edith Blumhofer, *Restoring the Faith: The Assemblies of God, Pentecostalism, and American Culture* (Urbana, Illinois: University of Illinois Press, 1993), 61.

65. MacRobert, *Black Roots and White Racism*, 60.

66. Blumhofer, *Restoring the Faith*, 81.

67. Blumhofer, *Restoring the Faith*, 61.
68. MacRobert, *Black Roots and White Racism*, 68.
69. MacRobert, *Black Roots and White Racism*, 68.
70. MacRobert, *Black Roots and White Racism*, 76.
71. Two examples are the "finished work" controversy, mentioned above, which concerned the length of the process of sanctification, and the "Jesus only" debate over the proper baptismal formula to be used and its implications for the community's understanding of the Trinity.
72. MacRobert, *Black Roots and White Racism*, 88.
73. MacRobert, *Black Roots and White Racism*, 94.
74. MacRobert, *Black Roots and White Racism*, 93.
75. Walter Hollenweger, *The Pentecostals* (Minneapolis: Augsburg Publishing House, 1972), 506.
76. MacRobert, *Black Roots and White Racism*, 86.
77. Bard Thompson informs us that *The Apostolic Tradition of Hippolytus*, the ancient document on which many contemporary ecumenical liturgical reforms have been based, was written as a response to Montanist ecstatic rituals that placed priority on the present activity of the Spirit over the witness of and to the historical figure of Jesus, as well as to the similarly "problematic" Monarchial counter-proposals, that recognized only the personality of God the Father. Attributed to Hippolytus, a bishop of Rome, writing in *c.* 215, the *Tradition* urges the churches to follow a shared and stable liturgical tradition, which he, of course, takes it upon himself to define (*The Liturgies of the Western Church* (Philadelphia: Fortress Press, 1980), 13–19).
78. Tom F. Driver, *Liberating Rites: Understanding the Transformative Power of Ritual* (Boulder: Westview Press, 1998), 210.
79. Hollenweger, "Foreword", in MacRobert, *Black Roots and White Racism*, xiii–xiv.
80. Mark Francis, *Worship in Multicultural Community* (Collegeville: The Liturgical Press, 1991), 52.
81. H.N. McTyeire, *Masters and Slaves: Three Premier Essays* (Charleston, 1851, 38–9); quoted in Jones, "Biracial Fellowship", 56–7.

Notes to Chapter 5

1. The majority of African-American Christians were converted by frontier-revival evangelists who were a step removed from Wesleyan traditions. Wesley, in turn, was critical of Anglican practices, which had taken many of its theological premises from Geneva, the middle-ground of the sixteenth century break from medieval Roman Catholic practice.
2. Driver proposes a theological method that makes clear the interdependence of the teachings of the churches and human conscience. He writes:

I am thinking that my methodological proposal to locate christology within ethics and not prior to it is in fact what has always gone on in the history of theology. Our human situation, I suggest, is such that we cannot avoid adopting some ethical stance or another in the situations in which we find ourselves. This necessity, and the ideas we form of what actions are good, underlie and shape our teaching about Christ. The question, "Who is Jesus?" is a mirror question: Whatever we answer reveals the state of our conscience. In this sense, which is an exceedingly important one, Jesus is not the source of Christian conscience and not the form or content of it, but he instead reveals it for what it is. The attempts of Christians to hide their conscience behind Jesus, making him responsible for their decisions and looking to him to forgive moral failure, does not fool the world. Actions and failures to act which cannot be justified by conscience cannot be justified by Christ either. Nor by God. To put God above conscience amounts to putting God below it. Nothing can be better than what is good. (*Christ in a Changing World: Toward an Ethical Christology* (New York: Crossroad, 1981), 23).

3. Driver, *Christ in a Changing World*, 13.
4. Rosemary Radford Ruether, *Faith and Fratricide* (New York: Seabury Press, 1974).
5. Driver, *Christ in a Changing World*, 36.
6. Driver, *Christ in a Changing World*, 168.
7. Victor Turner proposes that ritual functions in a dialectical relation to the structures of society as an "anti-structure". He writes:

    ... for individuals and groups, social life is a type of dialectical process that involves successive experience of high and low, communitas and structure, homogeneity and differentiation, equality and inequality. The passage from lower to higher status is through a limbo of statuslessness. In such a process, the opposites, as it were, constitute one another and are mutually indispensable. (*The Ritual Process: Structure and Anti-structure* (Ithaca, New York: Cornell University Press, 1977), 97).

8. Again, I look to Turner who expands the notion of "liminality" first proposed by Arnold Van Gennep. Van Gennep saw "liminality" as one stage in the larger frame of "rites of passage" (*The Rites of Passage*, trans. Monika B. Vizedom and Gabrielle L. Caffee (Chicago: University of Chicago, 1960)). Turner proposed that the entire ritual process has a liminal quality in relation to the social order (*From Ritual to Theater: The Human Seriousness of Play* (New York: PAJ Publications, 1982)). See also Driver's use of Van Gennep and Turner in *Liberating Rites: Understanding the Transformative Power of Ritual* (Boulder: Westview Press, 1998), 152–91 and 227–38.
9. Examples of liturgical theologies that emphasize eschatology include Gordon Lathrop, *Holy Things* (Minneapolis: Augsburg Fortress, 1993) and Don Saliers, *Worship as Theology: Foretaste of Glory Divine* (Nashville: Abingdon, 1994). Texts that highlight the relationship of worship and ethics include Kathleen Hughes and Mark Francis (eds), *Living No Longer For Ourselves: Liturgy and Justice in the Nineties* (Collegeville: The Liturgical Press, 1991) and Edward M. Grosz (ed.), *Liturgy and Social Justice: Celebrating Rites—Proclaiming Rights* (Collegeville: The Liturgical Press, 1989).
10. James Cone emphasizes the eschatological dimension of African-American traditions in "Sanctification, Liberation, and Black Worship", in *Theology Today*, 35 (July 1978), 140–41).

11. Driver, *Liberating Rites*, 131–2 and passim.

12. Catherine Bell emphasizes the ways in which ritual systems form individuals into citizens of specific social orders through the comportment of their bodies. She writes:

> The ultimate purpose of ritualization is neither the immediate goals avowed by the community or the officiant nor the more abstract functions of social solidarity and conflict resolution: it is nothing other than the production of ritualized agents, persons who have instinctive knowledge of these schemes embedded in their bodies, in their sense of reality, and in their understanding of how to act in ways that both maintain and qualify the complex microrelations of power. Such practical knowledge is not an inflexible set of assumptions, beliefs, or body postures; rather, it is the ability to deploy, play, and manipulate basic schemes in ways that appropriate and condition experience effectively. It is a mastery that experiences itself as relatively empowered, not as conditioned or molded. (*Ritual Theory Ritual Practice* (New York: Oxford, 1992), 221).

13. Virgil Funk declares the reform movement dead with the institutionalization of changes embodied in Vatican II and challenges those who pursue further re-vitalization to begin a new movement in "The Liturgical Movement (1830–1969)", in Peter Fink (ed.), *The New Dictionary of Sacramental Worship* (Collegeville: The Liturgical Press, 1990), 695–715.

14. See Hughes Oliphant Old, *Patristic Roots of Reformed Worship* (Zurich: Theologischer Verlag, 1975).

15. As one example, see Charles Baird, *Eutaxia, The Presbyterian Liturgies: Historical Sketches* (New York: M.W. Dodd, 1855).

16. Dom Gregory Dix, *The Shape of the Liturgy* (Westminster: Dacre Press, 1945).

17. Lathrop, *Holy Things*, 79–80.

18. Tom Driver, e-mail correspondence with the author, New York, January 1998.

19. James H. Cone, "Sanctification", 139.

20. In her criticism of the abuses of the doctrine of the Word of God to silence victims of exclusion within the church, Ann Kirkus Wetherilt suggests this juxtaposition (*That They May be Many: Voices of Women, Echoes of God* (New York: Continuum, 1994)).

21. Chupungco, *Liturgical Inculturation: Sacramentals, Religiosity, and Catechesis* (Collegeville: The Liturgical Press, 1992).

22. Chupungco speaks of three methods of inculturation: "dynamic equivalence", "creative assimilation", and "organic progression". He acknowledges another method, "liturgical creativity", that goes beyond inculturation to the formation of new rites. He notes that instances for liturgical creativity will be rare, however (*Liturgical Inculturation*, 37–54).

23. See also D. R. Whitt's reflections on the limits and possibilities for liturgical inculturation in relation to the African-American Roman Catholic experience that remain after the publication of the "Fourth Instruction for the Right Application of the Conciliar Constitution on the Liturgy" by the Congregation for Divine Worship ("*Varietates Legitimae* and an African-American Liturgical Tradition" in *Worship*, 71:6 (November 1997), 504–537).

24. Chupungco, *Liturgical Inculturation*, 19.
25. See Lathrop, *Holy Things*, 35 (note 9).
26. Paul Bradshaw, "The Homogenization of Christian Liturgy-Ancient and Modern: Presidential Address", in *Studia Liturgica*, 26:1 (1996), 15.
27. As an example, see Thomas Schattauer, "How does worship relate to the cultures of North America?", in *Open Questions in Worship: What does multicultural worship look like?*, ed. Gordon Lathrop (Minneapolis: Augsburg Fortress, 1996), 8–9.
28. See Driver, *Christ in a Changing World*, 152–64.
29. James White, *Protestant Worship: Traditions in Transition* (Louisville: Westminster/John Knox Press, 1989), 212–13.
30. Adrienne Rich, *A Wild Patience Has Taken Me This Far* (New York: W.W. Norton, 1981), 3–5. Marjorie Procter-Smith connects Rich's lament to liturgy, specifically in connection to feminist liturgical proposals in her book, *In Her Own Rite: Constructing Feminist Liturgical Tradition* (Nashville: Abingdon, 1990), 13.
31. Juan L. Segundo, *The Sacraments Today*, trans. John Drury (Maryknoll: Orbis Books, 1974), 61–62; quoted in Driver, *Liberating Rites*, 204.

Bibliography

Ahlstrom, Sydney E. (1972), *A Religious History of the American People*, New Haven: Yale University Press.

Baird, Charles Washington (1855), *Eutaxia, or the Presbyterian Liturgies: Historical Sketches*, New York: M.W. Dodd.

Bartleman, Frank (1980), *Azusa Street: The Roots of modern day Pentecost*, Plainfield, New Jersey: Logos International (originally published 1925).

Beck, Carolyn Stickney (1989), *Our Own Vine and Fig Tree: The Persistence of the Mother Bethel Family*, New York: AMS Press.

Bell, Catherine (1992), *Ritual Theory Ritual Practice*, New York: Oxford.

Berry, Mary, and John Blassingame (1982), *Long Memory: The Black Experience in America*, New York: Oxford University Press.

Blumhofer, Edith (1993), *Restoring the Faith: The Assemblies of God, Pentecostalism, and American Culture*, Urbana, Illinois: University of Illinois Press.

Boles, John (1988), "Introduction", in John Boles (ed.), *Masters and Slaves in the House of the Lord: Race and Religion in the American South, 1740–1870*, Lexington: University Press of Kentucky.

Bradshaw, Paul (1996), "The Homogenization of Christian Liturgy—Ancient and Modern: Presidential Address", *Studia Liturgica*, 26 (1), 1–15.

—— (2002), *The Search for the Origins of Christian Liturgy: Sources and Methods for the Study of Early Liturgy*, 2nd edn, Oxford: Oxford University Press.

Brown, Kenneth (1992), *Holy Ground: A Study of the American Camp Meeting*, New York: Garland Publishing, Limited.

Butler, Alfloyd (1980), *The Africanization of Christianity*, New York: Carlton.

Calvin, John (1975), "Short Treatise on the Holy Supper of Our Lord Jesus Christ", in John Dillenberger (ed.), *John Calvin: Selections from His Writings*, Missoula, Montana: Scholar's Press, 507–541 (originally published 1540).

—— (1960) *Institutes of the Christian Religion*, ed. John T. McNeill, Philadelphia: Westminster Press (originally published 1559).

Chupungco, Anscar (1992), *Liturgical Inculturation: Sacramentals, Religiosity, and Catechesis*, Collegeville: A Pueblo Book.

Collins, Mary (1993), "Principles of Feminist Liturgy", in Marjorie Procter-Smith and Janet R. Walton (eds), *Women at Worship: Interpretations of North American Diversity*, Louisville: Westminster/John Knox, 9–26.

Cone, James Hal (1991), *Martin, Malcolm, and America: A Dream or A Nightmare*, Maryknoll: Orbis Books.

—— (1986), "Black Worship", in Cheslyn Jones, Geoffrey Wainwright, and Edward Yarnold (eds), *The Study of Spirituality*, New York: Oxford University Press, 481–490.

—— (1978), "Sanctification, Liberation and Black Worship", *Theology Today*, 35 (July), 139–152.

—— (1972), *The Spirituals and the Blues: An Interpretation*, New York: The Seabury Press.

Costen, Melva W. (1993), *African American Christian Worship*, Nashville: Abingdon Press.

Cowling, Cedric (1995), *The Saving Remnant: Religion and the Settling of New England*, Urbana, Illinois: University of Illinois Press.

Crawford, Evans (1995), *The Hum: Call and Response in African-American Preaching*, Nashville: Abingdon.

Daniels, David D. (1994), "The Cultural Renewal of Slave Religion: Charles Price Jones and the Emergence of the Holiness Movement in Mississippi, 1865–1901", unpublished PhD thesis, Union Theological Seminary in the City of New York.

Davies, Horton (1990), *The Worship of the American Puritans, 1629–1730*, New York: Peter Lang.

Dillenberger, John (1975), "An Introduction to John Calvin", in John Dillenberger (ed.), *John Calvin: Selections from his writings*, Missoula, Montana: Scholar's Press, 1–20.

Dix, Gregory (1945), *The Shape of the Liturgy*, Westminster: Dacre Press.

Driver, Tom F. (1998), *Liberating Rites: Understanding the Transformative Power of Ritual*, Boulder, Colorado: Westview Press (previously published as (1991), *The Magic of Ritual: Our Need for Liberating Rites that Transform Our Lives and Our Communities*, San Francisco: HarperSanFrancisco).

—— (1981), *Christ in a Changing World: Toward an Ethical Christology*, New York: Crossroad.

DuBois, W. E. B. (1965), *The Souls of Black Folk*, in John Hope Franklin (ed.), *Three Negro Classics*, New York: Avon Books, 207–389 (originally published 1903).

Dvorak, Kathleen L. (1991), *An African-American Exodus: The Segregation of the Southern Churches*, Brooklyn: Carlson Publications Inc.

Edwards, Jonathan (1995), *A Faithful Narrative of the Surprising Work of God*, in John E. Smith, Harry S. Stout, and Kenneth P. Minkema (eds), *A Jonathan Edwards Reader*, New Haven: Yale University Press, 57–87 (originally published 1735).

—— (1995), "A Treatise Concerning the Religious Affections", in John E. Smith, Harry S. Stout, and Kenneth P. Minkema (eds), *A Jonathan Edwards Reader*, New Haven: Yale University Press, 137–171 (originally published 1746).

—— (1995), "Letter to Thomas Foxcroft", in John E. Smith, Harry S. Stout, and Kenneth P. Minkema (eds), *A Jonathan Edwards Reader*, New Haven: Yale University Press, 307–311 (originally published 24 May 1749).

Fink, Peter (1994), "Diversity in Communion; or, Whatever Happened to *BEM?*", *Proceedings of the North American Academy of Liturgy*, 3–17.

Finney, Charles Grandison (1968), *Revivals in Religion*, Chicago: Moody Press (originally published 1868).

Francis, Mark (1991), *Worship in Multicultural Community*, Collegeville: The Liturgical Press.

Frazier, E. Franklin (1964), *The Negro Church in America*, New York: Schoken Books.

Funk, Virgil (1990), "The Liturgical Movement (1830–1969)", in Peter Fink (ed.), *The New Dictionary of Sacramental Worship*, Collegeville: The Liturgical Press, 695–715.

Gallay, Allen (1988), "Planters and Slaves in the Great Awakening", in John Boles, (ed.), *Masters and Slaves in the House of the Lord: Race and Religion in the American South, 1740–1870*, Lexington, Kentucky: University Press of Kentucky.

Genovese, Eugene (1974), *Roll, Jordan, Roll: The World the Slaves Made*, New York: Pantheon Books.

George, Carol (1973), *Segregated Sabbaths: Richard Allen and the Emergence of Independent Black Churches 1760–1840*, New York: Oxford University Press.

Gilkes, Cheryl Townsend (1985), "Together in Harness: women's traditions in the Sanctified Church", *Signs: Journal of Women in Culture and Society*, 10:4 (Summer), 678–699.

Grimes, Ronald L. (1990), *Ritual Criticism: Case Studies in Its Practice, Essays on Its Theory*, Columbia, South Carolina: University of South Carolina.

Grosz, Edward M. (ed.) (1989), *Liturgy and Social Justice: Celebrating Rites— Proclaiming Rights*, Collegeville: The Liturgical Press.

Gutierrez, Gustavo (1988), *A Theology of Liberation: History, Politics, and Salvation*, revised edn, trans. Sister Caridad Inda and John Eagleson, Maryknoll: Orbis Books.

Hatch, Nathan O. (1989), *The Democratization of American Christianity*, New Haven: Yale University Press.

Hendricks, Obery M., Jr. (1999), "'I am the Holy Dope Dealer': The Problem with Gospel Music Today", in *African American Worship: Faith Looking Forward: The Journal of the Interdenominational Theological Center*, 27: 1 & 2, (Fall 1999/Spring 2000), 7–59.

Herskovitz, Melville (1958), *Myth of the Negro Past*, Boston: Beacon Press, (originally published 1941).

Hollenweger, Walter (1988), "Foreword", in Iain MacRobert, *The Black Roots and White Racism of Early Pentecostalism in the United States of America*, New York: St. Martin's Press.

—— (1972), *The Pentecostals*, Minneapolis: Augsburg Publishing House.

Hughes, Kathleen, and Francis, Mark (eds) (1991), *Living No Longer For Ourselves: Liturgy and Justice in the Nineties*, Collegeville: The Liturgical Press.

Hurston, Zora Neale (1981), *The Sanctified Church: The Folklore Writings of Zora Neale Hurston*, compiler Toni Cade Bambara, Berkeley: Turtle Island.

Isaac, Rhys (1980), *The Transformation of Virginia 1740–1790*, Chapel Hill: University of North Carolina Press.

Jasper, R.C.D., and Cuming, G.J. (eds) (1990), *Prayers of the Eucharist: Early and Reformed*, Collegeville: The Liturgical Press.

Johnson, Charles Albert (1955), *The Frontier Camp Meeting*, Dallas: SMU Press.

Jones, Charles Colcock (1834), *A Catechism for Colored Persons*, n.p.

—— (1969), *Religious Instruction of the Negroes in the United States*, New York: Negro Universities Press (originally published 1842).

Jones, Larry (1988), "Biracial Fellowship in Antebellum Baptist Churches", in John Boles (ed.), *Masters and Slaves in the House of the Lord: Race and Religion in the American South, 1740–1870*, Lexington, Kentucky: University Press of Kentucky.

Kavanagh, Aidan (1992), *On Liturgical Theology*, Collegeville: The Liturgical Press.

Klauser, Theodor (1979), *A Short History of the Western Liturgy: An account and some reflections*, 2nd edn, trans. John Halliburton, Oxford: Oxford University Press (originally published 1965).

Lambert, Frank (1994), *"Pedlar in Divinity": George Whitefield and the Transatlantic Revivals, 1737–1770*, Princeton: Princeton University Press.

Lammers, Ann (1982), "The Rev. Absalom Jones and the Episcopal Church: Christian Theology and Black Consciousness in a New Alliance", *Historical Magazine of the Protestant Episcopal Church*, 51:2 (June), 159–184.

Lathrop, Gordon (1993), *Holy Things: A Liturgical Theology*, Minneapolis: Augsburg Fortress.

Lewis, I.M. (1989), *Ecstatic Religion: A Study of Shamanism and Spirit Possession*, 2nd edn, London: Routledge.

Lincoln, C. Eric, and Lawrence H. Mamiya (1990), *The Black Church in the African American Experience*, Durham, North Carolina: Duke University Press.

MacRobert, Iain (1988), *The Black Roots and White Racism of Early Pentecostalism in the United States of America*, New York: St. Martin's Press.

Maultsby, Portia K. (1993), "Music in the African American Church", in Larry G. Murphy, J. Gordon Melton, and Gary L. Ward (eds), *The Encyclopedia of African-American Religions*, New York: Garland Publishing, Inc., 519–524.

Maynard-Reid, Pedrito U. (2000), *Diverse Worship: African-American, Caribbean & Hispanic Perspectives*, Downers Grove, Illinois: InterVarsity Press.

McGrath, Alistar E. (1988), *Reformation Thought: An Introduction*, Oxford: Basil Blackwell.

Melton, Julius (1967), *Presbyterian Worship in America: Changing Patterns since 1787*, Richmond, Virginia: John Knox Press.

Miller, Robert Oates (1985), *Harry Emerson Fosdick: Preacher, Pastor, Prophet*, New York: Oxford University Press.

Mitchell, Henry H. (1990), *Black Preaching: The Recovery of a Powerful Art*, Nashville: Abingdon.

Monroe, Irene (1993), "The Ache Sisters: Discovering the Power of the Erotic in Ritual", in Marjorie Procter-Smith and Janet R. Walton (eds), *Women at Worship: Interpretations of North American Diversity*, Louisville: Westminster/John Knox, 127–135.

Murphy, Joseph (1994), *Working the Spirit: Ceremonies of the African Diaspora*, Boston: Beacon Press.

Niebuhr, H. Richard (1929), *The Social Sources of Denominationalism*, New York: Holt and Co.

Niebuhr, Reinhold (1932), *Moral Man and Immoral Society: A Study in Ethics and Politics*, New York: Charles Scribner's Sons.

Old, Hughes Oliphant (1975), *Patristic Roots of Reformed Worship*, Zurich: Theologischer Verlag.

Ortiz, Manuel (1996), *One New People: Models for developing a Multiethnic Church*, Downers Grove, Illinois: InterVarsity Press.

Presbyterian Church, USA (1993), *Book of Common Worship*, Louisville: Westminster/John Knox Press.

Paris, Peter (1995), *The Spirituality of African Peoples: The Search for a Common Moral Discourse*, Minneapolis: Fortress Press.

Pendo, Mina (1957), *A Brief History of the Riverside Church*, New York: The Riverside Church.

Pitts, Walter (1993), *Old Ship of Zion: The Afro-Baptist Ritual in the African Diaspora*, New York: Oxford University Press.

Powell, Annie Ruth (1993), "Hold on to Your Dream: African-American Protestant Worship", in Marjorie Procter-Smith and Janet R. Walton (eds), *Women at Worship: Interpretations of North American Diversity*, Louisville: Westminster/John Knox, 43–53.

Procter-Smith, Marjorie (1995), *Praying with Our Eyes Open: Engendering Feminist Liturgical Prayer*, Nashville: Abingdon.

——— (1990), *In Her Own Rite: Constructing Feminist Liturgical Tradition*, Nashville: Abingdon.

Raboteau, Albert J. (1978), *Slave Religion: The "Invisible Institution" in the Antebellum South*, Oxford and New York: Oxford University Press, 1978.

Rauschenbusch, Walter (1909), *For God and the People: Prayers of the Social Awakening*, Nashville: Abingdon.

Reimers, David (1965), *White Protestantism and the Negro*, New York: Oxford University Press.

Rich, Adrienne (1985), *A Wild Patience Has Taken Me This Far*, New York: W.W. Norton.

Riverside Church (n.d.), *Acting On Faith*, New York City: The Riverside Church, (videocassette).

Ruether, Rosemary Radford (1974), *Faith and Fratricide*, New York: Seabury Press.

Ryan, Halford (1989), *Harry Emerson Fosdick: Persuasive Preacher*, New York: Greenwood Press.

Saliers, Don E. (1994), *Worship as Theology: Foretaste of Glory Divine*, Nashville: Abingdon.

Schattauer, Thomas (1996), "How does worship relate to the cultures of North America?", in Gordon Lathrop (ed.), *Open Questions in Worship: What does multicultural worship look like?*, Minneapolis: Augsburg Fortress.

Segundo, Juan L. (1974), *The Sacraments Today*, trans. John Drury, Maryknoll: Orbis Books.

Smith, Hilrie Shelton, Handy, Robert T. and Loetscher, Leffert A. (eds) (1960), *American Christianity: An Historical Interpretation with Representative Documents*, vol. 1, New York: Charles Scribner's Sons.

Smith, John, Harry S. Stout, and Kenneth P. Minkema (1995), "Editors' Introduction", in John E. Smith, Harry S. Stout, and Kenneth P. Minkema (eds), *A Jonathan Edwards Reader*, New Haven: Yale University Press, vii–xl.

Sobel, Mechal (1987), *The World They Made Together: Black and White Values in Eighteenth Century Virginia*, Princeton: Princeton University Press.

Sparks, Randy (1988), "Religion in Amite County, Mississippi, 1800–1861", in John Boles (ed.), *Masters and Slaves in the House of the Lord: Race and Religion in the American South, 1740–1870*, Lexington, Kentucky: University Press of Kentucky.

Spencer, Jon Michael (1995), *Sing a New Song: Liberating Black Hymnody*, Minneapolis: Fortress Press.

Stout, Harry S. (1991), *The Divine Dramatist: George Whitefield and the Rise of Modern Evangelicalism*, Grand Rapids: Eerdmanns.

Synan, Vinson (ed.) (1975), *Aspects of Pentecostal-Charismatic Origins*, Plainfield, New Jersey: Logos International.

Taft, Robert (1984), *Beyond East and West: Problems in Liturgical Understanding*, Washington: The Pastoral Press.

Thompson, Bard (ed.) (1980), *Liturgies of the Western Church*, Philadelphia: Fortress Press.

Thompson, E. P. (1964), *The Making of the English Working Class*, New York: Pantheon Books.

Thorne, Leo S. (ed.) (1983), *Prayers from Riverside,* New York: The Pilgrim Press.

Tinney, James (1976), "William J. Seymour: Father of Modern Day Pentecostalism", *Journal of the Interdenominational Theological Center*, 4:1 (Fall), 34–44.

Turner, Victor (1982), *From Ritual to Theater: The Human Seriousness of Play*, New York: PAJ Publications.

—— (1977), *The Ritual Process: Structure and Anti-structure*, Ithaca, New York: Cornell University Press.

Van Gennep, Arnold (1960), *The Rites of Passage*, trans. Monika B. Vizedom and Gabrielle L. Caffee, Chicago: University of Chicago Press (originally published 1908).

Vogt, Von Ogden (1921), *Art and Religion*, New Haven: Yale University Press.

Walker, Williston, Richard A. Norris, David W. Lotz and Robert T. Handy (1985), *A History of the Christian Church*, 4th edn, New York: Charles Scribner's Sons.

Walker, Wyatt Tee (1984), *The Soul of Black Worship*, New York: Martin Luther King Fellows Press.

Walton, Janet (1991), "The Missing Element of Women's Experience", in Paul F. Bradshaw, and Lawrence A. Hoffman (eds), *The Changing Face of Jewish and Christian Worship*, Notre Dame: Notre Dame University Press, 199–217.

—— (2000), *Feminist Liturgy: A Matter of Justice*, Collegeville: The Liturgical Press.

Washington, James M. (1986), *Frustrated Fellowship: The Black Baptist Quest for Social Power*, Macon: Mercer University Press.

Weber, Max (1958), *The Protestant Ethic and The Spirit of Capitalism*, New York: Charles Scribner's Sons, (originally published 1904–5).

West, Cornel (1993), *Race Matters*, Boston: Beacon.

Wetherilt, Ann Kirkus (1994), *That They May be Many: Voices of Women, Echoes of God*, New York: Continuum.

White, James (1989), *Protestant Worship: Traditions in Transition*, Louisville: Westminster/John Knox Press.

Whitt, D. R. (1997), "*Varietates Legitimae* and an African-American Liturgical Tradition", *Worship*, 71:6 (November), 504–537.

Williams, Delores (1993), "Rituals of Resistance in Womanist Worship", in Marjorie Procter-Smith and Janet R. Walton (eds), *Women at Worship: Interpretations of North American Diversity*, Louisville: Westminster/John Knox, 215–223.

Wilmore, Gayraud S. (1984), *Black Religion and Black Radicalism: An Interpretation of the Religious History of Afro-American People*, 2nd edn, Maryknoll: Orbis Books.

Wolterstorff, Nicholas (1992), "The Reformed Liturgy", in Donald K. McKim (ed.), *Major Themes in the Reformed Tradition,* Grand Rapids: Eerdmanns, 273–304.

Woodson, Carter (1972), *The History of the Negro Church*, Washington, DC: Associated Publishers.

World Council of Churches (1982), *Baptism, Eucharist and Ministry*, Faith and Order Paper No. 111. Geneva: World Council of Churches.

Index

division by race of 117–19
founding revival on Azusa Street 38–40
as initially racially mixed 85
Neo-Pentecostals and 44, 101
also see names of particular churches/
    denominations
Pentecostal worship/liturgies 15, 38–44, 76,
    83–87
  as biracial 101, 113–19, 120
  music in 47
  preaching in 41
  principles of 40–2, 84–5
  white vs. black 36
Pitts, Walter 26
"Plan for Union" 68
plantation missions 101, 109–113, 120
Powell, Adam Clayton, Jr. 34
Powell, Adam Clayton, Sr. 34
Powell, Annie Ruth 150n127
pragmatic/pragmatist,
  as principle of worship 31, 79–82
Prayers from Riverside (Thorne) 8–9
preaching
  in African-American churches 31, 33
  at camp meetings 32, 79–82
  style of Fosdick 6
  in Pentecostal worship 40–2, 84–5
  slave conversion and revival, 21
Presbyterian Church (USA) 52
Presbyterian churches/denominations 23–4,
    52, 66–70
  Anglican threat to 70
  Old School and New School in 66–70,
    82, 129
  restorationism in 72–3
  revivalism and 66–70
  schism and reunion in 70, 82
  service books in 73
Procter-Smith, Marjorie 74–5, 155n104,
    165n30
Protestant liturgical traditions, US
  Fosdick's interpretation 6
  and racism 134–5
  as "river" 91–101, 93fl.1
  and social power 127–9
  as source for African-American and
    European-American worship 92
Puritan/Puritanism 54, 58–62, 75, 77, 98
  Baptists, slaves and, 22–3

and Edwards 64
and Enlightenment 62
principles of worship 59–61
and revivalism 64–6
weaknesses in worship 61–2
worship in 58–62

Quaker worship
  Richard Allen, Free African Society
    and, 29
Quakers 51, 101

Raboteau, Albert J. 19, 23–4, 37, 102, 105,
    108, 110, 112, 142n9, 142n13,
    143n20, 150n140
race(s)
  cycles of segregation and integration in
    worship around 121
  Seymour vs. Parham on 115
  worship that fosters integration of
    104–5, 106–9, 113–116
  worship that fosters segregation by 4,
    105–6, 106–9, 121, 122–4, 160n28
racism
  African-American worship as critique
    of 49
  in founding of US 91
  praying our way out of 137
  revivalist preaching and critique of 33
  as shaping worship 134–5
  worship and 121–2, 125–9
Rauschenbusch, Walter 71–2
Reconstruction 38, 40, 114
Reformation, The Protestant 52
Reformed churches/denominations
  and Enlightenment 62–3
  also see Presbyterian churches/denomi-
    nations and Lutheran churches/de-
    nominations
Reformed worship/liturgical traditions
  Fosdick interpretation of 6
  Genevan roots of 55–58
  order of service at Riverside Church as 9
  Roundtable "spine" as 14
Reimers, David 160n28
revivals/revivalism 23, 30–34, 66–70
  biracial camp meetings and 103–6
  camp meetings as form of 79–82
  frequency of 131